RELIGIOUS PROPERTY DISPUTES AND THE LAW

House of God, Laws of Man

DANIEL P. DALTON

Cover design by Tahiti Spears/ABA Design

Printed in the United States of America.

25 24 23 22 21   5 4 3 2 1

Library of Congress CIP

Discounts are available for books ordered in bulk. Special consideration is given to state bars, CLE programs, and other bar-related organizations. Inquire at Book Publishing, ABA Publishing, American Bar Association, 321 N. Clark Street, Chicago, Illinois 60654-7598.

www.shopABA.org

For Peggy

Only we two are one
Wallace Stevens

About the Author

A founder of Detroit-based Dalton & Tomich PLC, Daniel P. Dalton has developed a national reputation as a tenacious and strategic litigator representing clients in religious property disputes related to local churches leaving denominations and retaining property and in representing religious organizations in land use and zoning litigation.

An accomplished speaker and legal writer, Dan is the author of *Litigating Religious Land Use Cases*. Originally published by the American Bar Association in 2014 and updated for a second edition in 2016, the book is a guide for religious entities and the attorneys who represent them. He is an active member of the Michigan Bar Association and the Federal Bar Association and is a lifetime member of the American Bar Foundation. Upon graduation from law school, he was a clerk for the Michigan Supreme Court.

Among his many legal honors, Dan is a multiple Michigan Super Lawyer and Business magazine Top Lawyer honoree, recognized in the areas of zoning and land use. In 2010, he was named to the prestigious Leaders in the Law by the trade journal *Michigan Lawyers Weekly*. Dan is regularly sought out by the media for stories on his high-profile cases or topical religious land use issues and has been quoted in the *National Catholic Reporter*, *The Atlantic*, *The Wall Street Journal*, *The Washington Post*, *USA Today*, *Christianity Today*, *The Detroit News*, the *Atlanta Journal-Constitution*, and *The Tennessean* among others.

Dan holds a juris doctor from the University of Detroit Mercy School of Law, where he is a member of the Dean's Advisory Board of Directors, and a bachelor of arts degree from Western Michigan University. He is actively engaged in his church—Trinity Church, an Evangelical Presbyterian Church near Plymouth, Michigan. He was a citizen leader for the city of Plymouth, where he held roles on the city Planning Commission and zoning board and also served three terms as an elected official on the city commission. In his free time, Dan is an avid swimmer.

Also by Daniel P. Dalton
Litigating Religious Land Use Cases, 2014
Litigating Religious Land Use Cases, Second Edition, 2016

Contents

Reviews

"RLUIPA is the great equalizer when religious expression is corralled by local land use laws, particularly where a religious congregation's space needs are suppressed—or worse, completely banned by artfully interpreted zoning laws. RLUIPA holds local vested land interests and their elected representatives accountable to one of the founding ideals of our great country: religious tolerance and inclusion. We owe Mr. Dalton our deepest gratitude, for he championed our Catholic high school's cause and saw us through by contesting and prevailing against the will of our current mayor."
Mr. Dasan Mahadevan
Former Chief Financial Officer
Academy of Our Lady of Peace
San Diego, California

"Thoughtful. Creative. Insightful. Informative. Well-researched. This book embodies all the attributes of Dan Dalton the author and Dan Dalton the lawyer. It brings to light the history of zoning as applied to religious land use and the current state of the law as applied to all religious uses today throughout the United States. A must read for anyone dealing with religious land use issues or practicing in this area of the law."
Mr. Ricky Edmiston
Douglas Church
Ruston, Louisiana

"RLUIPA has become a passion for Dan Dalton. Dan is the authority on land use issues. His book is filled with solid content and practical case studies. The distilled nuggets are pure gold! This needs to be read by anyone thinking about litigating land use cases."
Reverend Rose Schwab
Shawnee Mission Unitarian Universalist Church
Lenexa, Kansas

"Dan Dalton's book is a long-overdue resource for attorneys who represent religious organizations. For the first time, attorneys who may never have litigated a religious land use case before will have a soup-to-nuts primer on how to bring their case, what claims to raise, and how to think about settlement. The book is a unique and welcome contribution."
Pastor Donald Thrasher
Northside Church
Jackson, Tennessee

"Essential to living with integrity in the realm of a pastor is to practice what we preach. You have in your hands the fruits of one who decided to "preach" what he practices—and he practices well. With growing recognition around the country as one who knows what he's talking about, Dan Dalton has been gracious to share these fruits of his labor, and we are the beneficiaries. I assure you that the confidence he instills within those he represents in the courtroom is rooted in legal substance and savvy, the very things you will find herein."
Dr. John G. Grenfell III
Senior Pastor
First United Methodist Church
St. Clair, Michigan

"In his new book, Dan Dalton has done what many others cannot: he has written a thorough, detailed account of how to handle complex religious land use cases in a manner all can understand and thus benefit from. His writing style and wealth of knowledge make this a perfect book for attorneys who already practice in this realm, those who are looking to obtain

a basic understanding of this unique area of law, or law students learning the ins and outs of this complicated area of law. Well-done!"
Robert Thomas
Woodlawn Church
Panama City Beach, Florida

"Time and money represents the Jericho Wall of church leaders today desiring to expand their ministries in an ever-increasing, unsympathetic government environment. In resolving the barriers that allow the church and state to reach agreement, attorney Dan Dalton has provided a meaningful tool for both attorney and church leader that not only educates them regarding RLUIPA laws but also minimizes their learning curve, thus reducing stress, lost time and financial resources."
The Reverend Demetrius Booker
Lead Pastor
Lighthouse Community Church
Redford Township, Michigan

"Mr. Dalton's expertise and experience helped us through a very difficult legal journey, ultimately achieving a favorable outcome. His personal interest in helping our church went above and beyond just the call of duty. His understanding of both legal and spiritual matters seems to uniquely qualify him to do what he is doing in this very important field of litigation!"
Ronnie Holmes
Senior Pastor
Church of the Open Door
Waco, Texas

"I met Dan Dalton during a dark time for our church. He was recommended as the leading RLUIPA attorney in the nation. He demonstrated wisdom, expertise, a gentle nature, a calming interrelational skill, genuineness, and a humble demeanor, while at the same time being sharp, forthright, strong, assertive, and fully respected by the other side's attorneys and judge throughout the case. Dan successfully guided us through a minefield that had been unevenly stacked against us. Dan managed the legal details, while we continued to do church. He even attended church social events to answer questions and mingle with our church family. He was loved and appreciated by our church leaders and our congregation. Never one time during a yearlong litigation process did Dan demonstrate anything other than Christ-like professionalism. Today, our church continues to grow, we are nearing the completion of our 60,000-square-foot building, I have become the president of the Chamber of Commerce, and I am gladly welcomed in our City Hall. I have become an influencer within our community and our county. How Dan managed himself, managed our case, and represented our church set the table for me and our church to be where we are today."

Tim Rhodus
Lead Pastor, Cross Church
Carlinville and Staunton, Illinois

Acknowledgments

No book is written alone. And every story is inspired by a life event. This is especially true in the work and world that I have lived in the past 20 years. I have been litigating religious land use cases and religious property disputes for nearly two decades and am extremely grateful to the clients, friends, peers, and colleagues who have encouraged me along the way. You have inspired me and made me a better person through our work together.

My gratitude begins with my family. It has been my wife, Peggy, and our daughters, Abby and Amy, along with my son-in-law, Michael, who have inspired me to develop the potential of the ideas in this book, then rethink my questions, theories, and assumptions, which has allowed me to broaden my lens beyond work. Peggy's grace, love, advice, and humor have guided me every step of the way through this book. She has believed in me, patiently listened to the stories of the cases that I have litigated and the cases that I have read, and provided the patience that I have needed, along with the much-needed comment, criticism, and encouragement along the way. I love and appreciate Peggy so very much.

As always, it has been an honor to work with members of Dalton & Tomich PLC on evaluating and litigating religious property disputes. These professionals have offered the ideal blend of challenge and support in both working on cases and in reviewing and commenting on my ideas in this book. This treatise was enhanced by the meticulous work of my colleagues Zana Tomich, Noel Sterett, Lawrence Opalewski Jr., Chris Lund, Sorin Leahu, Adel Nucho, Emily Traister, and Zak Walsh, who worked with me to pursue religious liberty for religious entities and preserve the property of local churches in religious property disputes. I especially thank my partner, Ms. Zana Tomich, who has embraced religious property as an area of the law and has encouraged the development of the religious property law dispute practice area.

To the editors and friends who offered a review of the book, thank you. Sarah Craig has been incredibly patient with me through this long slog of writing, editing, peer review, rewriting, editing, and the publication process. Thank you, Sarah, for encouraging me along the way. I am especially grateful to the patience of Robert Allen whose comments and insights have made this a better book and me a better lawyer. I cannot thank him enough for enriching every section of the book, for providing suggestions on flow, and refinement on language. I also thank the anonymous peer reviewer whose feedback further improved the manuscript.

Much of this book would not have been written without the wisdom of friends and acquaintances. I am grateful to J. Ted Gillary and Pete Wilson for their coaching, encouragement, friendship, and wisdom. I appreciate the decades of mentoring from Randall Pentiuk, the friendship of Miles Hart, who went above and beyond to amplify complexity in diversified thought when evaluating the weighty concepts discussed in this treatise.

A number of key ideas regarding the content in tone of the book benefited immeasurably from conversations with Maurilio Amorim, Jordyn Wilson, and Kristen Shoates, my friends at the A Group in Nashville, Tennessee, who were exceedingly generous in their comments and criticism, the review of ideas, and the unfailingly brilliant suggestions in improving this book. And I cannot thank Barbara Fornasiero and our friends at EA Focus enough for enriching every section of the book with suggestions on flow and refinement on language.

As I finished writing this book during the pandemic, I have come to appreciate the value of the conversations that I have had with clients who helped shape the ideas of this book, the law, and the communities in which they serve. So much of this work could not have been done without them. To the clients who retained the firm to assist you in your land use matters, thank you for allowing me to represent you. Please know that all of you inspire me every day. You have played a role in writing this book, as your story has become this book.

I truly hope that you will find this book helpful. Please send your comments to ddalton@daltontomich.com to help make the next version of this book better than this one.

Introduction

This book on religious property law covers three narrow issues of religious property disputes: (1) the local church versus a denomination over the ownership of land and real property when the church leaves the denomination, (2) the ownership of religious property within an independent church, and (3) the religious entity versus a local community engaged in a land use and zoning dispute.

This book is intentionally a general overview of the law in these three areas. The reason is that the law continues to be developed in decisions state by state, federal circuit by circuit. Federal statutory and constitutional issues have a role to play in land use and zoning disputes. And state property, trust, and corporate law typically cover the answers to most of the questions as they relate to property disputes between the local church and denominations as well as intra-church disputes. No decision seems to be final, as state courts, for example, reach opposite conclusions on the same issue of the law all the time. That is why I can provide only a general overview of the law.

My goal is to provide you a starting point for your research, discussion, and deliberation of these three significant and narrow issues.

The first part of this book covers litigating the ownership of local church property for the church that wishes to leave a denomination, but the denomination will not release the church with its property—property that the church paid for with no help from the denomination—based on an asserted "trust clause." Given the recent trend of declining membership and allegiance to mainline denominations, the issue has become front and center over time.

The second part of this book builds on the first part—namely, the role of a court when evaluating religious property disputes within an independent congregation. That is, a church, temple, mosque, or synagogue that is not affiliated with a denomination.

The third part of this book covers land use and zoning for religious entities. I have previously written two books on litigating land use and zoning cases that cover this topic in greater detail.[1] This section provides an overview to give you an idea how to identify a religious land use case on behalf of a religious entity pursuant to the Religious Land Use and Institutionalized Persons Act (RLUIPA),[2] the U.S. and state constitutions, and other federal and state statutory claims. These claims can serve as an effective tool to protect the property interests and creed of religious organizations.

I hope you find this book interesting and helpful in your search for understanding and resolving religious property disputes in the United States.

1. *Litigating Religious Land Use Cases*, 2d ed., can be found at https://www.americanbar.org/products/inv/book/252179232/.

2. 42 U.S.C. §§ 2000cc *et seq.* (2000).

Part I

Religious Property Disputes

Chapter 1

Religious Property Disputes between Local Churches and Denominations

When religious organizations divide into factions, local church property becomes the central point of contention. Religious property disputes are decided by balancing federal constitutional claims, based on the Establishment and Free Exercise Clauses of the First Amendment, and individual state trust, property, and corporate laws. This is what the U.S. Supreme Court envisioned when it created the "neutral principles of law, developed for use in all property disputes" in *Jones v. Wolf.*[1]

The neutral-principles approach is intended to be "completely secular in operation" and "rel[ies] exclusively on objective, well-established concepts of trust and property law familiar to lawyers and judges."[2] The high court opined that by applying neutral principles, substantial constitutional benefits would occur. That is, the neutral-principles approach "promises to free civil courts completely from entanglement in questions of religious doctrine, polity and practice."[3]

In the ensuing 40 years, the application of neutral principles to religious property disputes by state courts has been mixed at best. As of this writing,

1. 443 U.S. 595, 99 S. Ct. 3020, 61 L. Ed. 2d 775 (1979), quoting Presbyterian Church v. Hull Church, 393 U.S. 440, 449 (1969).
2. 443 U.S. at 603.
3. *Id.*

six states continue to apply a form of deference, and the rest of the states apply either "strict neutral principals" of law or a "hybrid" version of "neutral principals of law."[4]

This has left a considerable amount of confusion over how to approach religious property disputes. As a result, a church that is part of a denomination in one state can leave the denomination and keep its property, although other local churches in the same denomination cannot retain their property when they leave. Therefore, it is critical to know the historical background of the law involving religious property and the application of the "neutral principles of law" by each state before planning a response to disaffiliating from a denomination.

I. The Establishment Clause and Religious Property Disputes

The history of religious growth in the United States can be traced to the frequency of schism within religious organizations. This is to be expected where the Establishment Clause of the First Amendment allows individuals to worship freely and where the Free Exercise Clause absolutely protects the right to believe whatever one chooses. The result is that the United States is a country of immense religious diversity.

Many historians trace the reason that so many people left their homes in Europe in the 17th and 18th centuries to live in the American Colonies to the ability to worship freely.[5] That is, the ability to freely worship in the religious traditions of their choice. Most Western European nations required their citizens to worship in one faith alone, with nations using state funding to pay for religious property and priests.[6] Those who objected

4. Hawaii, Idaho, Nevada, New Mexico, North Dakota, Oklahoma, Oregon, Rhode Island, Vermont and Wyoming have not adopted a standard for religious property. West Virginia applies a strict deference standard. And the remaining states apply either strict neutral principles or a hybrid neutral principles of law when considering religious property disputes. See footnotes 143 to 210.

5. FRANCIS J. BREMER, THE PURITAN EXPERIMENT: NEW ENGLAND SOCIETY FROM BRADFORD TO EDWARDS (Univ. Press of New England rev. ed. 1995).

6. *Id.*

to state-sanctioned religions then left the "old world," arrived in the new world, and created local governments, ensuring that religion could not be "established" by the state and that individuals could freely worship based on their sincerely held religious beliefs.[7]

By the early 1830s, all states included Establishment Clauses within their constitutions.[8] The state founders believed that regulating religious institutions should be limited at best as religious practice serving the individual, and rejected the notion that the state should support and compel religious worship in one church or denomination.[9] In addition, laity rejected the power that clergy had over the operation of the local church, its property, and its membership.[10]

Thus, with the exception of Virginia,[11] the original colonies provided that religious institutions could not be incorporated and could not own land.[12] Property was to be owned by "trustees" elected by the local church whose role included governance.[13] When states later allowed religious societies to incorporate, the legislatures provided that the laity controlled the governance of the local church, not the clergy.[14] The goal was to place control in those who were elected by their fellow church members, thereby limiting the power of clergy and denominations to impose conditions on congregations that they had not agreed to.[15]

A. The Supreme Court's First Religious Property Dispute: Methodist and Slavery (1854)

The power of religious convictions led American religious believers in opposite directions over slavery and the religious status of those enslaved. Like

7. *Id.*

8. Sarah Barringer Gordon, *The First Disestablishment: Limits on Church Power and Property before the Civil War*, 162 U. PENN L. REV. 162, 307, 313 (2014).

9. *Id.*

10. *Id.*

11. Falwell v. Miller, 203 F. Supp. 2d 624, 632 (W.D. Va. 2002).

12. Paul G. Kauper & Stephen C. Ellis, *Religious Corporations and the Law*, 71(8) MICH. L. REV. 1499, 1505–09 (1973).

13. *Id.* at 1506.

14. *Id.*

15. *Id.*; Patty Gerstenblith, *Associational Structures of Religious Organizations*, BYU LAW REVIEW, Volume 1995, Article 5, Issue 2, Page 439 (1995).

the divisions of the local, state, and federal government over slavery, the same issues arose within denominations. The Methodist Episcopal Church, a predecessor to the United Methodist Church, addressed the issue before the U.S. Supreme Court in *Smith v. Swormstead.*[16]

By way of background, in 1844, the Methodists met in New York City for their General Conference,[17] the quadrennial annual meeting of laity and clergy delegates.[18] The central topic for discussion was slavery—namely, whether a bishop[19] should resign when he married into a family owning slaves, yet refused to release the enslaved.[20] The New England delegates to the General Conference argued that Bishop James Andrew[21] of Georgia must either give up the slaves or resign his position, as holding slaves violated the Book of Discipline.[22] The southern delegates responded that the Book of Discipline did not preclude the ownership of slaves but, rather, required clergy to release slaves "only when practicable and when liberated persons could enjoy their freedom."[23] As the bishop lived in Georgia, and Georgia did not allow slaves to be liberated, the bishop's supporters argued that slaves "could not enjoy their freedom"—and thus, he did not violate the Discipline.[24]

After two weeks of debate, the General Conference voted to order the bishop to release his slaves or be removed from his office.[25] In response,

16. 57 U.S. 288 (1854).

17. The United Methodist Church comprises "Conferences." The "General Conference" is a meeting that occurs every four years to consider matters related to inclusion or removal from the Book of Discipline, the rule book for Methodists. 2016 BOOK OF DISCIPLINE, Constitution § IV, paras. 23–27, at 32–33.

18. Minutes of the Annual Conference of the Methodist Episcopal Church, 1839–1844, at 477 (Drew University).

19. The sole function of bishops in the United Methodist Church is to provide spiritual and temporal support to local churches and pastoral staff and to enforce the rules set forth by the General Conference in the Book of Discipline. 2016 BOOK OF DISCIPLINE, at v.

20. DONALD G. MATHEWS, SLAVERY AND METHODISM: A CHAPTER IN AMERICAN MORALITY, 1780–1845, at 260–61 (1965).

21. *Id.*

22. The Book of Discipline of the United Methodist Church is the instrument that contains the laws, the plan, the polity, and the process by which its members govern themselves. 2016 BOOK OF DISCIPLINE, at v.

23. MATHEWS, *supra* note 20, at 252.

24. *Id.*

25. *Id.* at 264.

the southern delegates moved to separate from the denomination.[26] A committee formed soon after created a "plan of separation," allowing southern churches to leave and retain their property, and the delegates to the General Conference voted to approve the plan.[27] Thereafter, the southern delegates quickly organized the Methodist Episcopal Church, South. The following year, the local churches joined that entity and left the Methodist Episcopal Church with their property.[28] The northern delegates quickly heard from the members of their churches, who were outraged that the local southern churches could leave and retain their property.[29] Four years later, the Methodist Episcopal Church delegates met at their next General Conference and voted to abrogate the 1844 Plan of Separation, declaring all provisions null and void.[30]

Litigation soon followed. The issue was control of property—namely, the ownership of the Methodist publishing houses, which were, at the time, the largest publishing houses in the world.[31] To determine ownership, two cases were filed, one in New York City and the other in Cincinnati—the home of two publishing houses.[32]

The Southern Methodist denomination argued that anything that was not forbidden by state law or the internal Methodist constitution was permitted and could be left for the General Conference to determine.[33] The Northern Methodist denomination argued that both publishing houses were held "in trust" for the denomination, and as it was the survivor denomination, the publishing houses belonged to it.[34]

After a trial on the merits, a federal court in New York found for the southern church, concluding that the delegates to the 1844 General Conference had the authority to allow local churches to leave the denomination and keep their property and properly voted on the same through its rules

26. Minutes of the Annual Conference, *supra* note 18, at 477–83.
27. *Id.*
28. *Id.*
29. Mathews, *supra* note 20, at 264.
30. *Id.* at 270.
31. *Id.* at 272.
32. Bascom v. Lane, 2 F. Cas. 994 (C.C.D.N.Y. 1851) (No. 1089); Smith v. Swormstedt, 22 F. Cas. 663 (C.C.D. Ohio 1852); *rev'd*, 57 U.S. 288 (1854).
33. Smith v. Swormstedt, 22 F. Cas. 663 (C.C.D. Ohio 1852); *rev'd*, 57 U.S. 288 (1854).
34. *Id.*

with the Book of Discipline.[35] The federal court in Ohio, however, reached the opposite conclusion and ruled that the northern church owned the publishing houses because the delegates to the General Conference did not have the authority under the Methodist Constitution to release property to local churches.[36]

This set up the appeal to the U.S. Supreme Court, which reversed the trial court's decision.[37] In reaching its decision in favor of the Methodist Episcopal Church, South,[38] the Supreme Court focused on the powers of the General Conference, the highest authority in Methodism, which properly and voluntarily voted to divide itself.[39] The Court relied on the language of the Book of Discipline, which allowed the General Conference to vote to disaffiliate local churches.[40]

B. The Supreme Court Adopts "Deference" in Religious Property Disputes (1871)

Twenty years later, in the case of *Watson v. Jones*, the Supreme Court affirmed deference to denominational hierarchy in the context of a religious property dispute involving a local church leaving a denomination.[41] The *Watson* case arose from a schism within a local Presbyterian Church in Kentucky where the congregation split into two—one side opposing slavery and one condoning its practice.[42] The issue was which part of the local church could retain the property and lead the congregation: the one loyal to the denomination or the majority group within the church that opposed slavery.[43]

35. Bascom v. Lane, 2 F. Cas. 994 (C.C.D.N.Y. 1851) (No. 1089).
36. Smith v. Swormstedt, 22 F. Cas. 663 (C.C.D. Ohio 1852), *rev'd*, 57 U.S. 288 (1854).
37. Smith v. Swormstedt, 57 U.S. 288 (1854).
38. The United Methodist Church is a "connectional" denomination—a series of conferences (it is a form of conciliarism), each dealing with different concerns. 2018 Methodist Judicial Council Decision No. 1366, at 11. This is the opposite of a hierarchal form of governance. The Uniform Court of Appeals recognized the same in *Freedom Church v. Cent. Dist. Conf. of the Evangelical Free Church of America*, 2007 Uniform App. LEXIS 343, at *10, where it concluded that the EFCA is an association of "autonomous but interdependent congregations of like faith."
39. *Id.* at 304–05.
40. *Id.* at 308–09.
41. 80 U.S. (13 Wall.) 679, 20 L. Ed. 666 (1871).
42. 80 U.S. at 717.
43. *Id.* at 717–18.

In evaluating this religious property dispute between the denomination and a local congregation, the Supreme Court noted that for congregational—that is, independent, stand-alone—churches undergoing a schism into "distinct and conflicting bodies, the rights of such bodies to the use of the property must be determined by the ordinary principles which govern voluntary associations," meaning state law.[44] In such circumstances, if no trust was previously imposed upon the property when purchased or given, the court would not imply one; the majority would keep the property; and "[t]he minority, in choosing to separate themselves into a distinct body and refusing to recognize the authority of the governing body, can claim no rights in the property from the fact that they had once been members of the church or congregation."[45]

But the Supreme Court treated a local church's membership in a hierarchical church—part of a large and general organization of some religious denomination that is "more or less intimately connected by religious views and ecclesiastical government"—differently.[46] The court acknowledged that the property's legal documents did not indicate its disposition and affirmed that the property was purchased for the use of a religious congregation, "and so long as any existing religious congregation can be ascertained to be that congregation or its regular and legitimate successor, it is entitled to the use of the property."[47]

Instead of looking to the rules that govern corporate entities to determine identity or succession, the *Watson* Court stated that in cases involving a hierarchical church,[48] "We are bound to look at the fact that the local congregation is itself but a member of a much larger and more important religious organization and is under its government and control and is bound by its orders and judgments" with regard to "questions of discipline; or of

44. *Id.* at 724–25.

45. *Id.* at 725.

46. *Id.* at 726.

47. *Id.*

48. The court did not, and has never, defined what a "hierarchal" church is. Rather, it identified the "Protestant Episcopal" church as one of the "large and influential bodies [with] . . . a body of constitutional and ecclesiastical law of its own, to be found in [its] written organic laws, [its] books of discipline, in [its] collections of precedents, in [its] usage and customs, which as to each constitute a system of ecclesiastical law and religious faith that tasks the ablest minds to become familiar with." *Watson*, 80 U.S. at 729.

faith; or ecclesiastical rule, custom or law" that have been decided by the highest of the hierarchical church's judicatories, and to accept those decisions as final and binding "in all cases of ecclesiastical cognizance."[49] Thus, in resolving the matter in favor of the local faction that had remained with the national, hierarchical church, the Court concluded,

> Whatever may have been the case before the Kentucky court, the appellants in the case presented to us have separated themselves wholly from the church organization to which they belonged when this controversy commenced. They now deny its authority, denounce its action and refuse to abide by its judgments. They have first erected themselves into a new organization and have since joined themselves to another totally different, if not hostile, to the one to which they belonged when the difficulty first began.[50]

C. The Supreme Court Introduces "Neutral Principles" (1969)

Nearly a century later, the Supreme Court introduced the concept of using "neutral principles of state law" when evaluating all religious property disputes in *Presbyterian Church v. Mary Elizabeth Blue Hull Memorial Presbyterian Church*.[51] In *Blue Hull*, the membership of two local churches, under the leadership of their ministers and most of their ruling elders, voted to withdraw and reconstitute themselves as autonomous organizations after they concluded that some of the national church's actions and pronouncements violated the organization's constitution and departed from the doctrine and practice that were in force at the time they affiliated.[52] The state courts considered the implied trust theory and integrated a departure-from-doctrine element that allowed a jury to conclude that the local churches could retain their property.[53]

---

49. *Id.* at 726–27, 729.
50. *Id.* at 734.
51. 393 U.S. 40, 89 S. Ct. 601, 21 L. Ed. 2d 658 (1969).
52. *Id.* at 42–43.
53. *Id.* at 443–44, 449–50.

After the state court appeals were exhausted, the U.S. Supreme Court granted certiorari and acknowledged that although the First Amendment severely circumscribes the role that civil courts may play in resolving church property disputes, not all such disputes are precluded from the civil courts' consideration.[54] Specifically, the Supreme Court held that "there are neutral principles of law, developed for use in all property disputes, which can be applied without 'establishing' churches to which property is awarded."[55] But to do this, states, religious organizations, and individuals must structure relationships involving church property so as not to require the civil courts to resolve ecclesiastical questions.[56]

Accordingly, the Court reversed the decision of the state court as violating the First Amendment because the departure-from-doctrine element required the state court to determine matters at the very core of a religion—whether the general church's challenged actions departed substantially from prior doctrine pursuant to the court's interpretation of the doctrine's meaning and then, after assessing the relative significance to the religion of the tenets from which departure was found, whether the issue on which the general church departed "holds a place of such importance in the traditional theology as to require that the trust be terminated."[57] The Court remanded the case for further proceedings.[58]

On remand, the Georgia state court held that, in light of the Supreme Court's pronouncement on the departure-from-doctrine element, the implied-trust theory itself was no longer valid.[59] Accordingly, because no trust was created for the general church in the property's deed or was required by the general church's constitution, and because the general church had put no funds into the property, legal title to the property remained with the local churches.[60]

54. *Id.* at 447, 449.
55. *Id.* at 449.
56. *Id.*
57. *Id.* at 449–50.
58. *Id.* at 452.
59. Presbyterian Church in U.S. v. E. Heights Presbyterian Church, 225 Ga. 259, 167 S.E.2d 658, 659 (1969), *cert. denied*, 396 U.S. 1041, 90 S. Ct. 680, 24 L. Ed. 2d 685 (1970).
60. 167 S.E.2d 658 at 659–60.

D. The Supreme Court Adopts "Neutral Principles" for All Religious Property Disputes (1979)

A decade after *Blue Hull*, the Supreme Court took up the issue of religious property disputes in a case involving the ownership of church property after a schism in a local church affiliated with a hierarchical church organization.[61] In *Jones v. Wolf*, the Court acknowledged that the First Amendment "prohibits civil courts from resolving church property disputes on the basis of religious doctrine or practice."[62] It held that the neutral-principles approach was consistent with the federal Constitution when merely looking to the language of the deeds, the terms of the local church charters, state statutes, and the provisions of the constitution of the general church concerning the ownership and control of church property.[63]

The high Court approved of this methodology because before any dispute arises, a religious group could determine its priorities as to the disposition of church property and enshrine those priorities under the applicable civil law, making it easy both on themselves and the court system.[64] The Court cautioned, however, that in reviewing church documents, if the interpretation of instruments of ownership would require a civil court to resolve a religious controversy, then the court would have to defer to the resolution of the doctrinal issue by the authoritative ecclesiastical body.[65]

An oft-cited excerpt of *Jones v. Wolf* purportedly solidifying the legitimacy of denominational trust provisions reads as follows:

> At any time before the dispute erupts, the parties can ensure, if they so desire, that the faction loyal to the hierarchical church will retain the church property. They can modify the deeds or the corporate charter to include a right of reversion or trust in favor of the general church. Alternatively, the constitution of the general church can be made to recite an express trust in favor of the denominational church. The burden involved in taking such steps will be minimal. And the civil

61. Jones v. Wolf, 443 U.S. 595, 99 S. Ct. 3020, 61 L. Ed. 2d 775 (1979).
62. *Id.* at 602.
63. *Id.* at 602–03.
64. *Id.* at 603–04, 606.
65. *Id.* at 604.

courts will be bound to give effect to the result indicated by the parties, provided it is embodied in some legally cognizable form.[66]

A facial reading may suggest that a denomination may simply adopt an express trust and that courts will be bound to enforce that trust "provided it is embodied in some legally cognizable form."[67] This is not the case. The opinion does not state that one party—the denomination—can make such modification. To the contrary, it requires plural participation, meaning the *parties*—denomination and local congregation—have to have reached a mutually understood agreement.

A question most courts will ask in these cases, therefore, is whether the local congregation consented to the trust. Given that many churches have little opportunity to address terms of church property management, this may not be as simple a question as the denomination hopes. That being said, some courts may conclude that general consent to a denominational constitution equals consent to partake in a trust relationship. But it is important to remember that one normally cannot forfeit a property right without giving consent.

In addressing which faction was entitled to control local church property, the Supreme Court in *Jones* identified as a fact question for remand whether Georgia had adopted a presumptive rule of majority representation with regard to a voluntary religious association's being represented by the majority of its members, or whether the corporate charter or constitution of the general church set out how the identity of the local church was to be established if not by majority rule.[68] The *Jones* Court observed that if state law provided for the identity of the church to be determined according to the general hierarchical church's "laws and regulations," then the First Amendment would require the civil courts to give deference to the church's determination of the local church's identity.[69] The implicit corollary of this statement would be that if state law did not provide for the church's identity to be determined by the general hierarchical church's laws

66. Jones v. Wolf, 443 U.S. 595, 606, 99 S. Ct. 3020, 61 L. Ed. 2d 775 (1979).
67. *Id.*
68. *Id.* at 607–08.
69. *Id.* at 609.

and regulations, then the court would need to examine everything else to identify the property's owners.

Jones, therefore, instructs state courts to perform a review related to nonreligious doctrine, within the context of that state's law, of the language of the deeds and the provisions dealing with ownership and control of property contained within the local and general churches' governing documents—that is, the plain language to ascertain the parties' intent. But if we attempt to divine ownership from the church's ritual and liturgy of worship or the tenets of its faith or if interpreting the parties' documents would require us to resolve a faith-based controversy, then we veer into constitutionally prohibited territory.

II. The State Law Used for Neutral Principles

While many similarities exist in trust law amongst the states, it is important to remember that each state, whether through jurisprudence or statutory instruction, creates its own standards for trust law. A particular state's stance on the creation and revocability of express and implied trusts is one of the most important things to consider for the local church. In most states, trusts are in fact revocable. In others, they may not be. Most commonly, only the settlor will be able to modify or revoke an extant trust. But, in any event, rules and exceptions tend to exist and must be analyzed closely for alignment with your situation.

Trusts are essentially a conditional transfer of property. Like contracts, trusts are dependent on mutual consent.[70] In trust law, the one creating a trust is referred to as the settlor. The settlor transfers property to a trustee under certain agreed conditions, creating a fiduciary duty for the trustee. This means that the trustee has a responsibility to abide by the terms of the trust in fulfilling the prescribed duties to specified beneficiaries.

It is important to keep in mind that the express trust is not the only obstacle. Courts have refused to recognize the trust clause as binding and

70. An exception is the remedial "constructive" trust. John H. Langbein, *The Contractarian Basis of the Law of Trusts*, 105 Yale L.J. 625, 650 (1995).

have still gone on to find that local church property was held in trust in favor of the denomination on related but different grounds. They do so under an "implied trust" doctrine that comes in two forms: constructive and resulting. Escaping a court finding of implied trust can be difficult. In some states—Indiana, for example—mere affiliation within a hierarchical church can function as a "foundation" of an implied trust.[71] Courts may nonetheless find an implied trust in favor of either the denomination or the local congregation.[72] But a local congregation should have an understanding of what courts are looking for under these doctrines.

With a conceptual understanding of trusts, a careful reading of the Supreme Court's *Jones* decision becomes all the more important. Courts will then consider a variety of factors to determine which party is the equitable owner. Accordingly, local churches should closely scrutinize their ties to the denomination to show that the general church has an unreasonable claim to the local property.

Resulting trusts are a bit more specific. They focus on the transaction that created the property interest. In essence, a resulting trust posits that property belongs first to those that paid for it.[73] A denomination that financially supported a congregation's land use may successfully establish a resulting trust in its favor, entitling it to said property. By contrast, a congregation that operated through financial independence may be able to fend off a denomination's resulting trust claim. Congregations should have a working understanding of how these principles play out in litigated disputes.

A. State Trust Law

1. A Trust Must Be Created in a "Legally Cognizable Form"

Quoting the decision of the Supreme Court in *Jones v. Wolf*,[74] the court said a trust may arise in favor of a hierarchical religious organization through a provision in the organization's governing documents, "provided it is embodied in some legally cognizable form."[75] As Justice Souter recently explained,

71. Emberry Cmty. Church v. Bloomington Dist., 482 N.E.2d 288, 293 (Ind. Ct. App. 1985).

72. Notes, *Judicial Intervention in Disputes over the Use of Church Property*, 75 HARV. L. REV. 1142 (1962).

73. 76 AM. JUR. 2D *Trusts* § 166 (1992).

74. 443 U.S. 595, 606 (1979).

75. *Id.*

"legally cognizable" means "including provisions in deeds and corporate charters spelling out reversionary rights or express trust benefits"—"options available to religious organizations as readily as to their secular counterparts."[76] "[T]hese common instruments for establishing ownership and control . . . most readily enable a court to apply the required neutral principles in evaluating disputed property claims," for such "contractual arrangements between the contending parties deserve the same preference as secular grounds for judgment."[77] The neutral-principles approach thus minimizes "judicial intrusion" into the actions of "religious bodies."[78]

Therefore, in accordance with long-standing principles of trust law as reflected in abundant case law, the Restatement of Trusts, the leading treatises and the Uniform Trust Code that has been adopted by a majority of the states, the starting point in the analysis is to determine if the purported trust was created in a "legally cognizable form." That is, has the denomination established an express trust under state law. Most states have adopted a form of the Uniform Trust Code,[79] which sets forth the following elements needed to create an express trust:

A. A trust is created only if:[80]

The settlor has capacity to create a trust.

The settlor indicates an intention to create the trust.

The trust has a definite beneficiary or is:

1. A charitable trust
2. A trust for the care of an animal, as provided in Section 408, or
3. A trust for a noncharitable purpose, as provided in Section 409

The trustee has duties to perform and . . .

---

76. Congregation Jeshuat Israel, 866 F.3d at 58 (emphasis added).

77. *Id.*

78. *Id.*

79. Reference to the Uniform Trust Code (U.T.C.) in this book is to the 2010 version drafted by the National Conference of Commissioners on Uniform State Laws and by it Approved and Recommended for enactment in all states at its annual conference meeting July 28 through Aug. 4, 2000. The hyperlink for the UTC and a chart setting forth the states and dates of adoption is found at http://bit.ly/3rQBRhI.

80. U.T.C. § 402.

The same person is not the sole trustee and sole beneficiary

B. A beneficiary is definite if the beneficiary can be ascertained now or in the future, subject to any applicable rule against perpetuities.

C. The power of a trustee to select a beneficiary from an indefinite class is valid. If the power is not exercised within a reasonable time, the power fails and the property subject to the power passes to the people who would have taken the property had the power not been conferred.

From this, several core principles should be considered when determining whether an express trust is present. First, "[i]n order to constitute an express trust, there must be either explicit language to that effect or circumstances which show with reasonable certainty that a trust was intended to be created."[81] In other words, no trust exists unless the purported settlor manifests an intention to create the purported trust.[82] In most states, the intent of a settlor is determined by examining the "four corners of the trust document."[83] To that end, "[t]he declaration must be reasonably certain in its material terms. If the language is so vague, indefinite, or equivocal that any one of the elements is left in uncertainty, the trust must fail."[84]

Next, in most states, in order for an express trust to be enforceable, it must be in writing and signed by the settlor,[85] contain a definite description of the property to be conveyed, and must fund the trust.[86] An express trust in land typically cannot be created or proved by a "parol evidence."[87] So, while a person can establish a trust for his or her own benefit, he or she must own the property that is transferred in order to create the trust.[88]

81. Woods v. Stull, 182 Va. 888, 902; 30 S.E.2d 675 (1944).

82. U.T.C. § 402(A)(2); Mills v. Gray, 147 Tex. 33, 210 S.W.2d 985, 987 (1948).

83. Shriner's Hosp. for Crippled Children of Tex. v. Stahl, 610 S.W. 2d 147, 151 (Tex. 1980).

84. *Id.*

85. Mo. Rev. Stat. Ann. § 456.4-407.

86. Edgar v. Fitzpatrick, 377 S.W.2d 314, 318 (Mo. banc 1964). The *Edgar* court found that the grantor did not make a later manifestation of intent to create a trust after he acquired more property, and thus it could not determine what was the property of the trust.

87. Woodard v. Cohron, 137 S.W.2d 497, 498 (1940).

88. Wise v. Haynes, 103 S.W.2d 477, 483 (Tex. Civ. App. 1937).

Further, a beneficiary cannot wish a trust into existence, divesting an unwitting settlor of the settlor's property,[89] and cannot unilaterally name itself as a beneficiary of a trust involving another entity's property.[90] The declarations of a beneficiary are not competent to establish a trust.[91] When examining a purported trust, all terms of the trust must be harmonized to properly give effect to all parts.[92] And, if possible, a court will construe the trust to give effect to all provisions so that no provision is rendered meaningless.[93] If the language of a trust is clear and expresses the intent of the settlor, it is unnecessary to construe the instrument, as it speaks to itself.[94] If, on the other hand, the instrument is uncertain or "reasonably susceptible to more than one meaning," the instrument is ambiguous.[95]

In sum, to prove the existence of an express trust, a party must establish the settlor's capacity to create a trust, an intent to create a trust, a definite beneficiary (unless charitable), the existence of duties for the trustee to perform, and that the trustee is not the sole beneficiary.

An implied trust comes in two forms: resulting and constructive. A resulting trust "arises from a transfer of property under circumstances showing that the transferee was not intended to take the beneficial interest."[96] Resulting trusts have been termed "intention-enforcing" trusts, to distinguish them from the other type of implied trust, the constructive or "fraud-rectifying" trust.[97] While "the resulting trust carries out the inferred intent of the parties, the constructive trust defeats or prevents the wrongful act of one of them."[98] In addition, "[a] resulting trust is founded upon presumption or inference that the person in whom the title vests intends to hold it

89. Jewett v. Capital Nat'l Bank, 618 S.W.2d 109, 112 (Tex. Civ. App. 1981); Hubbard v. Shankle, 138 S.W.3d 474, 484 (Tex. App. 2004).
90. Best Inv. Co. v. Hernandez, 479 S.W.2d 759, 763 (1972).
91. Wise v. Haynes, 103 S.W.2d 477, 483 (Tex. Civ. App. 1937).
92. Hutton v. Methodist Home, 615 S.W.2d 289, 292 (Tex. Civ. App. 1981).
93. Myrick v. Moody, 802 S.W.2d 735, 738 (Tex. App. 1990).
94. *Hurly*, 98 S.W.2d at 310.
95. *Myrick*, 802 S.W.2d at 738.
96. *In re* Estate of Nichols, 856 S.W.2d 397, 401 (Tenn. 1993); Shiflet v. May, 49 Va. Cir. 542, 547 (Cir. Ct. 1998).
97. 856 S.W.2d at 401.
98. *Id.*

for the benefit of the cestui; and intention—whether presumed, implied or supposed by the law—is always an element of resulting trust."[99]

Resulting trusts in land are of two general types: (1) those where a purchase has been made and the legal estate is conveyed or transferred to one party, but the purchase price is paid by another party; and (2) those where there is a gift by deed or will to a donee or grantee without pecuniary consideration coming from the grantee, but the intention appears, from the instrument itself, that the legal and beneficial estates are to be separated and that the grantee or donee is either to enjoy no beneficial interest or only a part of it.[100] Courts may impose a resulting trust as an equitable remedy to prevent unjust enrichment.

A constructive trust, on the other hand, is an equitable remedy created by operation of law to prevent a fraud or injustice.[101] In general, courts have imposed constructive trusts in four types of cases:

- Where a person procures the legal title to property in violation of some duty, express or implied, to the true owner.
- Where the title to property is obtained by fraud, duress, or other inequitable means.
- Where a person makes use of some relation of influence or confidence to obtain the legal title upon more advantageous terms than could otherwise have been obtained.
- Where a person acquires property with notice that another is entitled to its benefits.[102]

Technically, constructive trusts are not trusts at all but equitable devices employed by courts of equity. They arise by operation of law or, more accurately, by construction of the court, regardless and independent of any actual or presumed intention of the parties to create a trust. The constructive trust may be defined as the device used by chancery to compel one

99. *Id.* at 547.
100. Parker v. Blakeley, 93 S.W.2d 981, 988 (Mo. 1936).
101. Bank of Hampton Roads v. Powell, 292 Va. 10, 15; 785 S.E.2d 788 (2016).
102. Brown v. Brown, 152 S.W.3d 911, 916–19 (Mo. App. W. Dist. 2005) (internal citations and quotations omitted); Roach v. Renfro, 989 S.W.2d 335, 341 (Tenn. Ct. App. 1998).

who unfairly holds a property interest to convey that interest to another to whom it justly belongs.

In order to be entitled to the benefit of a constructive trust, a claimant's interest must be distinctly traced into the fund or other property that is to be made the subject of the trust.[103] In addition, the remedy of a constructive trust is generally available when legal remedies, such as monetary damages, would be insufficient.[104] Further, "a constructive trust may only be imposed against one who—by fraud, actual or constructive; by duress or abuse of confidence; by commission of wrong; or by any form of unconscionable conduct, artifice, concealment or questionable means—has obtained an interest in property which he ought not in equity or in good conscience retain."[105]

2. Revocation of Trust

The Uniform Trust Code provides that unless the terms of a trust expressly provide that the trust is irrevocable, the settlor may revoke or amend the trust.[106] Likewise, the settlor may revoke or amend a revocable trust:

- By substantial compliance with a method provided in the terms of the trust or . . .
- If the terms of the trust do not provide a method or the method provided in the terms is not expressly made exclusive by a later will or codicil that expressly refers to the trust or specifically devises property that would otherwise have passed according to the terms of the trust, or and other method manifesting clear and convincing evidence of the settlor's intent.[107]

The aforementioned statutory provisions are unambiguous.

Thus, if the local church has not signed a trust instrument declaring an irrevocable trust in favor of a denomination, these provisions of the U.T.C.

103. 152 S.W.3d at 916.
104. *Id.*
105. Livesay v. Keaton, 611 S.W.2d 581, 584 (Tenn. App. 1980).
106. U.T.C. § 602 (a).
107. *Id.* § 602 (c).

conclusively negate any claim by a denomination to an irrevocable and enforceable beneficial interest in the church's property.

The fact pattern of *Church of the Brethren v. Roann Church of the Brethren Inc.*[108] illustrates this point. The denomination, established in 1708, and the congregation, formed in Roann, Indiana, in 1835, affiliated in 1939 when the congregation began sending delegates to the denomination's annual conference.[109] The denomination recorded and published denomination polity in its Organization and Polity Manual, which could be revised yearly at the annual conference. The denomination, however, never bound local congregations to the Polity Manual, and it did not impose discipline for any given congregation's disharmony with denominational polity.[110] In 1945, the denomination issued a report that called for the use of restrictive covenants in individual congregations' deeds. And, in 1947, the denomination approved the placement of a requirement that all local churches include a denominational trust clause in its deeds as set forth in the denomination's Organization and Polity Manual.[111] Soon after, the denomination added the same requirement, noting that local churches needed to add the provision in their congregational constitutions.[112]

The Roann Church congregation acquired three parcels of land with money from member donations and an interest-bearing loan from the denomination, which the congregation later repaid in full, and did not include the trust clause language in its deeds. It also established several bank accounts at issue here, which were titled in the congregation's name. On the face of these assets, the denomination had no interest in the congregation's property, real or personal. However, in 2002, the local church amended its constitution to provide a method to amend its constitution and bylaws and included a modified version of the trust clause language but left the trust clause out of the deeds.[113]

Soon after, a dispute arose between the local church and the denomination. In 2010, the local church amended its bylaws and deleted the

108. 20 N.E.3d 906 (2014).
109. *Id.* at 907.
110. *Id.*
111. *Id.*
112. *Id.* at 908.
113. *Id.*

property ownership language in favor of the denomination's. Two years later, the membership voted to leave the denomination. In response to the local church's leaving the denomination, its leaders recorded an Affidavit of Transfer of Land with the Wabash County clerk to transfer title of the congregation's property to the denomination, then filed a complaint for declaratory and injunctive relief that asked the court to declare that the 2002 constitution created in its favor a trust—which, under then-existing Indiana law, was irrevocable. Moreover, it sought to enjoin the congregation's further use of the property. The congregation counterclaimed for slander of title because of the cloud on title that the affidavit created.[114]

The matter proceeded to trial, wherein the court found that the denomination failed to establish that the property of the local church was held in an express or implied trust for the denomination.[115] On appeal, the denomination argued that an express trust was created by the local church in 2002 when it amended its constitution to include a reference to the denomination. The Court of Appeals disagreed, applying neutral principles of law to the religious property dispute and concluding that nothing in the constitution "evinces a trust relationship."[116] Instead, the court held, "The relationship between the congregation and the denomination involved mutual benefits, none of which were specific to the Congregation's land. And these cited benefits are no different from those reciprocally flowing in a standard denomination-congregation relationship."[117] In other words, "the relevant language" does not implicate a fiduciary relationship and, therefore, "is not a clear and unequivocal statement of [the congregation's] intent to create a[n] [express] trust."[118]

More important, the court held that "even if the evidence showed that the congregation intended to create a trust in its 2002 constitution, that document expressly reserved an unqualified right to amend its provisions, which was a 'power to modify' equivalent to a 'power of revocation' with respect to any purported trust. . . . Consequently, we also hold that the

114. *Id.* at 909.
115. *Id.* at 910.
116. *Id.* at 912.
117. *Id.*
118. *Id.*

2010 constitution revoked the purported 2002 trust."[119] Accordingly, a local church can take steps to revoke a trust using state trust law guidelines.

Thus, in rejecting the express argument and later the implied trust argument, the court concluded that even if an express trust existed, a local church could revoke it—and in this case did revoke it—through its 2010 amendment to its constitution.

3. Reformation of Trust for Mistake

The Uniform Trust Code provides that a settlor can modify or terminate an express trust.[120] And a court may reform the terms of a trust, even if unambiguous, to conform the terms to the settlor's intention if it is proved by clear and convincing evidence that both the settlor's intent and the terms of the trust were affected by a mistake of fact or law, whether in expression or inducement.[121] Thus, a local church could petition a court to reform the trust to reflect the obvious intent of the local church for the property at issue to stay with the church's congregation and not pass to the denomination. The church would need to show, through sworn testimony by many people of faith, that at no time did the local church ever actually intend for any of the church's property to pass to the denomination in the event of the church's termination of its affiliation with the denomination.

The cornerstone of the interpretation of trusts is for a Court to determine, ". . . the meaning of a donative document is the donor's intention."[122] Thus, in the context of a religious property dispute with a denomination, if a local church never intended to create an enforceable, irrevocable trust or a beneficial interest by which the conference could demand all of the property of the church (or the fair market value of that property) in the event that the local church left the denomination, a court would properly reject a claim by a denomination for local property it never paid for, maintained, constructed, or created. Under the Uniform Trust Code, the terms of the trust may be reformed "to conform the terms to the settlor's intention if

119. *Id.* at 913.
120. U.T.C. § 415.
121. *Id.*
122. *See* Restatement (Third) of Property: Wills and Other Donative Transfers § 10.1 (2003).

it is proved through clear and convincing evidence that both the settlor's intent and the terms of the trust were affected by a mistake of fact or law, whether in expression or inducement."[123]

4. The Statute of Frauds Applied to Trust

Under most state laws,[124] a trust is only enforceable when it is evidenced by a written document, signed by the trustee conveying trust property.[125] A conveyance involving land must be in writing and signed by the owner.[126] As applied to a trust of land, the writing must also "manifest the trust intention and . . . reasonably identify the trust property, the beneficiaries and the purpose of the trust."[127] In this case, no writing signed by the Church meets these requirements. A trust in real property is enforceable only if written evidence exists of the trust's terms bearing the signature of the settlor or the settlor's authorized agent.[128] A trust in real property is enforceable only if written evidence exists of the trust's terms bearing the signature of the settlor or the settlor's authorized agent.[129]

5. Rule against Perpetuities Applied to Trust

One additional issue to consider, with respect to a denominational trust is the Rule Against Perpetuities. Under the Uniform Statutory Rule Against Perpetuities, a trust of unlimited duration that could give rise to a remote vesting of an interest in a denomination that is beyond the period allowed would violate the individual states' Rule Against Perpetuities.[130] As each state

123. U.T.C. § 415.

124. The requirement of a trust in writing is not universally accepted by all states. Virginia, for example, does not require a trust to be in writing. *See* VA. CODE ANN. § 64.2-725, "[e]xcept as required by a statute other than this chapter, a trust need not be evidenced by a trust instrument, but the creation of an oral trust and its terms may be established only by clear and convincing evidence." Gibbens v. Hardin, 239 Va. 425, 431; 389 S.E.2d 478 (1990).

125. RESTATEMENT (THIRD) OF TRUSTS § 22(1) (2003).

126. *Id.*

127. *Id.*

128. *See* TEX. PROP. CODE ANN. § 112.004; *see also* TEX. PROP. CODE ANN. § 111.003 (stating that trust statutes do not govern resulting, constructive, or business trusts or security instruments).

129. TEX. PROP. CODE ANN. § 112.004.

130. The Uniform Statutory Rule Against Perpetuities invalidates interest in properties that are intended to belong to somebody else at a future time but for which the actual determination of ownership cannot or will not be accomplished within a specific period of time.

has adopted its own Rule Against Perpetuities, it is important to examine the rule in light of state trust law requirements.

Under Virginia common law, for example, the rule against perpetuities provides that "an executory interest in property is void for remoteness if, at its creation, there exists a possibility, however remote or uncertain, that the interest will not vest within the period fixed by the rule."[131] Usually, "the period fixed by the rule is a life or lives in being plus 21 years and 10 months."[132] The Rule Against Perpetuities is a rule adopted in furtherance of public policy to prevent excessive restraints or limitations upon the alienation of an estate.[133] It is not a rule of construction "but a peremptory command of law," and its object is to defeat intention.[134] To remedy a perpetuities violation, the court would take evidence on what manner of permissible disposition would most closely approximate the church's intent.[135] In most circumstances, the facts demonstrate that a local church did not intend a beneficial interest in the denomination that would persist even if the local church withdrew from the denomination.[136]

B. State Corporate Law

A court must also consider a state's nonprofit or corporation law, along with its trust law, within the neutral-principles framework. Religious organizations are typically formed as nonprofit entities organized under state law. And, in most states, a religious corporation is a nonprofit, and a nonprofit may be the beneficiary of a trust.[137]

With the exception of West Virginia, each state has its own rules and regulations concerning incorporation and governance, all of which must be reviewed in light of the facts and circumstances of a case. For nonprofit

The Uniform Rule improves upon the common-law rule against perpetuities by including a "wait and see" provision that prevents automatic invalidation of property transfers. To learn more about the Uniform Statutory Rule Against Perpetuities and the states that have adopted it, see http://bit.ly/3mJheQr.

131. JVI Builders Inc. v. First Citizens Corp., 1995 Va. Cir. LEXIS 1401, at *16 (Cir. Ct. Dec. 12, 1995).

132. *Id.*

133. Hoover v. Jolley, 45 Va. Cir. 309, 315 (Cir. Ct. 1998).

134. *Id.*

135. *See* http://bit.ly/3mJheQr.

136. *Id.*

137. *See, e.g.*, Tex. Rev. Code § 252.015.

corporations, some states have adopted the Revised Model Nonprofit Corporation Act (MNCA) and the Revised Uniform Unincorporated Nonprofit Association Act (RUUNAA).

The two acts vary in the type of organizations they serve. The MNCA covers nonprofit corporations and the RUUNAA covers unincorporated nonprofit associations. The MNCA is legislation drafted by the Nonprofit Organizations Committee of the Business Law Section of the American Bar Association to provide legal guidelines for nonprofit corporations. The purpose of the legislation is to propose a framework for state law guidelines. Since the MNCA comes out of the Business Law Section, it's no surprise that it focuses on corporate law relevant to nonprofit corporations. As laws governing corporations change, the MNCA is revised. States vary in whether these changes are adopted as they occur.

To date, 37 states have adopted a version of the MNCA, including eight that have adopted the law in its entirety.[138] States that haven't adopted the MNCA follow the for-profit business law for their state. Often, the laws governing corporations in these states lack the nuance that protects nonprofits in states that have adopted the MNCA. A handful of states have rejected the MNCA and drafted their own.

A nonprofit organization is a group organized for purposes other than generating profit and in which no part of the organization's income is distributed to its members, directors, or officers.[139] Nonprofit organizations must be designated as nonprofit when created and may only pursue purposes permitted by statutes for nonprofit organizations.[140]

Nonprofit organizations include churches, public schools, public charities, public clinics and hospitals, political organizations, legal-aid societies, volunteer service organizations, labor unions, professional associations, research institutes, museums, and some governmental agencies. For federal tax purposes, an organization is exempt from taxation if it is organized and operated exclusively for religious, charitable, scientific, public safety, literary, or educational purposes; prevention of cruelty to children or animals;

---

138. *See* https://bit.ly/37OpuL4.
139. *Id.*
140. *Id.*

and/or to develop national or international sports.[141] Social Security tax is also currently optional, although 80 percent of the organizations elect to participate.[142]

III. The Application of Neutral Principles to Religious Property Cases

The case law continues to evolve with respect to how state courts apply neutral principles of law to religious property disputes. As of March 2021, a review of state law cases affirms that nine states have not addressed how religious property disputes are to be addressed, six states continue to apply a form of deference, and the rest of the states apply either "strict neutral principles" of law or a "hybrid" version of "neutral principles of law" that defers to church canons or denominational constitutions for certain religious organizations. The trend appears to be state courts heading toward the "strict neutral principles of law" approach. Only time will tell.

A. Strict Neutral Principles States[143]

Under the strict neutral-principles approach, courts resolve church property disputes by applying ordinary principles of property, trust, or contract law to civil legal documents, such as deeds, trust agreements, or contracts. Internal church rules are not enforced by the court unless they have been legally incorporated through a trust or otherwise. In other words, church property disputes are resolved just like property disputes within other voluntary

141. *Id.*

142. *Id.*

143. The following state courts apply "strict neutral principles" of law when evaluating the enforcement of denominational trust clauses. Haney's Chapel United Methodist Church v. The United Methodist Church, et. al., 716 So. 2d 1156, 1160 (Ala. 1998); Nelson v. Brewer, 238 N.E.3d 220 (Ill. 2019); The Episcopal Diocese of Fort Worth v. The Episcopal Church, 602 S.W.3d 417 (Tex. 2020); Hope Presbyterian Church of Rogue River v. Presbyterian Church, USA, 352 Or. 668, 291 P.3d 711 (Or. 2012); Heartland Presbytery v. Gashland Presbyterian Church, 364 S.W.3d 575, 589 (Mo. 2012); Brethren v. Roann Church of the Brethren Inc., 20 N.E.3d 906 (Ind. 2014); Carrollton Presbyterian Church v. Presbytery of S. La., 77 So. 3d 975, 981 (La. 2011); Arkansas Presbytery v. Hudson, 40 S.W.3d 301, 309–10 (Ark. 2001); Ohio Dist. Council Inc. of the Assemblies of God v. Speelman, 47 N.E.3d 954 (Ohio 2016); Church of God in Christ, Inc. v. Graham, 54 F.3d 522, 525–26 (8th Cir. 1995).

associations. Depending on the nature of the dispute and the claims of the parties, different principles of civil law may apply. For example, if a dispute arises over the language of a deed or the validity of a conveyance, courts will apply state property law.[107] If a dispute arises over an express or implied trust, courts will apply state trust law.[108] And, if a dispute arises over the validity of a contract or the locus of corporate control, courts will apply state contract or corporations law.[109]

Under this approach, church canons and constitutions are relevant only if they are "embodied in some legally cognizable form"[110]—that is, only if they comply with "the formalities" of property, trust, or contract law.[111] For example, a declaration of trust in church canons would be effective only if it met the ordinary requirements of state trust law—such as an intention by the settlor to create a trust, a reasonably ascertainable beneficiary, a trustee, and defined duties of the trustee.[112] Similarly, the course of conduct between the parties would be relevant only if it was made relevant under state law—such as when state law provides that an implied trust can be inferred from the conduct of the parties.[113]

In short, internal church rules and relationships are given the same weight as the internal rules and relationships of any other voluntary association.

That is not to say that the religious nature of a church is irrelevant. Constitutional restrictions remain in play, but they are the same two restrictions identified by the Supreme Court in Jones—namely, (1) civil courts cannot "resolv[e] church property disputes on the basis of religious doctrine and practice,"[114] and (2) state law must be "flexible enough to accommodate all forms of religious organization and polity."[115] So, for example, if a deed or trust agreement incorporates elements of church doctrine, a court must defer to church authorities on interpretation of the doctrine. Similarly, if state law makes it burdensome for a church to adopt a particular type of ownership structure, that law might be struck down as unconstitutional.[116]

1. Illinois

While the Illinois Supreme Court has not adopted any specific approach to be used in church property disputes and in fact never addressed the issue, the appellate court of Illinois did—several times. A survey of these cases, discussed next, leads to the following overall conclusion: first, an Illinois court will refuse to decide a case that requires a judicial interpretation of religious doctrine or church law, under the ecclesiastic abstention doctrine, which holds that the court lacks subject matter jurisdiction. However, where doctrinal controversy is not involved in the dispute, mandatory deference to religious authority is not required, and an Illinois court will apply the "neutral principles of law" approach, objectively examining pertinent church characteristics, constitutions and bylaws, deeds, state statutes, and other evidence to resolve the matter the same as it would a secular dispute.

In *Nelson v. Brewer*,[144] the court summarized the issue in the case, which reaches the merits, as follows: "whether the Circuit Court properly decided plaintiffs' claims under neutral principles of law or whether the Circuit Court lacked jurisdiction under the ecclesiastic abstention doctrine pursuant to the first amendment[.]"[145] The court concluded that the trial court properly applied the neutral principles of law and that the ecclesiastic abstention doctrine does not apply.[146] It summarized the law on whether the abstention doctrine applies and whether the court should apply the neutral principles approach as follows:

> The determining factor in applying the ecclesiastic abstention doctrine hinges upon the subject matter of the dispute. When the subject matter of a dispute is strictly and purely ecclesiastical in character regardless of the polity of the church, the civil court cannot exercise jurisdiction, including matters that concern theological controversy, church discipline, ecclesiastical government or the conformity of the members of the church to the standard of morals required of them. Accordingly, Illinois courts have generally refused to adjudicate cases requiring judicial interpretation of religious doctrine or church law where the governance structure is clearly hierarchical and the local group is clearly subordinate to the larger organization.
>
> However, Illinois courts have adopted the neutral-principles approach set forth in *Jones v. Wolf*, whereby a court may objectively examine pertinent church characteristics, constitutions, bylaws, deeds, statutes, and other evidence to resolve the matter as it would a secular dispute. In *Jones*,

144. Nelson v. Brewer, 138 N.E.3d 220 (Ill. App. 1st Dist. 2019), *appeal denied*, 132 N.E.3d 318 (Ill. 2019).

145. *Nelson*, 138 N.E.3d at 232.

146. *Id.*

the U.S. Supreme Court recognized the neutral-principles methodology as a constitutionally permissible way to resolve church property disputes. As a result, courts may decide whether disputed property belongs to the local church or general church by reference to objective, well-established concepts of trust and property law. This approach may be applied in resolving property disputes even with a hierarchical church organization, so long as the court does not decide a religious matter involving church doctrine, polity, or practice.

Simply put, if the analysis can be done in secular terms, the court should do so.[147]

2. Colorado

The Supreme Court of Colorado adopted the neutral principles of law in *Bishop & Diocese of Colo. v. Mote* after briefly discussing four decisions by the Colorado Court of Appeals that applied the neutral-principles approach.[148] In *Mote*, a dispute over the local church's property arose after the majority of the members decided to withdraw from the national church because of differences over doctrines.[149] The lower court found for the minority of members (who remained loyal to the general church), and the Court of Appeals applied the neutral principles of law and reversed—finding for the majority.[150] On appeal, the Supreme Court of Colorado agreed that the neutral principles of law should be used in resolving church property disputes but disagreed with the manner in which it was applied.[151] The proper manner to apply the approach is to "consider first, without the application of any presumption, whether the instruments of conveyance, church documents and other relevant evidence establish that the general church has rights of ownership or control over the disputed church property by reason of a trust, a reverter clause or some other basis."[152] "If, after

147. *Id.* at 234–35 (internal citations and quotations omitted).

148. Bishop & Diocese of Colo. v. Mote, 716 P.2d 85 (Colo. 1986); *see also* Bernson v. Koch, 35 Colo. App. 257, 534 P.2d 334 (1975); Bishop & Diocese of Colo. v. St. Paul's Episcopal Church of Central City, 80CA0317 (Dec. 26, 1980); Bishop & Diocese of Colo. v. Mote, 668 P.2d 948, 953 (Colo. Ct. App. 1983); Dickey v. Snodgrass, 673 P.2d 51 (Colo. App. 1983).

149. 716 P.2d at 87.

150. *Id.*

151. *Id.* at 99.

152. *Id.*

applying neutral principles of law, such rights of ownership or control are determined to be vested in the general church, there will be no need to assess how property of the local church is controlled. If, on the other hand, such an analysis results in a determination that ownership or control of the disputed property is vested in the local church, it then may be necessary to determine how control over that property is to be exercised."[153]

The court emphasized that no special presumptive rule of majority representation exists, which was something the Court of Appeals did. Rather, a Colorado court should look to "well-established principles of statutory and common law traditionally applied to determine who has legal control over any particular corporation or voluntary association and how freely or extensively that control can be exercised."[154] As an example, the court cited the Colorado Nonprofit Corporation Act, now known as the Colorado Revised Nonprofit Corporation Act.

Another thing the Colorado Supreme Court disagreed with is the "scope of the permissible inquiry" to the relevant evidence in the case. The Colorado Court of Appeals reviewed the record "only to determine whether the documentary evidence explicitly imposed an express trust over the property in favor of the general church."[155] This was done based on the proposition that "all the competent and relevant evidence" must "necessarily [be] documentary." The Colorado Supreme Court disagreed with this proposition. Although ultimately it might be that "the evidence determinative of the dispute is limited to documentary evidence," much of the "testimonial evidence concerning the interpretation of various documentary provisions and the historical relationship between the parish and the diocese has at least peripheral relevance and must be evaluated and weighed in arriving at a final resolution."[156] Courts should use a "general inquiry as to the locus and nature of control in the local organization."[157]

Under Colorado law, the intent to create a trust "can be inferred from the nature of property transactions, the circumstances surrounding the holding

153. *Id.*
154. *Id.* at 100.
155. *Id.*
156. *Id.* at 102.
157. *Id.*

and transfer of property, the particular documents or language employed and the conduct of the parties."[158] In *Mote*, it was undisputed that legal title to the disputed property is held by the local church, as no reference is made to the national church in the deeds, and none contain an indication of creating a trust.[159] It was also stipulated that the national church never paid for or provided any financial support to purchase the property, nor did it transfer the disputed property to the local church.[160]

Nevertheless, the court concluded that the local church's intent to "dedicate its property irrevocably" to the purposes of the national church was "expressed unambiguously" in the combination of the 1955 "articles of incorporation, the local church bylaws and the canons of the general church, to which the local church acceded in its articles at the time this dispute arose in 1976. This construction is reinforced by the conduct of the relevant officials of the local and general church."[161]

Starting with the articles of incorporation, although no explicit declaration of a trust was made, the first two clauses read together strongly indicated that the local church property was to be held for the benefit of the general church. Also, no provisions implicitly or explicitly expressed an intent to the contrary.[162] The court also noted that the parties stipulated that the rectors and vestry of St. Mary's Church have "acknowledged their status as a local unit within the Episcopal Church and have accepted the benefits of that affiliation for more than 40 years."[163] Moreover, the rector and members of St. Mary's have

> assumed an active role in diocesan affairs, particularly by sending representatives to the annual conventions of the diocese and by accepting appointments to various permanent bodies and positions within the diocese; that the local church submitted to the diocese annual reports concerning rites, salaries and the value of property; and that

158. *Id.* at 100.
159. *Id.* at 104.
160. *Id.*
161. *Id.*
162. *Id.*
163. *Id.*

the local church officials have sought the permission of the diocese before attempting to encumber parish property.[164]

As to the local church's bylaws, the court focused on Article II, which provided that, while the parish has control of its own local affairs, "nothing shall be done which conflicts with the canons of the church, either general or diocesan."[165] Exercising "unbridled control over church property by the local church," according to the court, would conflict with several provisions of the national church's constitution and canons.[166] For example, one of the canons provides a restriction on the local church's power and authority to encumber or alienate property without the written consent of the national church.

Accordingly, after reviewing the evidence in the record, the Supreme Court found that the Court of Appeals "erred when it held that the evidence does not show the imposition of a trust upon the real and personal property of [the local church] in favor of the general church."[167]

The *Mote* decision was distinguished in an unpublished opinion by the Colorado Court of Appeals, *Korean New Life Methodist Church v. Korean Methodist Church of the Ams.*[168] In *New Life*, the parties agreed that the local church was formed independently of the denomination, but they disputed whether the local church later submitted to the denomination's authority and how that question should be analyzed.[169] The court in *New Life* ultimately found for the local church. In its analysis, the *New Life* court distinguished *Mote* in four ways.

First, unlike *Mote*, the church's bylaws and articles of incorporation do not reference the denomination or its rules. Nor does either document expressly provide that the local church will abide by the denomination rules.

164. *Id.* at 105.
165. *Id.*
166. *Id.*
167. *Id.* at 103.
168. Korean New Life Methodist Church v. Korean Methodist Church of the Ams., No. 18 CA 1149, 2020 Colo. App. LEXIS 133 (Feb. 6, 2020) ("*New Life*").
169. *Id.* at *16–17.

And neither document has been amended to recognize the denomination or its authority over local churches since the local church was formed.[170]

Second, the evidence in *New Life* revealed that the local church attended to its own affairs, handled its own finances, and selected its own church officials. For example, the bylaws and resolutions placed the church's financial control in two designated board members, which was contrary to the denomination rules that vest administrative authority and responsibility in the pastor.[171]

Third, the record revealed that the local church bought and sold at least two properties without notifying or seeking approval from the denomination. It was also shown that the local church mortgaged its existing property, again without notification to or approval from the denomination. Similarly, the local church never registered the property with the denomination, which was contrary to the denomination rules.[172]

Finally, local church's articles of incorporation allowed the church board—not the denomination—to charitably distribute church property upon dissolution, which supported the court's finding that the local church did not submit to the denomination.[173] Accordingly, the Court of Appeals affirmed the lower court's decision that the local church never ceded control or submitted to the denomination's authority.[174]

3. Missouri

In *Missouri Presbytery of Elijah Parish Lovejoy v. Jaeggi*,[175] the Missouri Supreme Court unequivocally adopted the neutral principles of law as the "exclusive method" for resolution of church property disputes.[176] This approach requires Missouri courts to rely solely on "well-established concepts of trust and property law," with the caveat that a court must not rely on "religious precepts" in interpreting the relevant documents, nor

170. *Id.* at *24.
171. *Id.*
172. *Id.* at *26.
173. *Id.*
174. *Id.* at *3.
175. 682 S.W.2d 465 (Mo. 1984).
176. *Id.* at 467.

will it "resolve a religious controversy."[177] The dispute in Elijah Parish was between the Presbytery of Elijah Parish Lovejoy, a presbytery of the United Presbyterian Church in the USA (the "national church"), and Memorial Presbyterian Church of St. Louis, a Missouri pro forma decree corporation (the "local church"). The court applied the neutral-principles approach and looked at (1) the deeds, (2) trust documents, (3) contributions, and (4) the Book of Order.[178]

Respectively, the court pointed out that the deeds "make no mention" of the national church, and none of the trust documents name it "as a beneficiary."[179] Moreover, regarding a contribution (i.e., a monetary gift) made by the national church—which was contingent on the local church's staying connected to the national church and was in fact secured by an interest in the land—the court found that the contribution gave the national church no "right to control all property upon disaffiliation."[180] Finally, none of the sections of the Book of Order, as it existed before the local church's disaffiliation, contain any "language expressly creating a trust in church property in favor of the national church."[181] Accordingly, the *Elijah Parish* court held that the property at issue belonged to the local church.

However, it is worth noting that the national church in *Elijah Parish* "made no effort to invoke § 42.08 [of the Book of Order] with regard to dissolution of the local church and indeed disclaim[ed] such intent. Thus, the dissolution provisions of § 62.11 [did] not come into play."[182] As such, the possibility that the national church could have invoked that provision and the effect it would have had on the dispute was unaddressed. Nonetheless, based on *Elijah Parish* and subsequent case law (discussed later), a Missouri court will inevitably rely on state property and trust law to determine who the rightful owner is in a church property dispute.

177. Colonial Presbyterian Church v. Heartland Presbytery, 375 S.W.3d 190, 195 (Mo. App. W. Dist. 2012) (citing Jones v. Wolf, 443 U.S. 595, 603 (1979)).
178. 682 S.W.2d at 473–74.
179. *Id.* at 473.
180. *Id.* at 474.
181. *Id.*
182. *Id.*

Thereafter, in *Heartland Presbytery v. Gashland Presbyterian Church*,[183] Gashland Presbyterian Church (the "local church") terminated its affiliation with the Presbyterian Church (USA) (the "national church") and with the Heartland Presbytery, the presbytery of the national church for the geographic region.[184] The Heartland Presbytery made several arguments that the local church's property is held in trust, all of which the court rejected.

First, Heartland Presbytery argued that—according to Article I of the Articles of Agreement—the local church was "connected with and ecclesiastically subject to" the national church and in fact "agreed to be bound by all of the provisions of the denomination's present and future constitutions."[185] The court concluded that the distinction is irrelevant because a Missouri court need not concern itself with the form of organization because the neutral-principles approach accommodates all forms of religious organization and polity.[186] Moreover, the "subject to" language is in the context of ecclesiastical matters, and a "property dispute does not present an 'ecclesiastical' question."[187] Finally, Article VII of the Articles of Agreement provided that title to property acquired by the local church "shall vest in the [local church] in its corporate capacity." "This language makes no reference to the acquisition of property in a representative or fiduciary capacity and does not contemplate the possession of any beneficial interest in [the local church's] property by other persons or entities."[188] Accordingly, based on the well-established neutral principles of trust law, there was no division of title, whereby the trustee holds legal title and the beneficiary holds equitable title.[189]

Heartland Presbytery next argued that in its bylaws, the local church "recognizes that the constitution of the Presbyterian Church (U.S.A.) is, in all of its provisions, obligatory upon it and its members."[190] Also, that nothing in the bylaws "shall nullify or contravene the provisions of the [national

183. 364 S.W.3d 575 (2012).
184. *Id.* at 577.
185. *Id.* at 585.
186. *Id.* (citing *Elijah Parish*).
187. *Id.*
188. *Id.* at 584.
189. *Id.* at 585 (citing Moore v. Moore, 189 S.W.3d 627, 636 (Mo. App. W.D. 2006)).
190. 364 S.W.3d at 587.

church's] constitution," and "they shall be construed only in conformity therewith."[191] In response, the court noted that interpreting these provisions in favor of Heartland Presbytery would be inconsistent with the Articles of Agreement. But, even if they were consistent, these "general" statements, such as the constitution is "obligatory upon" the local church, are insufficient to create an express trust.[192] Finally, Heartland Presbytery argued that the court in *Elijah Parish* left open the question that the Book of Order will be binding on the local church because the Property-Trust Clause was not in place at the time the local congregation terminated its association.[193]

Again, rooting its analysis in the fundamental principles of property and trust law, the court rejected the argument because the Book of Order is not binding on the local church "without some effective expression of [the local church's] agreement to be bound by those provisions[.]"[194]

4. Texas

In *Masterson v. The Episcopal Church Diocese of Northwest Texas*,[195] the Texas Supreme Court addressed what happens to property when a majority of the membership of a local church votes to withdraw from a denomination.[196] Pursuant to the bylaws, the local church held a meeting in November 2006, seeking, among other things, to amend the corporate bylaws to remove all references to The Episcopal Church (TEC) and the diocese and to revoke any trusts that may have been imposed on any of the corporation's property by TEC, the diocese, or the original trustees.[197] After the resolutions passed by majority vote, amended articles of incorporation changing the corporate name from "The Episcopal Church of the Good Shepherd" to the "Anglican Church of the Good Shepherd" were filed.[198] In conjunction

---

191. *Id.*

192. *Id.* at 588.

193. *Id.* at 591.

194. *Id.*; *see also* Church of God in Christ Inc. v. Graham, 54 F.3d 522, 526 (8th Cir. 1995) (holding that the provisions of the local church's articles and "the language of the deeds vesting title and control over the property in the hands of the local congregation" were "particularly damaging to the [national church's] claims" that the local church was bound by the property-disposition provisions of the denomination's constitution).

195. 422 S.W.3d 594 (Tex. 2013), *cert. denied*, 135 S. Ct. 435 (2014).

196. 422 S.W.3d at 596.

197. *Id.* at 598.

198. *Id.*

with these acts, the majority of the church's members withdrew from the diocese and TEC and retained possession of the parish property.[199]

After reviewing both its own and U.S. Supreme Court precedent, the Texas Supreme Court acknowledged the neutral-principles methodology as the sole applicable methodology, requiring courts to decide non-ecclesiastical issues such as property ownership based on the same neutral principles of law applicable to other entities while deferring to religious entities' decisions on ecclesiastical and church polity issues.[200] The court concluded that the question of identifying who owns the property is not necessarily inextricably linked to or determined by ecclesiastical matters, explaining that "[t]here is a difference between (1) the bishop's determining which worshipers are loyal to the diocese and TEC, whether those worshipers constituted a parish and whether a parish properly established a vestry and (2) whether the corporation's bylaws were complied with when the vote occurred to disassociate the corporation from the diocese and TEC."[201] That is, the court concluded that a corporation, with its secular existence derived from state law and its articles of incorporation and bylaws, is subject to a neutral-principles determination.[202] In remanding the case to the trial court, the Texas Supreme Court instructed the trial court as follows:

Absent specific, lawful provisions in a corporation's articles of incorporation or bylaws otherwise, whether and how a corporation's directors or those entitled to control its affairs can change its articles of incorporation and bylaws are secular, not ecclesiastical, matters; and an external entity—under the former or current statutory scheme—is not empowered to amend them absent specific, lawful provision in the corporate documents.[203] More directly, the court held that the TEC-affiliated bishop could, as an ecclesiastical matter, determine which faction of believers was recognized by and was the "true" church loyal to the diocese and TEC, and courts must defer to such ecclesiastical decisions. But his decision identifying the loyal faction as the continuing parish does not necessarily determine the property

199. *Id.*
200. *Id.* at 596, 601–07.
201. *Id.*
202. *Id.*
203. *Id.* at 609–10.

ownership issue, and his decisions on secular legal questions, such as the validity of the parish members' vote to amend the bylaws and articles of incorporation, are not entitled to deference.[204] Thus, if the title to the real property is in the corporation's name, and the language of the deeds does not provide for an express trust in favor of The Episcopal Church or the diocese, then the corporation owns the property.[205]

With respect to TEC trust clause, the Dennis Canon, the court found that it could not be enforceable under Texas law. The TEC parties argue that the Dennis Canon sets forth an enforceable, irrevocable trust for TEC under Texas trust law, as well as under *Jones v. Wolf*, irrespective of state law requirements. They further argue that even if a trust was not established for TEC in the Dennis Canon, the deeds of various properties set forth trusts for the congregations. However, Texas law requires a writing signed by the settlor or the settlor's agent to create a trust with regard to real property.[206] Further, Texas law provides that a proposed beneficiary cannot unilaterally name itself as the beneficiary of a trust involving another entity's property.[207] Because, under Texas law, an entity that does not own the property to be held in trust cannot establish a trust for itself simply by decreeing that it is the beneficiary of a trust, the Dennis Canon, by itself, did not establish a trust under Texas law.[208] In *Masterson*, the Texas Supreme Court did not determine whether the Dennis Canon imposed a trust but stated that even assuming that it had created one, its terms did not make it expressly irrevocable.[209]

---

204. *Id.* at 610.

205. *Id.*

206. TEX. PROP. CODE ANN. § 112.004.

207. *Id.* § 111.004(14) (defining "settlor" as a person who creates a trust or contributes property to a trustee of a trust; "settlor" means the same as "grantor" and "trustor"), § 112.001 (defining the methods of creating a trust: through a property owner's declaration, inter vivos transfer, or testamentary transfer, through the power of appointment to another person as trustee for the donee of the power or for a third person, or through a promise to another person whose rights under the promise are to be held in trust for a third person), § 112.005 ("A trust cannot be created unless there is trust property.").

208. *Masterson*, 422 S.W.3d at 611–13.

209. 422 S.W.3d at 613.

B. Hybrid Neutral Principles States[210]

Under the hybrid neutral-principles approach, internal church rules and relationships are almost always dispositive. Although courts may discuss the ordinary requirements of property, trust, or contract law, they hold that internal church rules govern property ownership even when those rules do not comply with the necessary formalities of civil law.

1. Tennessee

The Tennessee Supreme Court adopted the hybrid neutral-principles approach to religious property disputes in *Church of God in Christ Inc. v. L.M. Haley Ministries Inc.*[211] The Church of God in Christ (COGIC) is a national denomination with a hierarchical structure.[212] The Gospel Center Temple COGIC was a local church and member of COGIC that "declared its willingness to submit to and abide by the government of COGIC,"[213] including COGIC's Official Manual, the denomination's government document. Temple COGIC acquired title to real property in 2000, and the deed by which it acquired title did not list COGIC as having any interest in the property. However, COGIC's Official Manual provides:

---

210. The following state courts apply "hybrid neutral principles" of law when evaluating the enforcement of denominational trust clauses. Church of God in Christ Inc. v. L.M. Haley Ministries Inc., 531 S.W.3d 146, 170 (Tenn. 2017); Heartland Presbytery v. Presbyterian Church of Stanley Inc., 53 Kan. App. 2d (Kan. 2017); Peters Creek United Presbyterian Church v. Washington Presbytery of Pennsylvania, 90 A.3d 95 (Pa. 2014); Falls Church v. Protestant Episcopal Church in the United States, 285 Va. 651, 740 S.E.2d 530 (Va. 2013); Rector, Wardens, Vestrymen of Christ Church in Savannah v. Bishop of Episcopal Diocese of Georgia Inc., 290 Ga. 95 (Ga. 2011); Presbytery of Hudson River of Presbyterian Church (USA) v. Trustees of First Presbyterian Church & Congregation of Ridgeberry, 72 A.D.3d 78, 895 N.Y.S.2d 417 (N.Y. 2010); Lamont Cmty. Church v. Lamont Christian Reformed Church, 285 Mich. App. 602 (Mich. 2009); *In re* Episcopal Church Cases, 198 P.3d 66, 80–81 (Cal. 2009); Fonken v. Cmty. Church of Kamrar, 339 N.W.2d 810, 818–19 (Iowa 1983); E. Lake Methodist Episcopal Church Inc. v. Trs. of the Peninsula-Delaware Annual Conference of the United Methodist Church Inc., 731 A.2d 798, 810 (Del. 1999); From the Heart Church Ministries Inc. v. Philadelphia-Baltimore Annual Conference, 184 Md. App. 11, 964 A.2d 215 (Md. 2009); Mills v. Baldwin, 377 So. 2d 971 (Fla. 1979); Episcopal Church in Diocese of Connecticut v. Gauss, 302 Conn. 408, 28 A.3d 302 (Conn. 2011).

211. 531 S.W.3d 146 (Tenn. 2017).

212. *See also* Church of God in Christ Inc. v. Middle City Church of God in Christ, 774 S.W.2d 950, 951 (Tenn. Ct. App. 1989) (stating that local member churches of COGIC operate as a part of a "connectional system"); Convention of Protestant Episcopal Church in Diocese of Tenn. v. Rector, Wardens, & Vestryman of St. Andrew's Parrish, No. M2010-01474-COA-R3-CV, 2012 Tenn. App. LEXIS 274, at *20 n.16 (stating that "connectional" and "hierarchical" mean the same thing).

213. *Haley*, *supra*, 531 S.W. 3d at 148.

> Real estate or other property may be acquired by purchase, gift[,] devise, or otherwise, by local churches. Where real or personal property is acquired by deed, the instrument of conveyance shall contain the following clause, to wit; The said property is held in trust for the use and benefit of the members of the Church of God in Christ . . . and subject to the charter, constitution, laws and doctrines of said church, now in full force and effect, or as they may be hereafter amended, changed or modifies [sic] by the General Assembly of said church.

After Temple COGIC's founding pastor, L.M. Haley, died, the denomination's supervising or jurisdictional bishop assumed the pastorship. A majority of Temple COGIC's members were dissatisfied with the bishop's move to assume the pastorship and voted to transfer to another ecclesiastical jurisdiction within COGIC, but the denomination would not recognize or approve the vote. Thereafter, the disaffected members incorporated a new church called Gospel Center Temple Church Moscow Inc., which was not organized as a COGIC church. Some of the disaffected members held themselves out as the sole trustees of Temple COGIC and by quitclaim deed transferred the real property titled to Temple COGIC to the Moscow church. After the quitclaim deed was executed, the Moscow church barred the jurisdictional bishop and pastor of Temple COGIC from entering the premises. A lawsuit followed.

While *Haley* holds that Tennessee courts may consider "any relevant statutes, the language of the deeds and any other documents of conveyance, charters and articles of incorporation and any provisions regarding property ownership that may be included in the local or hierarchical church constitutions or governing documents," the court began and concluded its analysis without giving any weight to relevant Tennessee statutes or even the language of the deeds.[214] The court concluded that the local church's real property was held in trust for COGIC based solely on the following:

214. 531 S.W.3d at 170 (Tenn. 2017).

- COGIC is a hierarchical denomination.
- COGIC's governing documents included a provision indicating that real property of local member churches was held in trust for the denomination.
- Temple COGIC had agreed and demonstrated its intent to be bound by COGIC's governing documents when it decided to become a local member church of COGIC.[215]

There was no discussion in *Haley* of what constituted a valid trust under Tennessee law and no weight given to the fact that the deeds did not contain any trust language in favor of the denomination, COGIC. And, while Tennessee has a history of applying the strict neutral-principles approach,[216] the Tennessee Supreme Court in *Haley* muddied the waters and made it more difficult for local congregations by adopting what it called the "hybrid neutral-principles approach." According to *Haley*, Tennessee courts may consider any relevant statutes; the language of the deeds and any other documents of conveyance, charters, and articles of incorporation; and any provisions regarding property ownership that may be included in the local or hierarchical church constitutions or governing documents. But under the neutral-principles approach approved as constitutionally permissible, the court concluded that "a civil court must enforce a trust in favor of the hierarchical church, even if the trust language appears only in the constitution or governing documents of the hierarchical religious organization."[217]

2. California

Before 2009, the leading case in church property disputes was the California Court of Appeal's decision in *Protestant Episcopal Church v. Barker*, which emphasized that California "has rejected the hierarchical theory as the basis for resolution of church property disputes and has adopted in its place neutral principles of law."[218] In *Barker*, four local churches disaffiliated

215. *Id.* at 173.

216. Before *Haley*, the Tennessee Court of Appeals had applied a strict neutral-principles approach in several church property cases. Fairmount Presbyterian Church Inc. v. Presbytery of Holston of the Presbyterian Church of U.S., 531 S.W.2d 301, 306 (Tenn. Ct. App. 1975).

217. 531 S.W.3d at 170 (Tenn. 2017).

218. Protestant Episcopal Church v. Barker, 115 Cal. App. 3d 599, 614 (1981).

themselves from the Episcopal Church's national organization and sought to take their parish property with them.[219] The court rejected the deference theory, applied the neutral-principles of law approach of *Jones v. Wolf*, and held that property disputes should be resolved through an examination of (1) the manner of holding title; (2) the articles of incorporation of the local churches; (3) the constitution, canons, and rules of the general church; and (4) relevant state statutes.[220] Applying the neutral-principles approach, the court found that three of the four churches did not hold their local property in express trust for the benefit of the national church.[221]

Thereafter, the California Legislature enacted subsections (c) and (d) of Nonprofit Religious Corporation Law section 9142. These subsections provide, in relevant part, the following:

> c. No assets of a religious corporation are or shall be deemed to be impressed with any trust, express or implied, statutory or at common law unless one of the following applies:
>
> (1) Unless, and only to the extent that, the assets were received by the corporation with an express commitment by resolution of its board of directors to so hold those assets in trust.
>
> (2) Unless, and only to the extent that, the articles or bylaws of the corporation, or the governing instruments of a superior religious body or general church of which the corporation is a member, so expressly provide.
>
> (3) Unless, and only to the extent that, the donor expressly imposed a trust in writing at the time of the gift or donation.
>
> d. Trusts created by paragraph (2) of subdivision (c) may be amended or dissolved by amendment from time to time to the articles, bylaws or governing instruments creating the trusts. . . .[222]

219. *Id.* at 607–11.
220. *Id.* at 620–25.
221. *Id.* at 625–26.
222. CAL. CORP. CODE ANN. § 9142(c)-(d).

The California Court of Appeals in *Cal-Nevada Annual Conference of the United Methodist Church v. St. Luke's United Methodist Church* interpreted the statute and concluded that the general church's governing instruments could and did not create a trust unilaterally.[223] In doing so, *St. Luke's* rejected the general church's argument that section 9142(c)(2) "enables a general church to create a trust in favor of itself, with the trust property being the local church's property . . . [and that] the general church (or 'superior religious body') can do this by so providing in the general church's governing instruments."[224] Such a reading, according to the court, would be "sharply at odds with other general principles of trust law."[225]

For example, nothing in trust law allows a nonowner to declare that an owner holds property as trustee for the nonowner. Conversely, the *St. Luke's* court opined, the statute appears to have been intended as a codification of *Barker* and that "[n]othing in *Barker* supports the view that a general church can create a trust in favor of itself simply by enacting a rule stating that a local church holds property in trust in favor of the general church."[226] Unfortunately, the interpretation of the statute and conclusion by *St. Luke's* was subsequently criticized by the Supreme Court of California in *Episcopal Church Cases*.[227]

In 2009, the Supreme Court of California in *Episcopal Church Cases* confirmed that civil courts should apply the neutral-principles approach and for the first time provided the analytical approach under which California courts are to proceed:

> State courts must not decide questions of religious doctrine; those are for the church to resolve. Accordingly, if resolution of a property dispute involves a point of doctrine, the court must defer to the position of the highest ecclesiastical authority that has decided the point. But to the extent the court can resolve a property dispute without reference to church doctrine, it should apply neutral principles of law. The

223. Cal-Nevada Annual Conference of the United Methodist Church v. St. Luke's United Methodist Church, 121 Cal. App. 4th 754, 769 (2004).
224. *Id.*
225. *Id.*
226. *Id.*
227. 45 Cal. 4th 467, 485 (2009).

> court should consider sources such as the deeds to the property in dispute, the local church's articles of incorporation, the general church's constitution, canons and rules, and relevant statutes, including statutes specifically concerning religious property, such as Corporations Code section 9142.[228]

Thus, a California court will look not only to the local church's documents (title instruments, articles of incorporation, etc.) but also to what the general church's constitution, canons, and rules have to say regarding church assets. Most significantly, a California court will also look to California Corporations Code Annotated section 9142, known as the Nonprofit Religious Corporations Law.

By way of background, in *Episcopal Church Cases*, when the local church sought permission from the Los Angeles Diocese to organize as a parish in 1947, the members promised in their application that the parish would be "forever held under and conform to and be bound by" the constitution and canons of the Episcopal Church.[229] Moreover, the local church's articles of incorporation, filed in 1949, provided that the constitution and canons, rules, regulations, and discipline of the Episcopal Church "for the time being shall, unless they be contrary to the laws of this state, always form a part of the bylaws and articles of incorporation of the corporation hereby formed and shall prevail against and govern anything herein contained that may appear repugnant to such constitutions, canons, rules, regulations and discipline."[230]

In 2004, the local church withdrew from the national organization after a doctrinal dispute and sought to establish ownership of the local church property.[231] In support of its position, the local church cited *Barker* and *St. Luke's* for the proposition that canon I.7.4 did not create a valid trust and that it is entitled to the disputed property. The court disagreed. First, the court noted that the trial court judgment in *Barker* was rendered (1) before the decision in *Jones v. Wolf*, (2) before canon I.7.4 was adopted

228. *Id.*
229. *Id.* at 474.
230. *Id.*
231. *Id.* at 475–76.

by the Episcopal Church and (3) before the California legislature enacted subsections (c) and (d) of section 9142.

Second, the court expressly disapproved *St. Luke's* statement that section 9142(c)(2) "does not authorize a general church to create a trust interest for itself . . . simply by issuing a rule declaring that such a trust exists."[232] According to *Episcopal Church Cases*, such a statement is inconsistent with the statute's plain language.[233] Instead, the court added, in a "hierarchically organized church, the 'general church' can impress a trust on a local religious corporation of which the local corporation is a 'member' if the governing instruments of that superior religious body so provide."[234] Moreover, the court noted that "subdivision (d) appears clearly to indicate that, under California law, a trust is created by compliance with any one of the alternatives set forth in subdivision (c)(2), and it can only be altered or dissolved by amending the creating instrument."[235]

In applying the neutral principles of law and section 9142 to the case before it, the court concluded that the general church, not the local church, owns the property in question. Although the deeds to the property have long been in the name of the local church: "That church agreed from the beginning of its existence to be part of the greater church and to be bound by its governing documents. These governing documents make clear that church property is held in trust for the general church and may be controlled by the local church only so long as that local church remains a part of the general church. When it disaffiliated from the general church, the local church did not have the right to take the church property with it."[236] Accordingly, the court observed that once the local church "left the general church, the property reverted to the general church."[237]

As seen earlier, the court's adoption and application of the neutral principles of law seemed to contradict its interpretation and application of section 9142. Although, at first glimpse, it seemed like the Supreme Court of California reached all the merits of the church property dispute, the court

232. *Id.* at 491.
233. *Id.*
234. *Id.* at 492.
235. *Id.* at 489.
236. *Id.* at 473.
237. *Id.* at 487 (concurring and dissenting opinion).

clarified its decision in *Rasmussen v. Super* (2001). There, the court clarified that "what [it] said [in *Episcopal Church Cases*] must be viewed in light of the case's procedural posture."[238] By way of background, on remand in the trial court (from *Episcopal Church Cases*), the local church "continue[d] to contend it owns the property, . . . rel[ying] largely on a 1991 letter that, it claim[ed], places ownership with the parish."[239] The general church filed a petition for writ of mandate in the Court of Appeal asking the court to, among other things, order the trial court to grant its motion for judgment on the pleadings.[240] The Court of Appeal granted the writ.

The court—understandably—viewed the Supreme Court of California's opinion in *Episcopal Church Cases* as "having resolved the property dispute for all purposes, leaving nothing for the trial court to do on remand but to dispose of the cases in favor of the Los Angeles Diocese and Episcopal Church."[241] But the Supreme Court of California disagreed and stated that the matter in *Episcopal Church Cases*:

> . . . was before us on a summary adjudication in favor of St. James Parish. Specifically, the trial court had (1) granted a motion to dismiss the action as a SLAPP[242] suit under Code of Civil Procedure section 425.16, and (2) sustained the demurrer. The former ruling meant the trial court had found that the action was a SLAPP suit—i.e., that the action arose out of protected activity and that the Los Angeles Diocese had not shown a probability it would prevail. The latter ruling meant the trial court had found the Episcopal Church had not stated facts sufficient to constitute a cause of action. We affirmed the judgment of the Court of Appeal, which had reversed these rulings.

---

238. Rasmussen v. Superior Court, 51 Cal. 4th 804, 808 (2001).

239. *Id.* at 807.

240. *Id.*

241. *Id.*

242. SLAPP stands for Strategic Lawsuit Against Public Participation. It refers to a lawsuit brought in an effort to intimidate a person or business into silence. California enacted an anti-SLAPP statute that allows defendants to seek dismissal of a complaint at the beginning of a lawsuit, before the expensive and time-consuming discovery process. The court will hold a hearing on the motion to determine whether the cases should be allowed to proceed. *See* CAL. CODE CIV. PROC. § 425.16.

But concluding, as the Court of Appeal and this court had done, that the action is not subject to dismissal as a SLAPP suit and that the demurrer should have been overruled does not mean the actions were finally decided in favor of the Los Angeles Diocese and the Episcopal Church. St. James Parish had not even filed an answer at that stage.[243] Thus, arguably, an avenue remains to argue that certain documents or evidence shows that a local church owns the property, notwithstanding the trust clause.

However, the Court of Appeal in *Iglesia Evangelica Latina Inc. v. S. P. Latin Am. Dist. of the Assemblies of God* decided a case in favor of the local church based on the failure to follow corporate law formalities. In *Iglesia Evangelica Latina*, the appellants, Juan Reyes individually and on behalf of *Iglesia Evangelica Latina* (IEL), prevailed against the Southern Pacific Latin American District of the Assemblies of God (SPLAD).[244] The national church there (Assemblies of God), a hierarchical church, is composed of three levels: the general council, the district councils, and a third level with two types of churches—(1) district council churches and (2) general council churches. District council churches are subject to direct control by their district councils, while general council churches have their own boards and operate independently.[245]

The local church initially incorporated as an independent church, subsequently affiliated with SPLAD as a district council church and finally affiliated with the national church as a general council church.[246] After certain allegations by one of IEL's board members were made against the assistant pastor, who was also a board member at the time, members of SPLAD and three out of the five board members of IEL held a meeting.[247] The meeting led to (1) the conclusion that SPLAD should take control and supervision of IEL, (2) a vote that the church should change its status from general counsel to district council, and (3) an assertion by SPLAD that IEL no longer had a board. Accordingly, two of the former IEL board members

243. 51 Cal. 4th at 808.
244. Iglesia Evangelica Latina Inc. v. S. Pac. Latin American Dist. of the Assemblies of God, 173 Cal. App. 4th 420, 424 (2009).
245. *Id.*
246. *Id.* at 425.
247. *Id.* at 427–28.

executed a grant deed transferring 16 properties held by IEL to SPLAD.[248] In response, members of IEL held an election and elected the assistant pastor and four other church members as the new IEL board.[249] A lawsuit followed.

In the lawsuit, one of the claims asserted by Reyes and IEL is a quit title claim to the property. The Court of Appeal granted judgment in favor of IEL and concluded, among other things, that

> SPLAD erroneously believed that because its hierarchical structure and governing documents permitted it to demote IEL to district council church status upon the request of a board member, it could ignore IEL's corporate form and applicable statutory and other corporate formalities in taking control of the church. The rule of deference to ecclesiastical decisions, such as to the decision to change IEL's status from general council church to district council church, does not require us to ignore IEL's secular corporate form.[250]

The court also found that, "even if IEL were demoted to district council status, this cannot amount to total surrender of corporate autonomy; and only voting members can elect a board, rendering SPLAD's election invalid."[251]

3. Delaware

In *East Lake Methodist Episcopal Church Inc. v. Trustees of the Peninsula-Delaware Annual Conference of the United Methodist Church Inc.*, the Delaware Supreme Court was called upon to "examine the legal standards that govern disputes over church property between local congregations and general ecclesiastical authorities."[252] But before delving into the details of the case, by way of summary, the Court of Chancery found that the congregation held title in trust for the benefit of the conference, using an implied-trust analysis. And, unfortunately, the Supreme Court of Delaware affirmed the decision. The case started when the trustees of the

248. *Id.* at 428.
249. *Id.* at 428–29.
250. *Id.* at 439–40.
251. *Id.* at 439.
252. East Lake Methodist Episcopal Church, Inc. v. Trustees of the Peninsula-Delaware Annual Conference of the United Methodist Church Inc., 731 A.2d 798, 800 (Del. 1999).

Peninsula-Delaware Annual Conference of the United Methodist Church Inc. sought an injunction to secure possession and control over personal and real property held and occupied by the East Lake Methodist Episcopal Church Inc.[253]

The lawsuit was based on a resolution adopted by the conference pursuant to the Book of Discipline, which authorized the discontinuation of further services at East Lake and the "transfer of control of the property to the Conference," which became effective on July 1, 1995.[254] Ultimately, the Court of Chancery found for the congregation, concluding that the Conference held "equitable title to the disputed property."[255] On appeal, the Supreme Court of Delaware first noted that "one must look to" the congregation's history "to determine its present legal status."[256] And it did.

In 1892, an untitled document naming certain individuals as trustees was filed with the recorder of deeds to form what would be known as East Lake M.E. Church.[257] That same year, the congregation acquired two parcels of land:

- The parcel that the current church structure sits on, through a deed naming East Lake M.E. Church as grantee
- An adjoining parcel of land, by a deed naming East Lake Methodist Episcopal Church as the grantee[258]

In 1905, the congregation revisited its 1892 incorporation efforts and filed two incorporation certificates.[259]

The first, titled "A Certificate of Incorporation of East Lake Methodist Episcopal Church" and dated December 5, 1905, was an attempt to incorporate under 27 Delaware Code section 101. The certificate provided that, for the purposes of being incorporated, "such additional notices were given according to the manner presented in the discipline, rules and regulations

253. *Id.* at 801.
254. *Id.*
255. *Id.*
256. *Id.*
257. *Id.* at 802.
258. *Id.*
259. *Id.*

of the Methodist Episcopal Church with which this said congregation is connected."[260]

The second, titled "Certificate of Incorporation of East Lake Methodist Episcopal Church Incorporated" and dated December 19, 1905, provided that the corporation was being organized pursuant to general corporation law and stated "a congregation of Christians having been organized . . . for the purpose of worshipping almighty God, according to the religion, faith, doctrines, rules, discipline and usages of the Methodist Episcopal Church in the United States of America. . . ."[261] On January 2, 1906, a confirmatory deed was recorded for the parcels acquired in 1892 with East Lake Methodist Episcopal Church Inc. as grantee, for the purpose of confirming and making good the title that may have been questionable because of the defective incorporation.[262]

On June 29, 1995, after the adoption of the resolution but before its effective date, the congregation executed a mortgage in favor of one of the congregation's trustees, reciting the current church property and parsonage as collateral. This mortgage was not authorized by the Conference and was viewed by the Court of Chancery as questionable.[263]

As explained more thoroughly later, based on the historical connection of the congregation with the Conference, the congregation's past conduct and actions, and the language in the certificate of incorporation and confirmatory deed, the Supreme Court of Delaware affirmed the Court of Chancery's finding of an implied trust. Specifically, the court noted that the incorporation certificate contained a dedication-of-purpose language, which recited the congregation's "intention to operate in accordance with the 'religion, faith, doctrines, rules, discipline and usages' of the predecessor to the United Methodist Church."[264] The court recognized that no trust language is contained in the deed. Nevertheless, it stated that "although the language of the deed carries great weight in determining whether a property has been devoted to the church or the local congregation, the deed itself is

260. *Id.*
261. *Id.*
262. *Id.*
263. *Id.* at 803.
264. *Id.* at 809.

not dispositive." According to the court, "the actions of the congregation dedicated the property to the hierarchical church."[265] In other words, the property "was dedicated by those who held it through their constant association with, and explicit recognition of, the parent church."[266]

Moreover, the court found it significant that previous transactions in which the congregation either conveyed or mortgaged portions of its property either "acknowledged the express-trust interest of the Conference or did not require the consent of the Conference."[267] Finally, the court noted that the confirmatory deed recited the congregation's connection with the Methodist Episcopal Church.[268] Accordingly, the Supreme Court of Delaware "agreed with the analysis conducted by the Court of Chancery under its neutral-principles-of-law approach" and noted the following:

> While the present trustees may desire to disassociate themselves and the congregation they purport to represent from the United Methodist Church, as presently constituted and organized, they are not free to nullify the affiliation accomplished by previous generations of East Lake church members over more than 100 years. More importantly, they may not negate the legal relationship established in the form of an implied trust based on the language of the conveyances, the recitals and the acknowledgments in the incorporation documents, and the adherence to the discipline of the parent church. Those documents, and the conduct of the members of East Lake over the course of many years, demonstrate a unity of purpose between the local church and the general church that the property held by the local church be dedicated to, and used for, the advancement of the interests of the United Methodist Church as governed by the Conference.[269]

265. *Id.*
266. *Id.* at 810.
267. *Id.*
268. *Id.*
269. *Id.*

4. The Problem with Hybrid Neutral Principles

There is no question that nonreligious corporations can avail themselves of the benefits and protections of state laws related to corporations, trusts, and property rights. But under the hybrid neutral-principles approach to the resolution of religious property disputes, certain religious congregations are deprived those public benefits and protections solely on account of their status as a congregation once affiliated with a hierarchical denomination.[270]

Contrary to how the hybrid neutral-principle courts interpreted *Jones*, the neutral-principles approach approved in *Jones* does not require civil courts to simply enforce a "trust" in favor of the hierarchical church when the purported trust is not "legally cognizable" or valid under state law.[271]

The hybrid neutral-principle court appears to rely on the following excerpt of *Jones v. Wolf*, which denominations often cite to support the

270. Religious property disputes have attracted a number of scholarly articles weighing in on various aspects of the tension between the First Amendment and state secular law. *See, e.g.*, Patty Gerstenblith, *Civil Court Resolution of Property Disputes among Religious Organizations*, 39 AM. U. L. REV. 513, 519–20 (1990) (observing that Supreme Court jurisprudence that grants greater deference in property disputes to hierarchical religious organizations than to congregational religious organizations "would seem to create a structural relationship violative of the establishment clause"); Jeffrey B. Hassler, Comment, *A Multitude of Sins? Constitutional Standards for Legal Resolution of Church Property Disputes in a Time of Escalating Intradenominational Strife*, 35 PEP. L. REV. 399, 455 (2008) ("Churches have not ordered their affairs in ways that lend themselves to easy civil court resolution."); R. Gregory Hyden, Comment, *Welcome to the Episcopal Church, Now Please Leave: An Analysis of the Supreme Court's Approved Methods of Settling Church Property Disputes in the Context of the Episcopal Church and How Courts Erroneously Ignore the Role of the Anglican Communion*, 44 WILLAMETTE L. REV. 541, 560 (2008) ("By ignoring the judicatory procedures outside of the national polity of the Episcopal Church, courts are not following the principles they set out for a hierarchical church in either a deference approach or a neutral principles approach."); Bernie D. Jones, *Litigating the Schism & Reforming the Canons: Orthodoxy, Property & the Modern Social Gospel of the Episcopal Church*, 42 GOLDEN GATE U. L. REV. 151, 215 (2012) (asserting that the property disputes within The Episcopal Church are about theology and proposing that ecclesiastical property courts would be more efficient to determine the Dennis Canon trust question); Valerie J. Munson, *Fraud on the Faithful? The Charitable Intentions of Members of Religious Congregations and the Peculiar Body of Law Governing Religious Property in the United States*, 44 RUTGERS L.J. 471, 509 (2014) (observing that history suggests that religion-based property disputes will always be around and that "the only constant in that body of law has been its utter inconsistency and uncertainty"); Sarah Barringer Gordon, *The First Dis-Establishment: Limits on Church Property Before the Civil War*, 162 U. PA. L. REV. 307, 313 (2014); Michael W. McConnell & Luke W. Goodrich, *On Resolving Church Property Dispute*, 58 ARIZ. L. REV. 307, 321–22 (2016) (observing the common pattern of church property disputes and the arguments made by each side).

271. *Jones*, 443 U.S. at 603–04.

legitimacy and enforceability of unilaterally adopted trust provisions. The excerpt reads as follows:

> At any time before the dispute erupts, the parties can ensure, if they so desire, that the faction loyal to the hierarchical church will retain the church property. They can modify the deeds or the corporate charter to include a right of reversion or trust in favor of the general church. Alternatively, the constitution of the general church can be made to recite an express trust in favor of the denominational church. The burden involved in taking such steps will be minimal. And the civil courts will be bound to give effect to the result indicated by the parties, provided it is embodied in some legally cognizable form.[272]

While at first blush this excerpt may suggest that a hierarchical denomination can unilaterally adopt an express-trust provision in its governing documents and demand the courts enforce it, this is not the case. *Jones* does not state that a single party, the denomination, can make such a modification and unilaterally claim an interest in property titled to the local church. To the contrary, *Jones* contemplates a situation in which the "parties"—that is, the denomination and the local church—reach a mutually understood agreement "before the dispute erupts" that the property would be held in trust for the denomination.

The hybrid neutral-principles understanding of the neutral-principles approach cannot be squared with either *Jones* or other precedents, which do not require courts to abandon neutral principles for the benefit of certain types of religion organizations. Rather, the hybrid approach ultimately guts both the court's teaching that "[t]he neutral-principles approach . . . obviates entirely the need for an analysis or examination of ecclesiastical polity or doctrine" and its assurance that "a state is constitutionally entitled to adopt neutral principles of law as a means of adjudicating a church property dispute."[273]

---

272. *Id.* at 606.
273. *Id.* at 604–05.

Under a proper reading of *Jones*, the enforceability of the relevant church rules turns on whether they are embodied in "legally cognizable form" under ordinary property, contract, and trust law.[274] The point of the neutral-principles approach is to avoid compelling courts to "defer to the resolution of the hierarchical church" or to its "laws and regulations."[275] Instead, the neutral-principles analysis "is completely secular"; "relies exclusively on objective, well-established concepts of trust and property law"; and facilitates "ordering private rights and obligations to reflect the intentions of the parties" as embodied in "legally cognizable form."[276]

Jones clearly provides that civil courts are free to apply the neutral principles of the state's property and trust laws to determine whether a trust was lawfully established, just as they would in any other case.[277] *Jones* specified that the neutral-principles approach "relies exclusively on objective, well-established concepts of trust and property law familiar to lawyers and judges," thereby producing outcomes reflecting the "intentions of the parties."[278]

In other words, courts may apply the neutral principles of state law to determine the existence of an enforceable trust, just like they would in any other property case. While church property disputes may require courts to "examine certain religious documents, such as a church constitution, for language of trust in favor of the general church," the Supreme Court held that courts may examine these documents so long as they take "special care to scrutinize the document in purely secular terms and not to rely on religious precepts in determining whether the document indicates that the parties have intended to create a trust."[279]

The threshold issue in the hybrid approach is whether a particular church is hierarchical or congregational. If a court using the hybrid approach finds that a church is hierarchical, then that church is entitled to direct the disposition of property in case of a schism with a lower burden than applies under state law and thus a lower burden than would apply to a nonhierarchical

274. *Id.* at 606.
275. *Id.* at 597, 609.
276. *Id.* at 603, 606.
277. *Id.*
278. *Id.* at 604.
279. *Id.*

church. The hybrid approach thus applies one set of property and trust rules for hierarchical denominations and a different set of property and trust rules for all other organizations.

Viewing the hybrid approach this way, it is clear that it actually inhibits the free exercise of religion by placing substantial pressure on individuals, families, and congregations in hierarchical denominations to stay in the denomination rather than follow their own sincerely held religious beliefs and faith commitments.[280] More people and congregations would leave denominations that no longer reflect their faith commitments if they were not afraid of losing their properties and were able to protect their properties just like any nonreligious entity can under state law. Under *Trinity Lutheran* and *Espinoza*, this unequal treatment and burden on religious exercise should be subject to strict scrutiny.

To satisfy strict scrutiny, government action "must advance 'interests of the highest order' and must be narrowly tailored in pursuit of those interests."[281] In *Espinoza v. Montana Department of Revenue*,[282] Montana argued that it had a compelling interest in ensuring the separation of church and state when it invalidated the scholarship program. But the Supreme Court rejected the argument and held that "creating greater separation of church and state than the federal Constitution requires 'cannot qualify as compelling' in the face of the infringement of free exercise here."[283]

Likewise, a denomination may argue that the hybrid neutral-principles approach is supported by the state's interest in ensuring the separation of church and state. But the Supreme Court, in both *Espinoza* and *Trinity Lutheran Church of Columbia, Inc. v. Comer*,[284] has already held that such an interest is not compelling. In sum, the "hybrid neutral-principles approach" is constitutionally infirm and would infringe upon a local church's free-exercise rights if it was applied in this case to deprive the local church of its properties.

---

280. St. Augustine Sch. v. Evers, 906 F.3d 591, 604–06 (7th Cir. 2018) (Ripple, J., dissenting) *vacated by, remanded by* St. Augustine Sch. v. Taylor, 2020 U.S. LEXIS 3528 (U.S., July 2, 2020).

281. Church of Lukumi Babalu Aye Inc. v. Hialeah, 508 U.S. 520, 546 (1993).

282. 104 S. Ct. 2246 (2020).

283. Trinity Lutheran Church of Columbia, Inc. v. Comer, 137 S. Ct. 2012, 2024 (2017).

284. *Id.*

Civil courts are poorly equipped to discern the often delicate balance between local and denominational authority, which is often contested and which varies from denomination to denomination. "[M]any religious polities fall somewhere between the two or change over time," and some religious organizations, particularly non-Christian ones, "cannot be located on a hierarchical-congregational spectrum at all."[285]

Further, notwithstanding a church's formal governance, which may or may not reflect how it actually operates, "a 'hierarchical' form alone offers little insight into" the particular question of "how any given church intends to hold property."[286] The hybrid approach thus forces courts to shoehorn churches into a dualistic hierarchical-versus-congregational paradigm that does not reflect the reality of how many religious organizations have chosen to organize themselves and structure their property ownership.

For example, if a legislature attempted to catalog "hierarchical" religious organizations and pass relaxed legal statutory rules only for their benefit, there is little doubt that its actions would run up against the First Amendment.[287] Yet, that is precisely what the hybrid approach requires the judiciary to do. It is a core First Amendment principle that "the government may not favor one religion over another."[288] Further, "inherent" in neutral principles is the "promise of non-entanglement and neutrality."[289] Yet, "[i]n the religiously diverse American context, many religious associations are neither 'congregational' nor 'hierarchical,' and it is no easy task for a court to determine where along the spectrum a given church lies."[290]

Clearly, the hybrid approach "puts a heavy thumb on the scales in favor of a more 'hierarchical' form of polity, contradicting the First Amendment rule that churches must remain free 'to decide for themselves, free from state

285. Maryland & Va. Eldership v. Church of God, 396 U.S. 367, 369, 90 S. Ct. 499, 24 L. Ed. 2d 582 (1970) (Brennan, J. concurring)

286. *Id.*

287. *Cf.* Goodson v. Northside Bible Church, 261 F. Supp. 99, 103–04 (S.D. Ala. 1966) (striking down a law "creat[ing] a legislative body of a 65% majority of adult members for local churches" and "grant[ing] to this legislative body the right, power and authority to change established systems of church ownership without regard to the ecclesiastical law of the denomination"), *aff'd*, 387 F.2d 534 (5th Cir. 1967).

288. Larson v. Valente, 456 U.S. 228, 244 (1982) (calling this rule "[t]he clearest command of the Establishment Clause").

289. *Jones*, 443 U.S. at 604.

290. McConnell & Goodrich, *supra* note 269, at 327–28.

interference, matters of church government.'"[291] "First Amendment values are plainly jeopardized when church property litigation is made to turn on the resolution by civil courts of controversies over religious doctrine and practice." And, "[i]f civil courts undertake to resolve such controversies in order to adjudicate the property dispute, the hazards are ever present of inhibiting the free development of religious doctrine."[292]

In addition, this "creates a one-way ratchet" for churches to become more hierarchical.[293] Denominations, even hierarchical ones, may have various reasons for giving local congregations more control, including a right of exit. A "right of exit can serve as a check on the denomination from running roughshod over the strongly held views of a minority, including on divisive theological issues."[294] Such a right also allows congregations to affiliate with a denomination safe in the knowledge that they can depart if deep differences arise, "mak[ing] it more likely that congregations will join in the first place."[295]

The hybrid approach, by contrast, leaves no room for such intermediate structures; "establishing a form of governance with a secure right of exit is not possible."[296] It is the "Hotel California" rule for local churches—they can check out any time they like, but they can never leave.[297] Thus, "[o]nce a church is deemed 'hierarchical,' all elements of denominational control must be enforced by the courts. But any elements of congregational control can be canceled by the denomination on a moment's notice, simply by changing the denomination's rules or adopting new interpretations of old rules."[298] In short, the hybrid approach ultimately "imposes more centralized forms of governance on churches than they may have agreed to."[299]

The hybrid approach cannot be defended as a religious "accommodation" of hierarchical denominations. Under this court's precedent, religious

291. Kedroff v. St. Nicholas Cathedral, 344 U.S. 94, 116 (1952).

292. Maryland & Va. Eldership v. Church of God, 396 U.S. 367, 369, 90 S. Ct. 499, 24 L. Ed. 2d 582 (1970) (Brennan, J. concurring)

293. McConnell & Goodrich, *supra* note 269, at 332.

294. *Id.* at 330.

295. *Id.*

296. *Id.* at 332.

297. https://genius.com/Eagles-hotel-california-lyrics.

298. McConnell & Goodrich, *supra* note 269, at 332.

299. *Id.*

accommodations are those that alleviate "a significant burden" on religious exercise.[300] As *Jones* confirmed, free exercise is not implicated by "neutral provisions of state law governing the manner in which churches own property"; the "burden" of complying with such provisions is "minimal."[301] Nor is this surprising. Recording interests in deeds is a common, everyday occurrence.

In fact, the hybrid approach itself imposes substantial burdens on local congregations, the distinct legal entities that hold title under civil law—including, among other things, the loss of their principal secular resource and the base for their ministries. Even where the burdens on third parties are far less severe, this court has held that states may not "vest in the governing bodies of churches" a "unilateral and absolute power" on "issues with significant economic and political implications" for others' property rights.[302]

In short, the hybrid approach is inconsistent with core First Amendment principles. It forces judges to answer a complex question of religious hierarchy that may have no answer—and certainly not an answer that civil courts are well equipped to provide. It incentivizes denominations to become more hierarchical, while discouraging local congregations from affiliating with them and from expanding their property or acting in accordance with their conscience as to whether to remain affiliated with their current denominations.

Under the hybrid approach to church property disputes, a congregation cannot easily avoid having its property expropriated by an affiliated denomination. The denomination can always transfer ownership, even retroactively, simply by passing unilateral rules at church conventions. It does not matter who holds title, what the donor of the property intended, who paid for and maintained the property, whether the denomination's interest is publicly recorded, what the rules were when the congregation joined the denomination, whether the congregation then held title in its own name or even whether the denomination then existed.

300. Corp. of Presiding Bishops v. Amos, 483 U.S. 327, 336; 107 S. Ct. 2862; 97 L. Ed. 2d 273 (1987).

301. 443 U.S. at 606.

302. Larkin v. Grendel's Den Inc., 459 U.S. 116, 117, 127 (1982).

Chapter 2

Property Disputes within an Independent Religious Organization

As frequently as divisions occur within denominations, the same amount of disputes arise within independent congregations, which gives rise to the same issue: Who retains the property of the church—mosque, temple, or synagogue—when an intra-church dispute arises? The U.S. Supreme Court has answered the question by relying again on neutral principles of law. It is true, of course, that courts cannot decide ecclesiastical issues. As the New Jersey Supreme Court has put it, "Civil courts lack jurisdiction over spiritual matters. . . ."[1] But it is essential to also understand that "[t]emporal matters of a church affecting civil or property rights, on the other hand, may be resolved by civil courts."[2] The general principle is that churches are just as entitled as nonreligious organizations to legal enforcement of their established internal procedures.

The question for many courts, however, is to what extent should the court look when evaluating the issue with respect to intra-church property disputes. Similar to denominational disputes, courts look at this issue on a case-by-case basis.

1. Chavis v. Rowe, 459 A.2d 674, 678 (1983).
2. *Id.*

I. The Supreme Court's Guidance on Intra-Church Disputes

The U.S. Supreme Court evaluated intra-church religious property disputes in *Serbian Eastern Orthodox Diocese v. Milivojevich*,[3] a case in which a defrocked bishop asked the civil court to declare him the "true diocesan bishop" of an undivided diocese. The dispute "essentially involve[d] not a church property dispute but a religious dispute, the resolution of which . . . is for ecclesiastical and not civil tribunals."[4] When the mother church in Russia removed Bishop Milivojevich from his post as head of the diocese and reorganized the diocese by dividing it into three parts, Milivojevich sued in Illinois state court to reverse the church's disciplinary and organizational determinations, asserting that the church's tribunal exceeded the scope of its authority under church law and therefore acted arbitrarily.[5]

The state court ruled in Milivojevich's favor, holding that the denomination violated its own procedures and internal regulations and lacked authority to divide the diocese. On appeal, the Supreme Court reversed, observing the state court's judgment "rest[ed] upon an impermissible rejection of the decisions of the highest ecclesiastical tribunals"[6] and impermissibly substituted its own inquiry into church polity. The high court explained:

> For civil courts to analyze whether the ecclesiastical actions of a church judicatory are in that sense "arbitrary" must inherently entail inquiry into the procedures that canon or ecclesiastical law supposedly requires the church judicatory to follow, or else into the substantive criteria by which they are supposedly to decide the ecclesiastical question. But this is exactly the inquiry that the First Amendment prohibits; recognition of such an exception would undermine the general rule that religious controversies are not the proper subject of civil court

3. Serbian E. Orthodox Diocese v. Milivojevich, 426 U.S. 696, 707–09 (1976).
4. *Id.* at 707.
5. *Id.*
6. *Id.*

inquiry and that a civil court must accept the ecclesiastical decisions of church tribunals as it finds them.[7]

The basic dispute in *Milivojevich* was control of the Eastern Orthodox Diocese for the United States of America and Canada, its property and assets.[8] But control of church property was merely an "incidental effect" of deciding who ran the church itself; church charters vested control in the denominational leader, and only the denomination had the authority to select its leader.[9] As the Court explained, "This case essentially involves not a church property dispute but a religious dispute the resolution of which under our cases is for ecclesiastical and not civil tribunals."[10]

Consistent with *Milivojevich*, "[C]ourts applying the neutral-principles methodology defer to religious entities' decisions on ecclesiastical and church polity issues, such as who may be members of the entities and whether to remove a bishop or pastor."[11] That is, what happens to the relationship between a hierarchical religious organization and a subordinate unit after a vote to disassociate "is an ecclesiastical matter over which civil courts generally do not have jurisdiction."[12] "But what happens to the property is not, unless the [local entity's] affairs have been ordered so that ecclesiastical decisions effectively determine the property issue."[13]

The relevant question becomes what "implicates religious doctrine or practice" and when is property "ordered so that ecclesiastical decisions effectively determine the property issue."[14] Denominations, for example, argue that ecclesiastical matters determine what happens to the property because (1) the dispute is essentially a question of church leadership, which is indisputably an ecclesiastical question, and (2) ecclesiastical decisions effectively determine the ownership of property.

7. *Id.* at 713.
8. *Id.* at 698.
9. *Id.* at 699, 701, 709–10.
10. *Id.* at 709.
11. *Id.*
12. *Id.* at 698.
13. *Id.* at 699, 701, 709–10.
14. *Id.* at 698.

However, as noted previously, issues of religious property ownership are not those of "purely ecclesiastic matters." Rather, the ownership of property is rooted in basic principles of contract law, trust law, property law, and corporate law. The adjudication of these issues requires the application of legal principles, not ecclesiastical ones. Although it is true that a court may not inquire into the validity of a religious belief or practice that prompts the challenged conduct,[15] a court, however, may apply neutral principles of law to decide an issue that does not implicate religious doctrine.[16]

Neutral principles "are wholly secular legal rules whose application to religious parties or disputes does not entail theological or doctrinal evaluations."[17] Only "when the underlying dispute turns on doctrine or polity" should a court refuse to enforce secular rights.[18] Thus, when courts are involved in intra-church disputes with no formal organized form of government—meaning, no bylaws, no constitution, no rules or polity, where the locus of control is ambiguous—the issue becomes to what extent may a court evaluate control.

The practical and constitutional problems that are presented by any method that relies on a judicial determination of ecclesiastical polity and a simplistic choice between only two alternatives, hierarchical or congregational, are apparent from the many inconsistent rulings that dot the judicial landscape.[19] That constitutional infirmity lies at the heart of the

15. United States v. Ballard, 322 U.S. 78 (1944).

16. *See* Elmora Hebrew Ctr. Inc. v. Fishman, 125 N.J. 404, 413, 419, 593 A.2d 725 (1991) (stating "religious parties or institutions are not . . . less entitled to civil adjudication of secular legal questions"); ("It is not proper for a trial court to refer civil issues to a religious tribunal in the first instance.").

17. *Id.* at 414–15, 593 A.2d 725.

18. Welter v. Seton Hall Univ., 128 N.J. 279, 293, 608 A.2d 206 (1992).

19. For example, Baptist churches have generally been found to be congregational in nature, Kent Greenawalt, *Hands Off! Civil Court Involvement in Conflicts over Religious Property*, 98 Colum. L. Rev. 1843, 1878 (1998), yet one modern court classified a Baptist church as hierarchical, Crumbley v. Solomon, 254 S.E.2d 330 (Ga. 1979); *see also* Chrapko v. Kobasa, 114 A. 254 (Pa. 1921) (holding that the Greek Catholic Church was connected with the Roman Catholic Church, despite evidence that the church was independently organized); Drozda v. Bassos, 23 N.Y.S.2d 544 (App. Div. 1940) (holding Greek Catholic Church to be an independent congregation, not united with the Roman Catholic Church, despite testimony indicating association); *compare* Mullins v. Elswick, 438 S.W.2d 496 (Ky. 1968) (holding Free Will Baptist Church is congregational because its governing power rests with members of the congregation), *with* W. Conference of Original Free Will Baptists of N.C. v. Miles, 129 S.E.2d 600 (N.C. 1963) (upholding a jury determination that a relationship between the local church

hierarchical-deference method. The base inquiry under that method is whether the church is, in fact, hierarchical. But that inquiry can become a snare. "For every Christian church and probably every religious organization, forms of government relate to doctrine. In religious institutions, government is not independent of belief; rather, it reflects an understanding of how God relates to human beings and how human beings seek religious truth."[20]

It was in part because of this heightened potential for constitutional violation that the U.S. Supreme Court in *Jones v. Wolf* strongly commended state court adoption of the neutral-principles of law method for use in resolving church property disputes. *Wolf* said the alternative method—of automatic deference to ecclesiastical authorities' assertion of a property trust—would involve more, not less, risk of civil court entanglement with religious doctrine, practice, and administration. In its critique of the dissenter's advocacy of the deference method, the majority opinion said:

> [C]ivil courts would always be required to examine the polity and administration of a church to determine which unit of government has ultimate control over church property. In some cases, this task would not prove to be difficult. But in others, the locus of control would be ambiguous, and a careful examination of the constitutions of the general and local church, as well as other relevant documents,

and a Conference appointed to decide matters of doctrine was enough to show Free Will Baptist churches have a hierarchical structure); *compare* Kemp v. Lentz, 68 N.E.2d 339 (Ohio Ct. App. 1943) (holding Church of the Brethren is congregational and that sending delegates to national conventions and giving money to a parent church does not mean it is hierarchical), *with* First Church of Brethren v. Snider, 79 A.2d 422 (Pa. 1951) (holding Church of the Brethren to be hierarchical because its affiliation with General Conference, and all ministers were duly ordained ministers of the Church of the Brethren); *compare* Hayman v. St. Martin's Evangelical Lutheran Church, 176 A.2d 772 (Md. 1962) (local church affiliated with Evangelical and Reformed Church through merger, but still held to be congregational), *with* Immanuel Evangelical Lutheran Church v. Fromm, 116 N.W.2d 766 (Mich. 1962) (holding church to be hierarchical because it "conducted business" as a part of the Evangelical and Reformed Church). As this illustrative recitation shows, courts find themselves reaching wildly inconsistent results in searching for a sort of jurisprudential Holy Grail. Cases such as these, where the locus of control is ambiguous, have beguiled courts into adjudicating questions of religious polity in violation of bedrock First Amendment.

20. Greenawalt, *supra* note 19, at 1877; *see also* Kathleen E. Reeder, *Whose Church Is It, Anyway? Property Disputes and Episcopal Church Splits*, 40 Colum. J.L. & Soc. Probs. 125, 130 (Winter 2006).

> would be necessary to ascertain the form of governance adopted by the members of the religious association. . . . In such cases, the suggested rule would appear to require "a searching and therefore impermissible inquiry into church polity."[21]

In contrast, the neutral-principles approach "obviates entirely the need for an analysis or examination of ecclesiastical polity or doctrine in settling church property disputes."[22] In *Jones v. Wolf*,[23] the U.S. Supreme Court permitted, but did not require, courts to apply the neutral-principles test and expressly noted the numerous advantages of that inquiry. But that was a generation ago. The intervening history over the past 40 years has not only demonstrated the practical advantages of neutral principles but also illuminated inherent problems with the hierarchical-deference methodology.

A church property rule designed for a more homogeneous, 19th-century America does not address the constitutional realities posed by religiously diverse 21st-century America. By contrast, the neutral-principles of law method, correctly understood, is sufficiently flexible to allow fair and constitutionally equal treatment to churches of all religious persuasions.[24] The neutral-principles approach, as its name suggests, levels the litigation playing field. And it does so in an admirably practical way that achieves a vitally important constitutional value. As the U.S. Supreme Court stated in *Board of Education of Kiryas Joel Village School District v. Grumet*, "[A]bsent the most unusual circumstances, one's religion ought not affect one's legal rights or duties or benefits."[25] Neutral-principles analysis avoids such constitutional difficulties and works to ensure fairness for all.

The Supreme Court noted in *Jones* that "[t]he primary advantages of the neutral-principles approach are that it is completely secular in operation and yet flexible enough to accommodate all forms of religious organization

---

21. Jones v. Wolf, 443 U.S. 595, 602, 605 (citing Serbian Orthodox Diocese, 426 U.S. at 723).

22. *Id.*

23. *Id.* at 602.

24. *See* Arlin M. Adams & William R. Hanlon, Jones v. Wolf: *Church Autonomy and the Religion Clauses of the First Amendment*, 128 U. Pa. L. Rev. 1291, 1294–95 (1980).

25. 512 U.S. 687, 715 (1994).

and polity."[26] For example, in denominations that are hierarchical for both theological and property purposes, such as the Roman Catholic Church, the potential for property disputes has largely been pretermitted by the vesting of title in the bishop.[27] That centralizing, dispute-avoidance tack is also employed by the Church of Jesus Christ of Latter-day Saints.[28] These churches would maintain current ownership structures under neutral principles by either holding title or using "appropriate reversionary clauses and trust provisions."[29]

At the other extreme, a clearly congregational denomination, such as Baptist churches, would continue to have disputes resolved as they have been in the past. All denominations would retain the prerogative through ordinary legal means to determine where property will end up in the event of a split.[30] The First Amendment "mandates governmental neutrality between religion and religion and between religion and nonreligion."[31]

In *Larson v. Valente*, the U.S. Supreme Court held that where a law violates the neutrality principle by discriminating among denominations, it becomes "suspect" and therefore subject to strict scrutiny.[32] The test for strict scrutiny requires that a compelling governmental interest exists to justify the discrimination, and that the law in question be narrowly tailored to further that interest.[33] A powerful governmental interest exists in giving religious bodies the power to rule autonomously. In order, though, to prevent judicial entanglement in ecclesiastical matters, the state's church property dispute-resolution methodology must be narrowly tailored—and the broad sweep of automatic deference to a denominational trust clause is, by definition, not narrowly tailored. Such automatic deference does

26. *Jones*, 443 U.S. at 603.

27. *See* Jeffrey B. Hassler, *A Multitude of Sins? Constitutional Standards for Legal Resolution of Church Property Disputes in a Time of Escalating Intradenominational Strife*, 35(2) Pepp. L. Rev. 399, 405–06 (2008).

28. *See id.* at 436.

29. *Jones*, 443 U.S. at 603.

30. *Id.* at 603–04.

31. Epperson v. Arkansas, 393 U.S. 97, 104 (1968); *see also* Everson v. Bd. of Educ., 330 U.S. 1 (1947); Zorach v. Clauson, 343 U.S. 306 (1952).

32. Larson v. Valente, 456 U.S. 228, 246 (1982); *see also* Corp. of Presiding Bishop of the Church of Jesus Christ of Latter-Day Saints v. Amos, 483 U.S. 327, 339 (1987).

33. *Larson* at 247.

nothing more than open the door for hierarchical churches to do what no other religious body can do.

Subsequent to *Jones*, the Supreme Court has consistently held that the government may not delegate decision-making authority to religious institutions. In *Larkin v. Grendel's Den*, the Court rejected a state law that gave churches a veto over neighboring applications for liquor licenses because the law "vest[ed] discretionary governmental powers in religious bodies."[34] The Massachusetts Legislature had granted churches a special benefit that it did not grant secular nonprofit organizations. The Court determined that the measure violated the Establishment Clause because it advanced religion by allowing churches to influence government use regulation.[35] This, however, is precisely the dubious function of hierarchical deference. It supplants the legislature's well-developed trust law and offers purportedly hierarchical churches—and no other organizations—the power to revoke the property rights of any subordinate parish or congregation.

Not only does this usurp governmental authority, but it also opens the door to the *Larkin* Court's fear that "the churches' power (ceded to them from the state) could be employed for explicitly religious goals."[36] Granting hierarchical religious bodies such untrammeled authority over property rights poses this exact risk, especially when the local churches have not expressly yielded such authority. The power to decide who owns property, a core power of civil government, would be vested in religious bodies, which history shows can and will use that power for their own purposes—to enforce imagined orthodoxy and to stifle dissent.

The result in *Larkin* would have been different if the churches' veto power had been included in local covenants, conditions, and restrictions that were voluntarily agreed upon by the surrounding property owners. Under those circumstances, the churches would have enjoyed veto power under neutral principles of contract law. In the same way, a local congregation is free to grant its religious denomination the contractual right to resolve property disputes. Yet, the denomination cannot assume this right without a proper legal instrument executed by the grantor—in this case, the

34. 459 U.S. 116, 122 (1982).
35. *Id.* at 120.
36. *Id.* at 125.

local congregation. Allowing religious organizations to unilaterally declare trusts in their own favor effectively delegates governmental authority to religious institutions, which would then become free to dictate results in a way other parties cannot. The First Amendment does not allow such a law.

Where appropriate, in some states, the other approach to church disputes is used regardless of the governing structure of a particular church, and it involves the application of neutral principles of law to determine disputed questions not implicating religious doctrine or practice.[37] This approach calls for the examination and interpretation of church documents such as deeds, constitutions, bylaws, and the like in accordance with wholly secular legal rules whose applications do not entail theological or doctrinal evaluations.[38] "The threshold requirement is a judicially protectable interest—whether it arises under the law of property, contract, corporations, tort or another area—presented for adjudication."[39]

In many of the cases where courts have refused to interpret church-governing documents, their rationale seems to turn on the underlying impact on such interpretation. For example, New Jersey courts will never interpret church bylaws regarding who can be a church member or church pastor.[40] Such an interpretation would clearly violate the First Amendment, because the court would essentially be deciding who is qualified to be a church member or pastor. Thus, in order for a New Jersey court to apply neutral principles to a church dispute, a party must be able to point the court to clear church governance documents that can be enforced and emphasize that no religious matter is affected.

37. Jones v. Wolf, 443 U.S. 595, 602, 99 S. Ct. 3020, 3025 (1979); Solid Rock Baptist Church v. Carlton, 347 N.J. Super. 180, 192, 789 A.2d 149, 156 (Super. Ct. App. Div. 2002).

38. *Jones*, 443 U.S. at 604, 99 S. Ct. at 3026, 61 L. Ed. 2d at 785; Elmora Hebrew Ctr. Inc. v. Fishman, 125 N.J. at 414–15, 593 A.2d 725. "Although judicial treatment of litigation involving religious entities sometimes may turn on the governance structure of the religious organization involved" that question is not determinative. Chomsky v. Sewitch, No. A-4767-11T2, 2013 N.J. Super. Unpub. LEXIS 1843, at *11 (Super. Ct. App. Div. July 23, 2013) (emphasis added); *see also* Trs. of the Alpine Methodist Episcopal Church v. N.J. United Methodist Church, No. A-4583-15T2, 2017 N.J. Super. Unpub. LEXIS 3127, at *28 (Super. Ct. App. Div. Dec. 19, 2017).

39. Chavis v. Rowe, 93 N.J. 103, 110, 459 A.2d 674 (1983).

40. Simons v. Lewis, No. A-4600-12T2, 2014 N.J. Super. Unpub. LEXIS 2381, at *22 (Super. Ct. App. Div. Oct. 2, 2014).

A few other states go a step further and will allow courts to interpret church bylaws by using neutral principles.[41] Missouri, in particular, has interpreted church bylaws on several occasions. In *First Missionary Baptist Church v. Rollins*, the court affirmed a circuit court's decision ordering a leadership election and determining that certain individuals were not church members and were therefore not eligible to vote.[42] In *Fast v. Smyth*, a case where competing factions were vying for control of a church facing trusteeship, a Missouri court held that a number of individuals were not properly made members of the church and, in turn, were properly denied the right to vote on church affairs.[43] However, Missouri is a distinct minority in this regard.

In *Hosanna-Tabor Evangelical Lutheran Church and School v. E.E.O.C.*,[44] Chief Justice Roberts was clear and unambiguous as to the applicability of the court's decision:

> The case before us is an employment discrimination suit brought on behalf of a minister, challenging her church's decision to fire her. Today we hold only that the ministerial exception bars such a suit. We express no view on whether the exception bars other types of suits, including actions by alleging breach of contract or tortious conduct by their religious employers. There will be time enough to address the applicability of the exception to other circumstances if and when they arise.[45]

Accordingly, the *Hosanna-Tabor* court's decision was limited to the applicability of the "ministerial exception" to employment discrimination suits.

---

41. Ervin v. Lilydale Progressive Missionary Baptist Church, 351 Ill. App. 3d 41, 46, 813 N.E.2d 1073, 286 Ill. Dec. 380 (2004) ("Conversely, where a complaint alleges that a church has violated its own bylaws, a civil court may exercise jurisdiction to decide whether the church has violated its bylaws."); Chen v. Tseng, No. 01-02-01005-CV, 2004 Tex. App. LEXIS 264, at *19–20 (Tex. App. Jan. 8, 2004) (interpreting and applying church bylaws); Beth Hamedrosh Hagodol Cemetary Ass'n v. Levy, 923 S.W.2d 439, 443 (Mo. App. E.D. 1996) ("In short, because the Church was incorporated under Missouri nonprofit law, it has submitted to the state courts all matters of a corporate nature."); *see also* Spirit & Truth Church v. Barnaby, 428 S.W.3d 764, 769 (Mo. Ct. App. 2014).

42. 199 S.W.3d 823.

43. 527 S.W.2d 673 (Mo. App. 1975).

44. 132 S. Ct. 694 (2012).

45. *Id.* at 710.

The Supreme Court specifically exempted breach-of-contract claims and tortious conduct from the ministerial exception.

In *McKelvey v. Pierce*,[46] the Supreme Court of New Jersey held, in pertinent part:

> The First Amendment *does not* immunize every legal claim against a religious institution and its members. The analysis in each case is fact-sensitive and claim-specific, requiring an assessment of every issue raised in terms of doctrinal and administrative intrusion and entanglement. In our view, the lower courts failed to engage in that kind of painstaking analysis and painted with too broad a brush when dismissing McKelvey's case in its entirety. We thus reverse and remand the case to the trial court to determine, on an issue-by-issue basis, whether any of McKelvey's claims may be adjudicated consistent with First Amendment principles.[47]

Further, "[a]lthough the church autonomy doctrine provides a shield against excessive government incursion on internal church management, it clearly cannot be applied blindly to all disputes involving church conduct or decisions."[48]

In *Minker v. Baltimore Annual Conference of United Methodist Church*,[49] the U.S. Court of Appeals for the District of Columbia Circuit permitted further review of an oral-contract claim, explaining that "[a] church is always free to burden its activities voluntarily through contracts, and such contracts are fully enforceable in civil court."[50] As recognized in *McKelvey* and *Minker*, it is premature to foreclose the breach-of-contract claim on a motion to dismiss. As set forth in *Minker*:

> [T]he [F]irst [A]mendment does not immunize the church from all temporal claims made against it. As we noted in *Costello Publishing*

46. 173 N.J. 26 (2002).
47. *See id.* at 32–33.
48. *Id.* at 44.
49. 894 F.2d 1354 (D.C. Cir. 1990).
50. *Id.* at 1359.

> *Co. v. Rotelle*, 670 F.2d 1035 (D.C. Cir. 1981), appellant need show only that some form of inquiry is permissible and some form of remedy is available to survive a motion to dismiss. . . . [We] noted that summary judgment was inappropriate because the trial court should at least consider the circumstances of the alleged activity to determine whether a religious concern existed and whether a nonintrusive remedy could be fashioned.[51]

As noted in *McKelvey*, the critical factor in the application of the ministerial exception to a given cause of action must be that resolution of the claim requires an impermissible inquiry into the propriety of a *decision* of core ecclesiastical concern—a decision, in other words, where the *dispute* truly is *religious*.

The First Amendment is not violated so long as resolution of a claim does not require the court to choose between competing interpretations of religious tenets or to interfere with a church's autonomy rights. Churches and their ministers are not above the law and may be held liable for tortuous conduct or contractual undertakings.[52]

Clearly, state courts have made it clear that local courts must step in to ensure that "established procedures of a religious organization, as proved, have been followed." In *Baugh v. Thomas*,[53] the New Jersey Supreme Court held that the established internal procedures of religious organizations, like those of other organizations, are legally enforceable; and that if churches fail to follow them, judicial intervention is both appropriate and required. William Baugh, who had been expelled from the First Baptist Church of South Orange, brought suit in the New Jersey courts challenging his expulsion as procedurally improper:

> According to plaintiff's amended complaint, 31 votes were cast against him and 25 in his favor. One vote against him was disqualified because the voter was delinquent in the payment of her dues. Plaintiff alleges

51. *Id.*
52. *McKelvey*, 173 N.J. at 54.
53. 265 A.2d 675, 677 (N.J. 1970); *see also* Alicea v. New Brunswick Theological Seminary, 581 A.2d 900, 908 (N.J. App. Div. 1990) ("[A] party may seek judicial relief based on a church's failure to follow its own procedures.").

> that two other members who voted against him should also have been disqualified for the same reason. This would change the vote to 28 against reinstatement and 25 in favor. He further alleges that four members who were present abstained. He contends that the votes of these four members should have been counted for him in accordance with the constitution of the church, since that document requires that abstentions should be counted as affirmative votes. Thus, by plaintiff's count, he should have been reinstated by a vote of 29 to 28.[54]

The lower New Jersey courts had dismissed Baugh's claims, reasoning that courts should not investigate whether an expulsion was proper. But the New Jersey Supreme Court reversed, saying Baugh's claim had to go forward. Crucially, Baugh did not challenge that the church *could* expel him, nor was Baugh challenging the specific reasons that the church had expelled him. Instead, Baugh sought judicial review of a narrower kind—over whether the church had complied with its own established procedures when it expelled him. Church bylaws and constitutions are written for a reason, Baugh pointed out. Both are ways that religious communities exercise their rights of self-governance. So, when a religious organization fails to follow its own procedures, judicial intervention is warranted—and, in fact, needed—to protect the rights of the true majority of the church.

The Supreme Court of New Jersey agreed, siding with Baugh in a unanimous opinion:

> We cannot, however, accept the proposition that civil courts lack jurisdiction to determine whether established procedures of a religious organization, as proved, have been followed where a member is expelled from that organization. . . . [E]xcept in cases involving religious doctrine, we can see no reason for treating religious organizations differently from other nonprofit voluntary associations. . . . In the present case, the plaintiff urges that the vote for reinstatement was improperly counted because it did not accord with established church procedure. He alleges that members who were ineligible to vote were included in the tally against him, and persons who abstained were not

54. 265 A.2d at 676.

> counted for him. In short, he contends that a tabulation of the votes which comported with church procedure would result in his reinstatement. . . . We conclude that plaintiff's amended complaint states a cause of action which our courts may properly hear in that it alleges an expulsion in violation of the church's established procedures.[55]

The Supreme Court concluded the case by ordering a remand for Baugh to have the opportunity to prove the allegations of his amended complaint.[56] *Baugh* has been widely followed. As the Appellate Division squarely and succinctly put it, "[A] party may seek judicial relief based on a church's failure to follow its own procedures."[57] One such case was the Appellate Division's decision in *Hardwick v. First Baptist Church of Perth Amboy*.[58]

Hardwick is a detailed case factually, but the legal principle it adopts is simple. A Baptist church had engaged in outreach to the surrounding Hispanic community, leading to a Hispanic sub-congregation within the larger church. Members of the Hispanic sub-congregation believed themselves members of that larger church. They pointed out, for example, how the former pastor had added them to the voting rolls. But, others in the church did not see members of the Hispanic sub-congregation as members. They pointed out that church bylaws required membership decisions to be approved both by the deacons and the general church membership, which had not happened.

They also contended that even if the members of the Hispanic sub-congregation had been made members, they were deleted from the voting rolls after they took steps to form a separate church. After an escalating dispute, a special general meeting was called. In that meeting, the members of the Hispanic sub-congregation were asked to leave the room, and the remaining church members declared them not to be members of the church. Soon after, the Hispanic sub-congregation was evicted from the building.[59]

55. *Id.* at 677–78.
56. *See id.* at 678 ("On this remand, the procedure which defendants allegedly breached must, of course, be proved by plaintiff.").
57. 581 A.2d at 908.
58. 524 A.2d 1298 (N.J. App. Div. 1987).
59. *Id.* at 1299–300.

In response, the members of the Hispanic sub-congregation filed suit, claiming that they were improperly expelled from the church. After all, the plaintiffs said, they were members of the church and thus entitled to participate in the expulsion vote against them. In response, the church—the defendant in the action—said that both the decision to exclude the plaintiffs from the room and the vote to expel them were beyond the purview of the New Jersey courts.

Following *Baugh*, the Appellate Division rejected the church's claim. The court found that it was entirely appropriate for the New Jersey courts to decide whether the church had followed its established procedures. As in *Baugh*, the court said judicial review was not merely appropriate but actually required.

> [I]f the issue is not resolved by the courts, what may have been a minority of the church membership could, by requesting the majority to leave the room, have appropriated the church, its property and the right to designate future members by a rump vote subject to no civil or ecclesiastical appeal.[60]

Hardwick concluded the case by remanding for fuller consideration of the plaintiff's claims that the defendant had not followed the procedures established in its bylaws and church constitution—"matter[s] well within its jurisdiction."[61] It is indeed true that although New Jersey courts have jurisdiction to ensure churches generally follow their own procedures, they still may not determine ecclesiastical issues. *Baugh* and *Hardwick* are both consistent with that principle. In fact, they adopt it explicitly.[62]

Thus, in *Baugh*, the plaintiff claimed that people ineligible to vote actually voted and that abstentions under established church rules had to be counted as votes in his favor.[63] In *Hardwick*, the claim was that people

60. *Id.* at 1301.

61. *Id.* at 1302.

62. *Baugh*, 265 A.2d at 677 ("It must be emphasized that there is no question of spiritual matters or church doctrine in the present case."); *Hardwick*, 524 A.2d at 1301 ("[T]he question of church membership is not one that is removed from the jurisdiction of the civil courts, even though the courts may not determine ecclesiastical issues.").

63. *Baugh*, 265 A.2d at 676.

prevented from voting actually had a right to vote.[64] In these two cases, the plaintiffs had the right to try to show that the "established procedure of a religious organization" has not "been followed."[65]

In *Chavis v. Rowe*,[66] the New Jersey Supreme Court held that courts could not inquire into whether a deacon was properly defrocked. "The procedure for removing a deacon is ambiguous," the court said, and could "be properly resolved only by going *beyond* the bylaws and the constitution of Calvary to a study of the purpose and the philosophy of congregational structure in general and of disciplining congregational deacons in particular."[67]

Another case also illustrates the line between ecclesiastical and non-ecclesiastical issues. In *Chomsky v. Sewitch*,[68] members of a synagogue challenged the sale of its Perth Amboy property. The court concluded that "secular matters affecting the civil or property rights of individuals—such as those pertaining to contractual obligations, church membership or corporate governance," the Appellate Division said—"may be addressed by civil courts so long as excessive entanglement with ecclesiastical and doctrinal matters does not occur."[69]

It was true that the lower court should not ask whether the property sale was consistent with Halacha (Jewish religious law based on the Talmud), which perhaps forbade selling synagogue property to non-Jews. But, the Appellate Division added, the lower court was right to examine whether the property sale was consistent with the synagogue's established internal procedures. Here, by asking only whether the bylaws and constitution had been complied with and staying out of ecclesiastical questions about Jewish religious law, the trial court had gotten it exactly right:

> The trial court did not decide any disputed questions of religious doctrine. Indeed, the issues resolved did not require the judge to go beyond the statutes or the bylaws and constitution of the congregation. Rather, he deliberately and expressly abstained from adjudication of,

64. *Hardwick*, 524 A.2d at 1299–300.
65. *Baugh*, 265 A.2d at 677.
66. 459 A.2d 674 (N.J. 1983).
67. *Id.* at 679 (emphasis added).
68. No. A-4767-11T2, 2013 WL 3791707 (N.J. App. Div. July 23, 2013).
69. *Id.* at *4.

and thereby avoided entanglement with, those claims which required resolution of religious questions, such as whether defendants' actions complied with the tenets of Halacha and whether the parties were required to submit their dispute to the beth din because the congregation was an Orthodox Jewish institution.[70]

The U.S. Supreme Court's decision in *Serbian Orthodox Diocese v. Milivojevich* is perfectly consistent with these decisions. As noted previously, in *Milivojevich*, the Supreme Court dismissed the suit of a bishop who claimed he was improperly defrocked by the Serbian Orthodox Church, just as the deacon in *Chavis* was defrocked. Investigating such a claim led Illinois courts to engage in extensive review of Serbian Orthodox religious beliefs. This, the court said, was improper—courts cannot decide internal religious disputes "where resolution of the disputes cannot be made without extensive inquiry by civil courts into religious law and polity."[71]

It is clear that church bylaws, articles of incorporation, and constitutions are legally enforceable. Religious organizations, after all, "come before us in the same attitude as other voluntary associations for benevolent or charitable purposes; and their rights of property, or of contract, are equally under the protection of the law."[72] Churches are entitled to govern themselves and are just as entitled to the law's protection of that self-governance as any other organization. And courts have the power to interpret and enforce the local church's bylaws, constitutions, and polity.

70. *Id.* at *5.

71. Serbian East Orthodox Diocese v. Milivojevich, 426 U.S. 696, 709-709, 96 S. Ct. 2372, 49 L. Ed. 2d 658 (1969).

72. Watson v. Jones, 80 U.S. 679, 714 (1871).

Part II

Religious Land Use and Zoning Law

Issues involving the use of religious land emerged centuries ago. In the Book of Ezra, found in the Old Testament of the Bible, is a brief discussion of how uses of religious land are governed by largely discretionary administrative proceedings prone to arbitrariness that can incentivize discriminatory treatment—intentional or not—in a way that the First Amendment shield cannot necessarily block with the same ease.

The concern with pretextual land use denials that provided one of the bases for the enactment of the Religious Land Use and Institutionalized Persons Act (RLUIPA) parallels the controversy in the Book of Ezra over constructing the Second Temple. By way of background, the Jewish people were taken captive and exiled to Babylon. Nehemiah—a chief servant of the King of Babylon, Cyrus the Great—asked him for permission to return to Jerusalem to rebuild the wall and the holy temple. The king granted his request, and Nehemiah returned, gathered the faithful, and rebuilt the wall. However, the local people who had occupied the land after the Jewish people were exiled to Babylon felt threatened by their works and tried to stop the temple from being rebuilt. When their attempts were blocked, they went to the king, alleging that the Jewish exiles were building the wall and the temple to block his ability to rule and collect taxes.

In many ways, the story of the Second Temple is symbolic of a religious land use case. A parcel or building is found in which to build a temple, but it is not in a condition to be used for religious purposes. It is clear that the issue of land use and zoning for local religious uses are not new. The arguments in opposition to the use are the same—too noisy, too much traffic, lighting is too bright, inadequate parking—yet they all boil down to one issue: the neighboring community does not want them in the area.

So why is there such animosity to uses of religious land? There are three main reasons:

1. Religious entities do not generate property taxes, resulting in the argument that churches are a "drain" on public resources.
2. A belief that churches take up valuable prime real estate in the community.
3. Religious discrimination.

It is clear that religious zoning is a centuries-old issue and one that will never go away. That is why a need exists for religious entities to rely on federal and state constitutional and statutory laws when considering religious uses.

Chapter 3

Religious Land Use and Zoning: Statutory Claims

I. RLUIPA: The Religious Land Use and Institutionalized Persons Act

A. Historical Background

The impetus behind the passage of the Religious Land Use and Institutionalized Persons Act (RLUIPA) stems from the Supreme Court's decision in *Employment Division v. Smith*, which marked a turning point in free exercise jurisprudence by shielding neutral laws of general applicability from violations of religious freedom. Congress responded to the *Smith* decision by passing the Religious Freedom Restoration Act[1] (RFRA) on November 16, 1993. RFRA was designed to prevent the federal and state governments from substantially burdening a person's free exercise rights unless the burden furthered a compelling interest and was the least-restrictive means of furthering that interest. In many respects, RFRA was meant to embrace a return to the *Sherbert* and *Yoder* line of cases—hence the "restoration" in the title of the act.

RFRA was introduced in the House by then-Representative Charles Schumer and attracted no fewer than 170 co-sponsors from both political parties. The bill was unanimously approved in committee, and after years of congressional hearings, the full House subsequently passed the bill by a

1. 42 U.S.C. § 2000bb.

unanimous vote.[2] Senators Orrin Hatch and Edward Kennedy jointly presented the chamber's companion bill. It garnered a bipartisan group of 58 co-sponsors and passed the full Senate by a vote of 97–3.[3] When RFRA was passed in 1993, the bill "was supported by one of the broadest coalitions in recent political history," with 66 religious and civil liberties groups, "including Christians, Jews, Muslims, Sikhs, Humanists and secular civil liberties organizations."[4]

In his signing, President Bill Clinton noted "what a broad coalition of Americans came together to make this bill a reality" and that "many of the people in the coalition worked together across ideological and religious

2. H.R. Rep. No. 103-88 (1993).

3. S. Rep. No. 103-111 (1993).

4. Douglas Laycock & Oliver S. Thomas, *Interpreting the Religious Freedom Restoration Act*, 73 TEX. L. REV. 209, 210, 244 (1994); *see also id.* at 201 n.9 ("The Coalition for the Free Exercise of Religion included: Agudath Israel of America; American Association of Christian Schools; American Civil Liberties Union; American Conference on Religious Movements; American Humanist Association; American Jewish Committee; American Jewish Congress; American Muslim Council; Americans for Democratic Action; Americans for Religious Liberty; Americans United for Separation of Church and State; Anti-Defamation League; Association of Christian Schools International; Association on American Indian Affairs; Baptist Joint Committee on Public Affairs; B'nai B'rith; Central Conference of American Rabbis; Christian Church (Disciples of Christ); Christian College Coalition; Christian Legal Society; Christian Life Commission of the Southern Baptist Convention; Christian Science Committee on Publication; Church of the Brethren; Church of Jesus Christ of Latter-day Saints; Church of Scientology International; Coalitions for America; Concerned Women for America; Council of Jewish Federations; Council on Religious Freedom; Episcopal Church; Evangelical Lutheran Church in America; Federation of Reconstructionist Congregations and Havurot; First Liberty Institute; Friends Committee on National Legislation; General Conference of Seventh-day Adventists; Guru Gobind Singh Foundation; Hadassah, The Women's Zionist Organization of America Inc.; Home School Legal Defense Association; House of Bishops of the Episcopal Church; International Institute for Religious Freedom; Japanese American Citizens League; Jesuit Social Ministries, National Office; Justice Fellowship; Mennonite Central Committee U.S.; NA'AMAT USA; National Association of Evangelicals; National Council of Churches; National Council of Jewish Women; National Drug Strategy Network; National Federation of Temple Sisterhoods; National Islamic Prison Foundation; National Jewish Commission on Law and Public Affairs; National Jewish Community Relations Advisory Council; National Sikh Center; Native American Church of North America; North American Council for Muslim Women; People for the American Way Action Fund; Presbyterian Church (USA), Social Justice and Peacemaking Unit; Rabbinical Council of America; Traditional Values Coalition; Union of American Hebrew Congregations; Union of Orthodox Jewish Congregations of America; Unitarian Universalist Association of Congregations; United Church of Christ, Office for Church in Society; United Methodist Church, Board of Church and Society; United Synagogue of Conservative Judaism. . . . The American Bar Association did not formally join the Coalition, but repeatedly endorsed the bill."); American Bar Association, Statement of Support for the Religious Freedom Restoration Act of 1993 (Mar. 11, 1993).

lines."[5] The president praised "the shared desire . . . to protect perhaps the most precious of all American liberties—religious freedom"—and even joked that "the power of God is such that even in legislative process miracles can happen."[6] Thus, RFRA essentially reinstated the pre-*Smith* "Sherbert test," which reigned from 1963 to 1990.

However, just three years later, in 1997, the Supreme Court struck down RFRA as an unconstitutional use of Congress's enforcement of powers.[7] The constitutionality of RFRA came before the court in *City of Boerne v. Flores*.[8] The case involved a dispute between a Texas town and the Catholic archbishop of the diocese that wanted to enlarge an existing building, resulting in a violation of local historic preservation laws.[9] The Court found that RFRA was unconstitutional as applied to the states based primarily on federalism concerns.[10] In reviewing the enactment of the law, the Court concluded that Congress offered limited evidence that state and local governments were systematically imperiling religious liberty. The Court suggested that evidence of the same could be sufficient to restore the compelling-interest test established by the Court in *Smith*.[11]

It is important to recognize that RFRA remains applicable against the federal government, even after *Flores*. It prohibits the government from substantially burdening a person's exercise of religion unless the government can prove that the burden furthers a "compelling government interest" and is the "least restrictive means" of furthering that interest.[12] RFRA is at the heart of the mandate cases challenging the requirement to provide contraceptives and abortion-inducing drugs to all employees, including those whose religious beliefs prohibit contraceptives and abortion, under

5. Statement by President on Signing the Religious Freedom Restoration Act of 1993 (Nov. 16, 1993).
6. *Id.*
7. City of Boerne v. Flores, 521 U.S. 507 (1997).
8. *Id.*
9. *Id.* at 520.
10. *Id.* at 523.
11. *Id.* at 525
12. O'Bryan v. Bureau of Prisons, 349 F.3d 399, 401 (7th Cir. 2003).

the Affordable Care Act.[13] Notably, several states—21 in all—have enacted their own versions of the Religious Freedom Restoration Act.

Soon after the *Flores* decision, Congress contemplated another statute, the Religious Liberty Protection Act (RLPA), which essentially mirrored the RFRA except that Congress based its authority to pass such legislation on its broad powers under the Commerce and Spending Clauses.[14] In looking at the issue, Congress investigated state and local burdens on religious freedom and amassed evidence in nine congressional hearings that took place over three years. This bill, however, never made it out of the Senate Judiciary Committee.[15]

With RFRA declared unconstitutional as applied to states, Congress determined that it was necessary to pass an additional law "to address 'those areas of law where the congressional record of religious discrimination and discretionary burden was the strongest': laws governing institutionalized persons (i.e., prisoners and persons in mental institutions) and land use laws."[16] In their joint statement to the Senate discussing RLUIPA, Senators Hatch and Kennedy observed:

> The right to assemble for worship is at the very core of the free exercise of religion. Churches and synagogues cannot function without a physical space adequate to their needs and consistent with their theological requirements. The right to build, buy or rent such a space is an indispensable adjunct of the core First Amendment right to assemble for religious purposes. [17]

Proponents of both statutes recognized that these laws would protect religious expression that is unpopular, poorly understood, or otherwise unable to receive protection through the political process. The president of the ACLU testified that "members of minority religious groups should not have to depend on accidents of political process to protect their fundamental

13. Michael Gryboski, *Supreme Court Schedules Arguments for Hobby Lobby Case*, CHRISTIAN POST (Jan. 13, 2014), http://bit.ly/2WJL7FX.
14. *See* S.2869, Bill Summary and Status for 106th Congress (2000).
15. *Id.*
16. *Id.*
17. 146 CONG. REC. S7774 (July 27, 2000) (emphasis added).

freedoms" and that without the passage of RFRA, religious liberty would be "[g]ravely [t]hreatened."[18] Representative Nadler noted that Congress's "experience in the three years since Smith . . . demonstrated that religious minorities—and even majority religions—have been placed at a tremendous disadvantage. . . . It was no accident that the framers of our Bill of Rights chose to place the free exercise of religion first among our fundamental freedoms. This House should do no less."[19]

In hearings focused on the context of religious land use, both statistical and anecdotal evidence demonstrated widespread resistance to churches in the zoning context.[20] Thus, RLUIPA was proposed. Like RFRA, it was enacted with overwhelming bipartisan support, passing both the House and Senate by unanimous consent,[21] and President Clinton signed it into law on September 22, 2000.[22] In his signing statement, Clinton expressly applauded "Sens. Kennedy, Hatch, Reid and Schumer and Reps. Canady and Nadler for their hard work in passing this legislation." He noted that RLUIPA "once again demonstrates that people of all political bents and faiths can work together for a common purpose that benefits all Americans."[23]

Though it is much more limited in scope than RFRA and RLPA, RLUIPA reestablished the Sherbert test to include "substantial burden" and "compelling governmental interest" standards that were displaced by the *Smith* decision in two areas: land use and religious practices in prisons.[24] In enacting RLUIPA's land use provisions, Congress relied in part on its authority under section 5 of the Fourteenth Amendment, which provides that Congress "shall have power to enforce this article by appropriate legislation" and the Spending and Commerce Clauses of the Constitution found in article

18. *Religious Freedom Restoration Act of 1991: Hearings on H.R. 2797 Before the S. Comm. on Civil and Constitutional Rights of the H. Comm. on the Judiciary*, 102d Cong., 2d Sess., at 64, 80 (1992).

19. Cong. Rec. H.R. 1308, at 2359–60 (May 11, 1993).

20. H.R. Rep. No. 106-219, at 18–24 (1999); 146 Cong. Rec. S7774, S7774 (daily ed. July 27, 2000), joint statement of Sen. Hatch and Sen. Kennedy noting "massive evidence" of widespread discrimination against churches [hereinafter Joint Statement].

21. *Id.*

22. Pub. L. No. 106-274, 114 Stat. 803 (2000).

23. Statement by President on Signing of Law S. 2869 (Sept. 22, 2000), 2000 WL 1371281, at *1.

24. *Id.*

1, section 8, clause 1.[25] In so doing, Congress was mindful of the Supreme Court's decision in *City of Boerne v. Flores*, which held that Congress lacked authority solely under section 5 to apply RFRA to governmental entities. Congress also sought to comply with *Flores* by compiling a legislative record that would satisfy *Flores*' "congruence and proportionality" test, even if RLUIPA were to exceed existing constitutional requirements in some way that Congress did not anticipate.[26]

Congress enacted RLUIPA's land use provisions to enforce, by statutory right, four constitutional prohibitions that Congress found states and localities were frequently violating in that context.[27] To a large extent, RLUIPA's land use provisions track the legal standards in one or more Supreme Court opinions.

B. The Legal Claims That Can Be Brought under RLUIPA

The litigation under RLUIPA reflects an ongoing clash between the legitimate authority of municipalities to regulate land use and the sincere land use needs of religious organizations in pursuing their missions.

The authority to regulate land use can be traced to the broad but limited state police power. Since the Tenth Amendment reserves powers not delegated to the federal government to the states, the states may exercise any nonfederal power within their own jurisdictional boundaries.[28] This authority to enact and enforce reasonable regulations furthering the general welfare is known as the police power. Under the police power, states may regulate their internal affairs on a general, but not particular, level pursuant to protection of the public interest.[29] Since at least the 1920s, courts have understood that zoning and other land use regulations can be a permissible use of police power.[30] Though expansive, police power, as courts have routinely noted, can still be exercised in arbitrary and oppressive ways in

---

25. *See* Joint Statement, *supra* note 20, at S7775.
26. See pp. 81–83, *infra*.
27. *See* Joint Statement, *supra* note 20, at S7775.
28. State police power is also bound by state constitutional provisions. *See, e.g.*, Garrett v. Faubus, 323 S.W.2d 877, 900–01 (Ark. 1959) (noting that it "is recognized everywhere that the police power of the State Legislature is limited by the State Constitution").
29. Lawton v. Steele, 152 U.S. 133, 137 (1894).
30. Vill. of Euclid v. Ambler Realty Co., 272 U.S. 365, 396–97 (1926).

particular cases, commonly necessitating judicial intervention.[31] Accordingly, Congress enacted RLUIPA as a vehicle for religious organizations to fend off these occasional abuses of municipal authority.[32]

As noted earlier, RLUIPA contains five claims under the same broad statutory umbrella, but each has distinct and separate elements that require their own attention. While a substantial-burden claim might be particularly reliant upon the facts, equal-terms claims might have more to do with the text of the local zoning ordinance. What follows is a review of each type of RLUIPA claim as well as multiple case discussions meant to give the reader a feel for how the cases have been treated in the courts.

1. Substantial Burden Cases

a. Substantial Burden—Jurisdiction

A religious entity may pursue a substantial-burden claim under RLUIPA when at least one of three jurisdictional tests are met: (1) the substantial burden is imposed in a federally funded program or activity; (2) the substantial burden affects, or removal of that burden would affect, interstate or foreign commerce; and (3) the substantial burden is imposed in the implementation of a land use regulation or system of regulations in which the government makes individualized assessments of the proposed uses for the property involved.[33]

This section contains two key phrases: land use regulation and individualized assessment. Congress defined land use regulation in RLUIPA as a

> zoning or land-marking law, or the application of such a law, that limits or restricts a claimant's use or development of land (including a structure affixed to land), if the claimant has an ownership, leasehold, easement, servitude or other property interest in the regulated land or a contract or option to acquire such an interest.[34]

---

31. Jacobson v. Massachusetts, 197 U.S. 11, 38 (1905).

32. Cutter v. Wilkinson, 544 U.S. 709, 714 (2005) (recognizing that "RLUIPA is the latest of long-running congressional efforts to accord religious exercise heightened protection from government-imposed burdens").

33. *See* 42 U.S.C. § 2000cc(a)(2).

34. 42 U.S.C. § 2000cc-5(5).

Under this definition, a government entity or agency implements a land use regulation when it acts pursuant to a zoning law that limits the manner in which a claimant may develop or use property in which the claimant has an interest.[35] With respect to the definition of individualized assessment, several circuits have established that zoning ordinances by their nature impose individual assessment regimes.[36] For this reason, the most common jurisdictional hook under which substantial-burden claims are asserted is the individualized assessment component.

b. Substantial Burden—Religious Beliefs

In order to affirm a religious use under RLUIPA, the court is limited to determining whether the claimant has a "sincere religious belief."[37] Congress did not define the term "religious institution" or "religious assembly" within RLUIPA, and few courts have actually performed a legal analysis as to whether a particular entity qualifies as a "religious assembly or institution" for purposes of RLUIPA. Nevertheless, the available case law and related guidance that address this topic seem to indicate the issue of whether an entity is a religious institution under RLUIPA is a question of fact. In two separate RLUIPA land uses cases, the Eleventh and Third Circuits both looked to the dictionary definitions of "assembly" and "institution" to deduce their ordinary meanings.[38] Certainly, whether a religious entity meets the dictionary definition of an "assembly" or "institution" is a question of fact that will largely depend on the specific factual circumstances surrounding that particular entity.

---

35. Second Baptist Church v. Gilpin Twp., 118 F. App'x 615, 617 (3d Cir. 2004); Church of Universal Love & Music v. Fayette Cnty., 2008 U.S. Dist. LEXIS 65564 (W.D. Pa. Aug. 26, 2008).

36. Freedom Baptist Church v. Twp. of Middleton, 204 F. Supp. 2d 857, 868 (E.D. Pa. 2002). *See also* Sts. Constantine & Helen Greek Orthodox Church v. City of New Berlin, 396 F.3d 895, 900 (7th Cir. 2005) ("[B]ecause these discretionary systems run the risk of religious discrimination, RLUIPA appropriately subjects burdens imposed pursuant to systems of individualized assessment to strict scrutiny.").

37. Church of the Hills of Twp. of Bedminster v. Twp. of Bedminster, 2006 WL 462674 (D.N.J. Feb. 24, 2006); Midrash Sephardi v. Town of Surfside, 366 F.3d 1214, 1225 (11th Cir. 2004).

38. 366 F.3d at 1230–31; Lighthouse Inst. for Evangelism Inc. v. City of Long Branch, 510 F.3d 253, 284 n.29 (3d Cir. 2007).

The U.S. Department of Justice has specifically recognized numerous entities that qualify as "religious assemblies or institutions" under RLUIPA, including:

- Houses of worship (churches, synagogues, mosques, and temples)
- Accessory religious uses such as fellowship halls, parish halls, and similar buildings or rooms used for meetings, religious education, and similar functions
- Individuals exercising their religion through use of property, such as home prayer gatherings or Bible studies
- Religious schools, even where the facilities are used for both secular and religious educational activities
- Religious camps
- Religious retreat centers
- Faith-based homeless shelters
- Faith-based soup kitchens
- Faith-based group homes
- Other faith-based social services[39]

Federal law and guidance from the U.S. Department of Justice seems to indicate that the determination of whether an entity qualifies as a religious institution under RLUIPA constitutes a question of fact. The Third Circuit delineated nine factors that a court should consider when determining whether an entity qualified as a "religious organization" under Title VII.[40] These nine factors are:

1. Whether the entity operates for a profit
2. Whether it produces a secular product
3. Whether the entity's articles of incorporation or other pertinent documents state a religious purpose
4. Whether it is owned, affiliated with, or financially supported by a formal religious entity such as a church or synagogue

39. https://bit.ly/3aFYr6u.
40. LeBoon v. Lancaster Jewish Cmty. Ctr. Ass'n, 503 F.3d 217, 226 (3d Cir. 2007).

5. Whether a formal religious entity participates in the management—for instance, by having representatives on the board of trustees
6. Whether the entity holds itself out to the public as secular or sectarian
7. Whether the entity regularly includes prayer or other forms of worship in its activities
8. Whether it includes religious instruction in its curriculum, to the extent it is an educational institution
9. Whether its membership is made up of co-religionists

The court emphasized that "not all factors will be relevant in all cases, and the weight given each factor may vary from case to case."[41] The court also noted that the Title VII exemption should not be denied to institutions simply because they might engage in some secular activities, might not adhere to the strictest tenets of their faith, or might not hire only coreligionists.[42]

The nine-factor LeBoon test used to determine whether an entity qualifies as a religious organization under Title VII could also be used to determine whether an entity qualifies as a "religious assembly or institution" under RLUIPA. As the Third Circuit stated, the analysis performed under this test involves weighing the specific facts in each case, not all nine of which will be applicable in every case.[43] Thus, the question of whether an entity is a religious institution under RLUIPA is a question of fact.

c. Substantial Burden—Identifying the Land Use Regulation

Courts have been entrusted to decide whether alleged injuries resulted from imposition or implementation of a land use regulation within the context of RLUIPA. Although the object of the statute extends to zoning and landmarking laws,[44] courts are continually commissioned to determine the breadth and peripheries of that object. Accordingly, they have refined and continue to refine the meaning of a land use regulation within the meaning

41. *Id.* at 227.
42. *Id.* at 229–30.
43. *Id.* at 226–27.
44. 42 U.S.C. § 2000cc-5(5).

of RLUIPA. Courts have ruled that a law's relation to land use does not necessarily render it a land use regulation for purposes of RLUIPA. In some contexts, building code regulations fall within the scope of RLUIPA.[45]

In *United States of America v. County of Culpepper, Virginia*, the complaint alleges that the county imposed a substantial burden on a Muslim congregation's exercise of religion and discriminated against the congregation when it refused the mosque a pump-and-haul permit to remove sewage from a septic tank to another area. The court found that the county considered 26 similar applications for commercial and religious uses and granted all of them permits.[46]

Whether RLUIPA extends to eminent domain has been a point of some dispute among courts.[47]

In *Cottonwood Christian Center v. Cypress Redevelopment Agency*,[48] the court found that RLUIPA applied to eminent domain proceedings.[49] The court found that the redevelopment agency's authority to exercise eminent domain was based on a zoning system that the city had developed, and this system "unquestionably 'limited or restricted' Cottonwood's 'use or development of land.'"[50] Based on this determination, the court found RLUIPA applicable to Cottonwood's land use issue, and it went through a full RLUIPA analysis before ultimately concluding that an injunction should be issued preventing the city from condemning Cottonwood's property.[51]

The case of *Fortress Bible Church v. Feiner*[52] addressed whether a state's environmental-quality law could constitute a land use regulation for purposes of RLUIPA. In 1998, Fortress Bible Church purchased a vacant piece of land in the town of Greenburgh, New York, on which the church intended to build a structure that could accommodate 500 worshippers and 150

45. United States of America v. Cnty. of Culpepper, Va., Case No. 3:16-cv-00083 (W.D. Va. 2017).

46. *Id.*

47. The Seventh Circuit Court of Appeals, however, has taken a different approach. St. John's United Church of Christ v. City of Chicago, 502 F.3d 616 (7th Cir. 2007).

48. 218 F. Supp. 2d 1203 (C.D. Cal. 2002).

49. *Id.* at 1222 n.9.

50. *Id.*

51. *Id.* at 1232.

52. Fortress Bible Church v. Feiner, No. 10-3634-cv, 2012 U.S. App. LEXIS 20019 (2d Cir. Sept. 24, 2012).

students.[53] The church first needed approval from the town before commencing its project. The construction plans the church submitted involved three discretionary land use approvals, and as a result they triggered New York's State Environmental Quality Review Act, or SEQRA.[54] SEQRA requires analyses of the potential environmental impacts of certain land use developments, including the effects of traffic and property access.[55] Beginning in 1998, the town conducted a nearly five-year review of the church's project. During this time, the church made various changes to its plans in an effort to comply with the town's requirements.[56] In mid-2003, when the plans had still not been approved, the church filed suit against the town under RLUIPA, among other claims.[57] The church also sought an order requiring the town to finish its SEQRA review and approve the church's project.[58]

After a 26-day bench trial, the district judge found that the town's actions violated RLUIPA.[59] The court further determined that the town acted in bad faith by using the SEQRA process as a means of blocking the church's development plans.[60] The court deemed the SEQRA review effectively approved and ordered the town to allow the church to proceed uninterrupted with its project.[61] The town appealed, and the Second Circuit affirmed the judgment.[62] The Second Circuit first rejected the town's contention that SEQRA is not a valid land use regulation under RLUIPA.[63] The court determined that while an environmental-quality law does not automatically implicate RLUIPA, it may do so when applied in a way to determine issues surrounding a land use proposal.[64]

Here, the town intertwined its SEQRA review process with its zoning regulations, specifically with respect to the church's review when it focused

53. *Id.* at *4.
54. *Id.* at *5.
55. *Id.* at *6.
56. *Id.* at *6–9.
57. *Id.* at *9.
58. *Id.*
59. *See* Fortress Bible Church v. Feiner, 734 F. Supp. 2d 409, 522–23 (S.D.N.Y. 2010).
60. *Id.* at 522.
61. *Id.* at 523.
62. Fortress Bible Church v. Feiner, 694 F.3d 208 (2d Cir. Sept. 24, 2012).
63. *Id.* at *12–13 (citing 42 U.S.C. § 2000cc(a)(1)).
64. *Id.* at *15–16.

on zoning issues rather than environmental issues.[65] The Second Circuit specifically noted that if RLUIPA did not apply to zoning actions conducted under the guise of an environmental-quality review, towns could essentially insulate their zoning decisions from all RLUIPA review.[66] Here, the town's actions substantially burdened the church's religious exercise, since the town's stated willingness to consider any modified plans from the church was disingenuous.[67]

This decision will have a significant impact on future RLUIPA decisions, given that states such as California, Washington, and Massachusetts have adopted similar environmental laws, and other states in the future will surely follow suit with similar measures. It also offers an exception to the general RLUIPA requirement that courts have espoused: only action "pursuant to a zoning or landmarking law" can be seen as a land use regulation.[68]

One other governmental action that has been deemed to fall within a land use regulation is the use of land use restrictive covenants imposed by a local economic development corporation, which restricted land to only secular assembly uses. In *Summit Church et al. v. The Randolph County Development Authority*,[69] the Sextons, owners of a Branson, Missouri-style live theater in a former railyard, contracted to sell the property to Summit Church, which had been leasing the property the prior four years. Upon learning of the sale, the development authority threatened a lawsuit to prevent the church from acquiring the property, claiming that churches are banned because the covenants allow only commercial land uses. The church sued, alleging a facial equal-terms claim.[70]

The court agreed with the church, concluding that in addition to the plentiful federal court precedent, many of the permitted uses in the railyard are nonreligious assemblies or institutions.[71] Libraries, theaters, parks,

65. *Id.* at *17–18.

66. *Id.* at *19 ("We decline to endorse a process that would allow a town to evade RLUIPA by what essentially amounts to a re-characterization of its zoning decision.").

67. *Id.* at *23.

68. Vision Church v. Vill. of Long Grove, 468 F.3d 975, 998 (7th Cir. 2006) (quoting Prater v. City of Burnside, 289 F.3d 417, 434 (6th Cir. 2002)) (internal quotation marks omitted).

69. Case No 2:15-cv-00082-JBP, Dkt. 39, filed 03/02/16, in the United States District Court for the Northern District of West Virginia, Elkins.

70. *Id.*

71. *Id.*

museums, restaurants, museums, convention centers, and public squares are all land uses that require people to assemble for some common purpose for a particular length of time. These are textbook "assembly" land uses, according to many federal courts and according to the common-sense understanding of the term.[72]

d. Substantial Burden—The Definitions

As the statutory text makes clear,[73] RLUIPA generally provides that government cannot impose a land use regulation in a manner that imposes a substantial burden on a religious institution or individual.[74] However, if the governmental entity can demonstrate that its regulation furthered a compelling governmental interest and was also the least-restrictive means of furthering that interest, the governmental action will be allowed to stand.[75] RLUIPA's legislative history reveals that Congress deliberately did not define "substantial burden" in the statutory language but, rather, intended that courts use the definition developed through Supreme Court jurisprudence.[76]

The substantial-burden provision is probably the most litigated part of the RLUIPA statute, primarily because the meaning of "substantial burden" has not been explicitly defined and remains fact-sensitive. In fact, courts have been more inclined to outline what could be a substantial burden under RLUIPA, as opposed to stating a plain definition.

Clearly, the courts have recognized that the statute is written such that what constitutes a substantial burden will depend on the facts of the case. As the District Court for the Southern District of New York has attested, "[S]uch burdens come in many forms."[77] And as will be seen, many of the

72. *Id.*

73. "No government shall impose or implement a land use regulation in a manner that imposes a substantial burden on the religious exercise of a person, including a religious assembly or institution, unless the government demonstrates that imposition of the burden on that person, assembly or institution is in furtherance of a compelling governmental interest and is the least restrictive means of furthering that compelling governmental interest."

74. 42 U.S.C. § 2000cc(a)(1).

75. *Id.* § 2000cc(a)(1)(A)–(B).

76. 146 CONG. REC. S7774 (July 27, 2000).

77. Congregation Rabbinical Coll. of Tartikov Inc. v. Vill. of Pomona, 2013 U.S. Dist. LEXIS 2207, at *159 (S.D.N.Y. 2013).

standards that courts have formulated for judging substantial-burden claims overlap and build on one another.

The following are a variety of decisions from courts around the country that demonstrate the different ways in which courts interpret the clause.

i. Undue Delay, Uncertainty, and Additional Costs Is a Substantial Burden

Like being left without a ready alternative, government action that not merely hinders religious exercise but unreasonably creates other complications for a religious organization can result in a substantial burden. This standard has commonly served as a vehicle for establishing a substantial burden without having to show that no other suitable locations exist and even when the government acted pursuant to a generally applicable and neutral land use regulation.[78] In turn, it offers both a reminder that discriminatory or hostile motives can often underlie zoning regulations or regulatory decisions.

In a 2005 case before the Seventh U.S. Circuit Court of Appeals, Judge Richard Posner set forth an oft-cited interpretation of the Substantial Burden Clause focusing on when government action with respect to religious land use can result in a substantial burden because of undue delay, uncertainty, and additional costs. In *Saints Constantine and Helen Greek Orthodox Church Inc. v. City of New Berlin*,[79] a Wisconsin church purchased a tract of land in the city that was zoned residential.[80] In its proposal to build on the land, the church sought rezoning of the parcel as well as a planned unit development (PUD) overlay ordinance to limit use of the parcel to church uses, to pacify concerns that the property if sold might instead be used for other institutional purposes.[81] While the New Berlin planning director recommended approval to the planning commission, the commission disagreed. Following the commission rejection, the city council voted down the church's proposal.[82] The city was apparently concerned that the PUD would

78. Bethel World Outreach v. Montgomery Cnty. Council, 706 F.3d 548, 557 (4th Cir. 2013) (noting that requiring individualized targeting to create a substantial burden under RLUIPA "would render the nondiscrimination provision superfluous.").

79. 396 F.3d 895 (7th Cir. 2005).

80. *Id.* at 898.

81. *Id.*

82. *Id.*

apply only to the church and not to later owners should the church sell the property, even though nothing in the PUD's text supported this belief.[83]

The New Berlin mayor gave the church two options to construct its new building:[84] The church could apply for a conditional-use permit, but it would expire in one year unless construction commenced. The second option was to apply for a PUD that "would overlie not an institutional rezoning but instead the existing residential zoning, so that if the church sold the parcel rather than building a church on it, . . . the buyer could not make an institutional use of the property because the property would revert to being rezoned residential." While the former option could destabilize fundraising efforts for church construction, the latter option would in fact replicate the already-proposed regulations but at the cost of further delay.[85] Hence, either way, the church faced uncertainty and undue delay, especially as it could be inferred that the mayor had intentionally tried to delay the church's proposed land use.[86]

Of course, the church's ensuing suit would have to demonstrate that the city's conduct imposed a substantial burden on the church's religious exercise.[87] The Seventh Circuit found that it did. "The church could have searched around for other parcels of land (though a lot more effort would have been involved in such a search than, as the city would have it, calling up some real estate agents), or it could have continued filing applications with the city." Nevertheless, "In either case," the court continued, "there would have been delay, uncertainty and expense." Hence, the court concluded that just because a burden "would not be insuperable would not make it insubstantial."[88] Because the facts were not disputed, the court saw no need in remanding the matter to trial. Rather, the court reversed the district court's grant of summary judgment in favor of the city, and it remanded with instructions for the district court to grant the church's requested relief.[89]

83. *Id.*
84. *Id.* at 899.
85. *Id.*
86. *Id.*
87. *Id.*
88. *Id.* at 901.
89. *Id.*

This decision stands in stark contrast to others that expressly state that religious land use applicants are subject to regulatory schemes just like any other applicant, even if the process is expensive and time-consuming. What perhaps tipped the scales in favor of the applicant in the case was the "whiff of bad faith" exhibited by city officials.[90]

Government may also impose a substantial burden on religious groups indirectly by enforcing generally applicable and neutral regulations lacking evidentiary justification that restrict property or by refusing to grant exceptions to those regulations. *Lighthouse Community Church of God v. City of Southfield*,[91] another case that I litigated, discussed RLUIPA's substantial-burden provision in the context of a city's refusal to grant permits based on the number of parking spaces at a religious institution. Lighthouse Community Church of God involved a Christian congregation in Southfield, Michigan, a suburb of Detroit. The congregation met in Detroit but wanted to relocate its worship facility closer to where most of its members lived.[92] The church found a building in a zoning district in Southfield that permitted churches, and it began considering whether to purchase it for a church.[93] However, the church needed a certificate of occupancy to operate as a church. The pastor began to meet with the city's zoning director, who initially supported the church's plans to purchase the property.[94] Based on the zoning director's representations, the church purchased the building.[95] The pastor later claimed he would never have purchased the building if the zoning director had not assured him that the building could be used as a church.[96]

Several months later, the city discovered that the church was using the building for religious services and sent a letter to the pastor indicating that the church would have to vacate the building because it did not have a certificate of occupancy permitting it to use the property as a church.[97] A state

90. *Id.*
91. 2007 WL 30280, No. 05-40220 (E.D. Mich. Jan. 3, 2007).
92. *Id.* at *1.
93. *Id.*
94. *Id.*
95. *Id.*
96. *Id.*
97. *Id.* at *2.

court later issued an order requiring the church to cease and desist using the building. The church was unable to obtain a certificate of occupancy mainly because the city required 95 parking spaces and the property had only 73.[98] Consequently, the church filed suit in federal court, claiming that the city's denial of the certificate of occupancy violated RLUIPA.[99]

In addressing the church's substantial-burden claim, the court disagreed with the city's position that the parking ordinance imposed no such burden because it did not directly prohibit using the building as a church but only prohibited use if there were not enough parking spaces.[100] The court noted that a land use regulation does not have to specifically target a religious exercise to create a substantial burden—and this is important for religious land use applicants and governmental officials alike to understand. Rather, "[A] land use regulation that is specifically blind to religious use of land can still substantially burden religious exercise."[101] Here, the parking ordinance effectively prohibited the church from using its building for religious exercise. The city had the ability to grant the church a variance to the parking requirement, but it did not do so because of unsubstantiated traffic and safety concerns.[102]

Echoing the city's argument in *Saints Constantine*, Southfield tried to maintain that since the church could relocate, its religious exercise had not been substantially burdened. However, again, in that previous case, the Seventh Circuit acknowledged that a government-imposed obligation to relocate can create a substantial burden. Similarly, here, in light of the city's needless variance application rejection, the court observed that "[w]orship services are fundamental to the practice and exercise of one's religious beliefs." Accordingly, forcing the church to sell its property and relocate would not create a "mere inconvenience" but rather a "substantial" burden on religious exercise.[103] Even assuming that Southfield's traffic and safety concerns were compelling, the court continued, the city had not demonstrated that imposing the regulation would further its purported

98. *Id.*
99. *Id.*
100. *Id.* at *8.
101. *Id.*
102. *Id.*
103. *Id.* at *9.

concerns, thereby failing the least-restrictive-means requirement. Based on this explanation, the court found that the church had established a prima facie case of a violation of RLUIPA's substantial-burden provision.[104]

Broadly speaking, a jurisdiction's denial of a land use proposal in demonstrably bad faith will ordinarily result in a substantial-burden finding because suffering any sort of undue delay, uncertainty, or cost is perhaps an inexorable consequence of being on the receiving end of undue government behavior. Take *Irshad Learning Center v. County of DuPage*[105] for instance. Irshad Learning Center, a Muslim religious and educational group in suburban Chicago, purchased property in 2008 to serve as a permanent home for its activities. The property was zoned residential, which authorizes operation of religious institutions with a conditional use permit.[106] Irshad applied for a conditional-use permit in 2008, resubmitting the application as a religious institution later that year after retaining counsel.[107]

After a series of hearings and public complaints, the Zoning Board of Appeals (ZBA) unanimously denied the application. In 2009, the County Development Committee (CDC) voted unanimously to remand the application to the ZBA to clarify its findings of fact. Still, the ZBA voted again to deny the application. On review, the CDC unanimously voted to amend the application, adding conditions.[108]

After examining the proposal again, the County Board decided to send the amendments to the ZBA for another review. Again, the ZBA voted unanimously to deny the application. The CDC then reviewed the matter and voted 3–1 to approve the application before the County Board rejected it 10–7. In response, Irshad filed suit under RLUIPA, state law, and the U.S. Constitution.[109]

The county claimed that Irshad had failed to present competent evidence during the ZBA hearings and that, inappropriately, only its attorney testified on its behalf. But the court was quick to point out that the ZBA's own regulations permit attorneys to offer testimony and field questions from the

104. *Id.*
105. 937 F. Supp. 2d 910 (N.D. Ill. 2013).
106. *Id.* at 914–15.
107. *Id.* at 918.
108. *Id.* at 918–26.
109. *Id.* at 926–31.

ZBA and that the ZBA was permitted to question any of Irshad's representatives.[110] The ZBA disputed that Irshad would use the property principally for religious purposes because certain activities could be characterized as social, cultural, and educational. To the court, however, this understanding was "arbitrary and capricious," especially because no authority supported that conclusion.[111]

There remained a dispute over the nature and intensity of the proposed use. Some evidence on record suggested that Irshad's prior activities at other locations exceeded occupancy limitations for the structure in question. But Irshad's attorney claimed that under the regulations pending approval, Irshad would enforce the requisite cap on occupancy at the new property. The county insisted that it did not engage in speculation over future use, but to the court this claim "makes sense only if one unreasonably believes, as the county insists, that [Irshad] sought to move 'all of their current activities' to the subject property."[112] With the power to take enforcement action if conditions were not met in practice, it appeared that the county "did not consider the application as it was submitted but, rather, speculated regarding future use," leaving open the question whether Irshad would ever be able to use the property as a religious institution.[113]

Irshad indicated a willingness to comply with mitigating conditions. It met with a county board member and added conditions to its application and insisted that it would comply, but the ZBA never recommended any conditions to alleviate its concerns. Irshad had therefore "expressed a willingness to meet the demands of both the professional planning staff and elected officials but had seen its request rebuffed nonetheless."[114] In turn, the county's "repeated errors, speculation and refusal to impose conditions" were arbitrary and unreasonable to the point that, in accord with *Saints Constantine*, they subjected Irshad to a substantial burden. Furthermore, the county did not offer a sufficiently justificatory compelling interest.[115]

110. *Id.* at 943.
111. *Id.* at 945.
112. *Id.* at 945–46.
113. *Id.* at 947.
114. *Id.* at 947–48.
115. *Id.* at 948.

By extension, hostility to long-term or permanent religious land use plans, even if approval for a shorter proposal is granted, can result in a finding of a substantial burden. In yet another significant case, *Grace Church of North County v. City of San Diego*,[116] the Southern District of California granted summary judgment in favor of Grace Church after it found that the city's enforcement of its land use regulation imposed a substantial burden on the church.

Grace Church was a nondenominational Christian church operating in the Rancho Bernardo area of San Diego.[117] The community was a central location for members of the church, which was trying to eventually find a permanent location there.[118] The church had been meeting at a high school, but its growing membership led it to seek a location with more space.[119] Grace Church decided to lease a facility in Rancho Bernardo on a long-term basis.[120] After a commercial broker evaluated the needs of the church and found no parcel available in the section of the city where zoning regulations permitted religious institutional use as a matter of right, the church found three sites that potentially met its needs within an industrial park.[121]

The industrial park zoning designation specified that nonindustrial uses, including the church use, were permitted if the owner obtained a conditional-use permit (CUP).[122] The church applied for a ten-year CUP from the city, matching the duration of the lease agreement.[123] City staff determined that the church's proposal did not conform with the community plan and then held a public hearing before the community planning board.[124] The board voted to recommend a denial of the CUP because the proposed use was not consistent with the community's land use plans.[125]

Next, a hearing took place at which city staff said they would support a CUP that had a limited term of not more than five years and that they could

116. 555 F. Supp. 2d 1126 (S.D. Cal. 2008).
117. *Id.* at 1129.
118. *Id.*
119. *Id.*
120. *Id.*
121. *Id.*
122. *Id.* at 1130.
123. *Id.* at 1130–31.
124. *Id.* at 1131.
125. *Id.*

not support an indefinite term because the city would consider such a term to be a permanent use that would conflict with the master plan.[126] Over the church's objections, the city approved a CUP for seven years.[127] The decision was partly based on the city's average CUP length being between ten and 20 years and the average CUP length in the Rancho Bernardo Industrial Park being between five and ten years.[128]

The Planning Commission then held two hearings at which the city planning staff stated its support for a five-year CUP, even though the city had recommended seven years.[129] The Planning Commission eventually approved a five-year CUP.[130]

Grace Church subsequently filed an RLUIPA action and moved for summary judgment under the substantial-burden provision.[131] In analyzing whether the city's regulations imposed a substantial burden, the court relied on the Ninth Circuit's decision in *Guru Nanak Sikh Society of Yuba City v. County of Sutter*,[132] which held that "[f]or a land use regulation to impose a substantial burden, it must be oppressive to a significantly great extent." And for the Ninth Circuit, substantially burdening a religious exercise means "impos[ing] a significantly great restriction or onus upon such exercise."[133] Further, the district court recognized Guru Nanak's concern that jurisdictions should not leave religious organizations "fraught with uncertainty" on future land use decisions,[134] and in turn crystallized an understanding that "uncertainty regarding the future constitutes a present and very real burden."[135]

In applying these principles to the facts, the court concluded that the mandatory CUP process established by the city and applied to Grace Church constituted a substantial burden on Grace Church's religious exercise.[136] In

126. *Id.*
127. *Id.* at 1132.
128. *Id.*
129. *Id.*
130. *Id.* at 1133.
131. *Id.* at 1134.
132. 456 F.3d 978 (9th Cir. 2006).
133. *Id.* at 985.
134. *Id.* at 991.
135. Grace Church, 555 F. Supp. 2d at 1136–37.
136. *Id.*

particular, "Grace Church experienced outright hostility to its application, decision-making that is seemingly arbitrary or pre-textual, and ignorance regarding the requirements of controlling federal law regarding the application of land use laws to religious institutions."[137] City officials expressed hostility toward a longer CUP and threatened that the CUP granted would not be renewed, creating a level of uncertainty "regarding the future that constitutes a present and very real burden on the church's religious exercise, since plaintiff does not know whether it will be able to remain at the Via Frontera property for the full term of its [10-year lease]."[138]

To the court, this was "precisely the situation" that produced a substantial-burden finding as in *Saints Constantine*. But the court also attributed the imposition of a substantial burden in part to practices of the Rancho Bernardo planning board, whose members had no legal training or knowledge of RLUIPA (which, to some extent, goes to the certain components, since religious land use applicants would be uncertain how government officials ignorant of RLUIPA would treat their applicants).[139]

The court then determined that the city did not demonstrate that preserving industrial lands for industrial uses qualified as a compelling interest.[140] The city also failed to demonstrate that it used the least restrictive means when enforcing its regulations.[141]

Establishing a reasonable expectation to use property for religious purposes often helps bolster a substantial-burden claim when facing delay, uncertainty, and additional costs.[142] In *Reaching Hearts International Inc. v. Prince George's County*,[143] the Fourth Circuit affirmed a Maryland district court determination that a municipality's refusal to change sewer and water classifications for a religious entity amounted to a substantial burden when the municipality had approved such reclassifications numerous times for secular organizations. The plaintiff was Reaching Hearts International,

137. *Id.*
138. *Id.* at 1137.
139. *Id.* at 1137–38.
140. *Id.* at 1140.
141. *Id.*
142. Eagle Cove Camp & Conference Center Inc. v. Town of Woodboro, 734 F.3d 673, 681 (7th Cir. 2013) (holding that delay, uncertainty, and expense alone do not shield a religious organization from reasonable land use restrictions).
143. 368 F. App'x 370 (4th Cir. 2010).

a Seventh-day Adventist congregation that purchased property in Prince George's County, Maryland, on which it intended to build a church and related facilities.[144] Although the zoning restrictions on the property permitted churches as a matter of right, Reaching Hearts was unable to obtain a change in the sewer and water classification for portions of the property. The county's denial of the reclassification of its property effectively prohibited the church from developing its worship center.[145]

Though many other properties had received county approval for sewer and water reclassifications, Reaching Hearts—the only church property—was denied such a reclassification.[146] Reaching Hearts unsuccessfully pursued an administrative remedy before filing suit, alleging that the county violated RLUIPA.[147] At trial, Reaching Hearts prevailed on its claims and obtained an award of more than $3.7 million in damages, as well as an injunction to enjoin the county from engaging in any potential future discriminatory conduct.[148]

On appeal, the Fourth Circuit affirmed the district court's decision upholding the jury verdict, concluding that the evidence Reaching Hearts presented in regard to the county's "anti-church animus was very strong."[149] The court further ruled that the jury had correctly found intentional discrimination on a prohibited ground and that the land use regulation imposed a substantial burden without satisfying strict scrutiny.[150] Like the church in *Saints Constantine*, Reaching Hearts had a reasonable expectation to use its property as a church and would thereby face undue financial stress if forced to proceed with protracted administrative review. That Reaching Hearts had already invested substantial sums of money in transitioning to the new location and would continue to have to make payments served to better frame the burden. In turn, the Fourth Circuit affirmed the district court's finding that the jury's finding of a substantial burden was properly based on evidence that the county's discriminatory denial of two sewer

144. *Id.* at 371.
145. *Id.*
146. *Id.*
147. *See* 42 U.S.C. § 2000cc (2000).
148. *Reaching Hearts*, 368 F. App'x at 372.
149. *Id.*
150. *Id.* at 372.

category change applications, as well as the church's expenditure of funds while facing delays and uncertainty, amounted to a substantial burden.[151]

An unreasonable expectation to use property for religious purposes, on the other hand, can be detrimental and perhaps fatal to a substantial-burden claim. Indeed, in *Andon LLC v. City of Newport News*,[152] Reconciling People Together in Faith Ministries, a small local religious congregation, wanted to expand by moving to a new property. It settled on a parcel within Newport News, Virginia. But under city ordinances, the location was ineligible to become a church because it was too close to residential property.[153] Knowing this, the congregation still entered into a lease to use the property. In conversations with city officials, the lessor, Andon LLC, was told that a variance application would be rejected. Still, Andon nevertheless applied for a variance, which was rejected, and it subsequently filed suit, alleging that Newport News placed a substantial burden on the congregation's religious exercise.[154]

The city of Newport News quickly moved to dismiss the case. It pointed out that the zoning ordinance was applied neutrally and that the congregation never had a reasonable expectation to use the property as a church.[155] It appeared, rather, that the congregation knew it was not a permitted use and that any burden on religious exercise could be attributed to the congregation's own inability to find a suitable location elsewhere. In fact, the congregation even conceded that it had not looked into all available alternatives.[156] Since, according to the court, costs associated with looking for an affordable location do not create a substantial burden, any delays, uncertainties, and expenses in this case are "both self-imposed and unclear."[157]

151. 584 F. Supp. 2d 766, 785–87 (D. Md. 2008).
152. 63 F. Supp. 3d 630 (E.D. Va. 2014).
153. *Id.* at 632–33.
154. *Id.* at 634.
155. *Id.* at 641.
156. *Id.* at 642.
157. *Id.*

ii. Substantial Pressure and Effectively Impracticable Tests

In some cases, courts have applied definitional understandings of "substantial burden" developed over the years[158] to elucidate the otherwise ambiguous term. One such understanding is the "substantial pressure" test, on display in *Living Water Church of God v. Charter Township of Meridian*,[159] a 2007 case in the Sixth Circuit. *Living Water* involved a Christian congregation that ran educational and day care ministries in Meridian Township, Michigan.[160] Living Water owned six acres in the township in an area zoned for single-family residential, medium density. To build a religious or educational institution in a residential zone, the township required a special-use permit. To construct a building larger than 25,000 square feet, the township required an additional special-use permit.[161]

In 1994, the township granted Living Water such a permit to build a single-story, 10,925-square-foot building to be used as a day care center for 40 children. Living Water then constructed and occupied the new building.[162] In 2000, the church applied for and received a special-use permit to build a 28,500-square-foot elementary school and increase its day care enrollment.[163] However, on March 7, 2001, the township informed Living Water that the 2000 special-use permit would expire in 12 days unless the church began construction or obtained an extension on its permit. Living Water requested an extension.[164]

Despite a past policy of freely granting extensions, the township denied the extension after its attorney claimed the township ordinances did not allow extensions.[165] Living Water resubmitted its 2000 permit application and later amended it to include a Christian education building totaling 34,989 square feet.[166] The township board granted a special-use permit for

158. Midrash Sephardi Inc. v. Town of Surfside, 366 F.3d 1214, 1226–27 (11th Cir. 2004) (noting the extent to which courts have applied different definitions of substantial burden over a period of several decades).

159. 258 F. App'x 729 (6th Cir. 2007).

160. *Id.* at 730.

161. *Id.*

162. *Id.*

163. *Id.*

164. *Id.*

165. *Id.* at 730–31.

166. *Id.* at 731.

the nonresidential use of a school in the residential district but denied any addition that resulted in a gross floor area exceeding 25,000 square feet.[167] The board explained that, compared with similar structures, the land was disproportionate to the facility's size, and the proposal was inconsistent with review criteria and standards for special use.[168]

Living Water sued, seeking an injunction restraining the township from enforcing its denial and a declaratory judgment that the township violated RLUIPA's substantial-burden provision.[169] After being removed to federal court, the district court found that Living Water's religious exercise had been substantially burdened absent a least-restrictive compelling government interest. The court focused its decision on the insufficient space for expansion and the issues and costs of having two locations for the church and school.[170]

The Sixth U.S. Circuit Court of Appeals reversed. At the heart of the court's debate was what constituted a substantial burden under RLUIPA. After an extensive survey of other federal circuit courts' interpretations of the phrase, the Sixth Circuit declined to set a bright-line test.[171] Nevertheless, the court suggested a question for determining whether a burden is substantial:

> [T]hough the government action may make religious exercise more expensive or difficult, does the government action place substantial pressure[172] on a religious institution to violate its religious beliefs or effectively bar a religious institution from using its property in the exercise of its religion?[173]

167. *Id.* at 732.
168. *Id.*
169. *Id.*
170. *Id.*
171. *Id.* at 737.
172. Courts have often used this language interchangeably with a test assessing the extent to which government action "coerced" a religious organization to act contrary to its religious beliefs. *See, e.g.*, Hudson v. Spencer, 2015 U.S. Dist. LEXIS 129304, at *8 (D. Mass. 2015) (noting that by government pressuring religious exercise to the point of creating a substantial burden, "the effects" of that government action also created "a tendency to coerce" a religious organization to violate its religious beliefs).
173. *Id.*

In this case, the court concluded that while denying the special-use permit did burden Living Water, the burden did not rise to the level of "substantial pressure" on the church to violate its religious beliefs or effectively bar it from using its property to exercise its religious beliefs.[174] The denial did not bar Living Water from operating the school on church property, nor did it prevent it from providing religious education and opportunities to worship at a newly constructed 14,075-square-foot school structure.[175]

Though some circuits have criticized this framework as too strict,[176] a land use regulation that squarely necessitates a choice as grave as either acting in conflict with religious beliefs or leaving a jurisdiction altogether has been found to exert pressure capable of establishing a substantial burden. In *Merced v. Kasson*,[177] the Fifth Circuit interpreted the application of RLUIPA's substantial-burden provision to the lesser-known religion of Santeria. In Merced, the plaintiff, a Santeria priest, filed suit against the city of Euless, Texas, and its officials, alleging that the city's ordinance prohibiting the keeping and slaughtering of animals violated his rights under RLUIPA and the Texas Religious Freedom Restoration Act.[178] Santeria is a religion that combines elements of both African tribal religion and Roman Catholicism.[179] An essential aspect of many Santeria rituals—including birth, marriage, death, and priest initiation ceremonies—is the sacrificing of live animals.[180]

Following a bench trial, the district court entered judgment for the city. But the Fifth Circuit reversed and found that the city's ordinances did impose a substantial burden on Merced's ability to practice his religion. The court determined that the district court's decision that Merced's religious practices were not substantially burdened was made in error. Merced's not testifying

174. *Id.* at 738.

175. *Id.*

176. *See, e.g.*, Bethel World Outreach v. Montgomery Cnty. Council, 706 F.3d 548, 555 (4th Cir. 2013) (arguing that land use regulations "will rarely, if ever, force the organization to violate its religious beliefs. . . . Thus, requiring a religious organization to prove that a land use regulation pressured it to violate its beliefs would be tantamount to eliminating RLUIPA's substantial burden protection in the land use context.").

177. 577 F.3d 578 (5th Cir. 2009).

178. *Id.* at 583.

179. *Id.* at 582.

180. *Id.*

as to whether the Santeria spirits instructed him to sacrifice animals at his home was an impermissible attempt by the judge "to evaluate the intricacies of a religious practice," given that "[t]he judiciary is ill-suited to opine on theological matters and should avoid doing so."[181] In addition, the record made clear that Merced was unable to initiate Santeria priests on his property because of the city's ordinances, and the inability to ordain new priests had the effect of barring the continuation of the Santeria religion.[182]

The court stressed that the burden on Merced's religious exercise was especially substantial because the city's decision forced him to choose between practicing Santeria and living in the city.[183] Additionally, Merced faced criminal prosecution if he performed a ritual that was essential to his religious beliefs.[184] Merced had proposed at least three alternatives that were less restrictive than the city's current ordinances, which the city did not even attempt to rebut.[185] Accordingly, the trial court's decision was reversed, and the court granted Merced an injunction that prevented the city from enforcing any ordinances that burden his sacrificing of animals for religious purposes.[186]

Some courts subscribe to a similar "effectively impracticable" test that originated with the Seventh Circuit in 2003.[187] In an unreported decision out of the Eastern District of North Carolina, the court in *Dixon v. Coats*[188] determined that a decision to rezone a six-block area in a city did not amount to a substantial burden when the rezoning meant that a church would not be an allowable use. The plaintiff owned property that he leased to several businesses and churches. But after a rezoning, one church lessee was no longer permitted to use its land.[189] After initially accommodating one of the plaintiff's other lessees, the city denied a second lessee's request

181. *Id.* at 590.
182. *Id.* at 590–91.
183. *Id.* at 591.
184. *Id.*
185. *Id.* at 595.
186. *Id.*
187. Civil Liberties for Urban Believers v. City of Chicago, 342 F.3d 752, 761 (7th Cir. 2003).
188. 5:08-CV-489-BR, 2010 WL 2347506 (E.D. N.C. June 9, 2010).
189. *Id.* at *1.

for a church, leading the plaintiff to file claims under RLUIPA and the First and Fourteenth Amendments.[190]

The court granted the city's motion for summary judgment on all claims. As to RLUIPA, while the plaintiff had standing, the fact that the zoning restriction applied to only a six-block area did not amount to a substantial burden.[191] In the court's view, no evidence of a substantial burden existed when plaintiffs could not demonstrate that zoning regulations restricting religious assemblies within a six-block area "render religious exercise effectively impracticable within the town as a whole."[192]

2. Equal Terms Claims

The Equal Terms Clause provides that "[n]o government shall impose or implement a land use regulation in a manner that treats a religious assembly or institution on less than equal terms with a nonreligious assembly or institution."[193] While a substantial-burden claim is focused on a particular plaintiff, Equal Terms claims are based on the treatment of one religious institution compared to similar secular institutions both under the plain language of a land use ordinance and in how that ordinance is applied to a religious organization. One must keep in mind that a claim pursuant to the Equal Terms Clause is an entirely separate matter from claims arising under the Substantial Burden Clause. Accordingly, a religious institution alleging an Equal Terms violation is not required to also demonstrate that a local government substantially burdened its religious exercise.

Facial Equal Terms claims have been infrequent since the birth of RLUIPA in 2000. This is somewhat self-explanatory due to the nature of land use discrimination cases. Most local ordinances do not, on their face, treat religious institutions on less than equal terms compared to secular institutions. Thus, Equal Terms cases are more likely to be fact-sensitive inquiries into how a local government applied its ordinances to religious organizations compared to entities that are similarly situated and nonreligious. Following are a number of cases that address both types of Equal Terms

190. *Id.* at *2–3.
191. *Id.* at *4–5.
192. *Id.* at *16.
193. 42 U.S.C. § 2000cc(b)(1).

claims—facial challenge and as-applied challenges. In brief, a facial challenge takes issue with the plain terms of an ordinance that treats religious organizations on less than equal terms compared to secular organizations. As-applied challenges contest the government's application of a zoning regulation as treating religious organizations worse than secular institutions.

a. Circuit Split on Application

At present, circuit courts are divided on the appropriate application of the Equal Terms provision. Most of this disagreement centers on what constitutes an assembly or institution, whether or when a similarly situated comparison is necessary and what level of scrutiny should be applied. Still, considerable overlap exists among the differing standards, with the Second Circuit going as far as claiming that the courts still "come to essentially the same result" despite "differences in the mechanism."[194] Nonetheless, as will be shown, the differences can lead to some confusion when litigating under Equal Terms.

The leading Equal Terms case is the 2004 Eleventh Circuit decision in *Midrash Sephardi Inc. v. Town of Surfside*.[195] A facial challenge case, *Midrash* advanced a broad and friendly understanding of appropriate comparators under the Equal Terms provision, to include assembles and institutions generally without requiring a similarly situated comparator. It also designated the strict scrutiny standard for treatment on less than equal terms. The case involved two Orthodox Jewish congregations operating in the business district of Surfside, Florida. The town's zoning scheme prohibited churches and synagogues within a business district but permitted "private clubs," among other secular uses. The town argued that its small business district was the only retail area the town had, and its tax base was essential to serve the needs of its residents.[196] The congregation eventually filed suit under RLUIPA, alleging that it was treated on less than equal terms compared to the secular uses that were permitted in the business district. The district court found for the town, but the appellate court reversed and found for the congregation on its Equal Terms claim.

194. Third Church of Christ v. City of New York, 626 F.3d 667, 670 (2d Cir. 2010).
195. 366 F.3d 1214 (11th Cir. 2004).
196. *Id.* at 1221–22.

The Eleventh Circuit began by analyzing the plain meaning of the terms "assembly" and "institution" and determined that private clubs and other nonreligious uses allowed in the zone constituted assemblies for purposes of RLUIPA.[197] Because both groups were assemblies under RLUIPA, the court next addressed whether the town treated the Jewish congregations differently from the secular uses. The court found that the town's zoning ordinance, on its face, treated religious assemblies on less than equal terms by excluding them from the business district when secular assemblies were permitted.[198]

In addition, the court determined that the zoning ordinance was not narrowly tailored, as it improperly distinguished between religious assemblies and similar secular entities that also did not further the town's stated goal of earning tax revenue to support its residents.[199]

One year later, the court, in an as-applied case, held that the application of a neutral statute could violate Equal Terms when a jurisdiction denies a religious land use having "comparable community impact" to a permitted secular land use.[200] The following year, it clarified that this framework does constrain Midrash, but only to the extent that as-applied challenges require more than a showing that a religious organization received less than equal treatment than a secular assembly or institution. Indeed, they require one to show that a religious organization was subject to less than equal treatment compared to a similarly situated secular assembly or institution.[201]

However, in 2007 the Third Circuit, "not persuaded by the reasoning of the 11th Circuit," took a more contextual approach to Equal Terms in *Lighthouse Institute for Evangelism v. City of Long Branch*.[202] Here the court required a similarly situated comparator even for facial challenges, but similar insofar as its effect on the purpose of applicable regulations. In particular, the court addressed whether the city violated RLUIPA's Equal

197. *Id.* at 1230.
198. *Id.* at 1234.
199. *Id.* at 1235.
200. Konikov v. Orange Cnty., 410 F.3d 1317, 1327–29 (11th Cir. 2005) (holding that enforcing a law to preclude religious organizations that met with similar frequency as would permitted secular gatherings violates equal terms).
201. Primera Iglesia Bautista Hispana v. Broward Cnty., 450 F.3d 1295, 1311 (11th Cir. 2006).
202. 510 F.3d 253, 268 (3d Cir. 2007).

Terms provisions by denying a church use in a given area based on concerns that the church would interfere with a state law prohibiting establishments with liquor licenses from being within 200 feet of a house of worship.

In 1994, the Lighthouse Institute for Evangelism, a Christian church, bought property in downtown Long Branch, New Jersey.[203] The city ordinances set forth a number of permitted uses in the area, such as theaters and assembly halls. However, a church was not listed as a permitted use.[204] Lighthouse wanted to open a building that would be used for various purposes, including as a church and soup kitchen, and to provide job skills classes.[205] Lighthouse tried to obtain a zoning permit to use the property as a church, a request that the city denied. In response, Lighthouse filed suit, claiming a variety of constitutional and other violations.[206] The district court dismissed all claims as either unexhausted or unripe.[207]

While the litigation was proceeding, Long Branch adopted a redevelopment plan that superseded its prior ordinances.[208] The plan was adopted to help redevelop an area of the city in the hopes of attracting more retail and service enterprises.[209] The plan allowed for theaters, dance studios, restaurants, bars, and other similar uses in one part of the city, while churches, schools, and governmental buildings were not listed as a permitted use in the very same section.[210] The design guidelines under the plan stated that "[a]ny uses not specifically listed" were prohibited.[211] The plan did not include an individual waiver procedure, but it could be amended by the city council.[212]

In November 2003, Lighthouse submitted a request to be designated as the developer for the property and also requested a waiver of the prohibition of church use. The request was denied.[213] The city council also denied an appeal because the proposed church use was not permitted and that

203. *Id.* at 256–57.
204. *Id.* at 257.
205. *Id.*
206. *Id.* at 257–58.
207. *Id.* at 258.
208. *Id.*
209. *Id.*
210. *Id.*
211. *Id.*
212. *Id.* at 259.
213. *Id.*

allowing a church in the proposed location would interfere with a state law prohibiting the issuance of liquor licenses within 200 feet of a house of worship.[214]

After RLUIPA was passed in September 2000, Lighthouse amended its complaint to state that the city's plan violated the Free Exercise Clause and RLUIPA.[215] The district court held that the ordinance and redevelopment plan did not violate RLUIPA's Equal Terms provision because Lighthouse did not show that it was being treated worse than a similarly situated secular entity.[216] The court also found that Lighthouse could not demonstrate that the city substantially burdened its exercise of religion.[217] Lighthouse appealed, and the Third Circuit found for the church on its facial Equal Terms claim.[218]

The Third Circuit determined that RLUIPA's Equal Terms provision requires a secular comparator that is similarly situated with respect to the purpose of the regulation in question and that it also operates on a strict liability standard as opposed to the Eleventh Circuit's adoption of strict scrutiny. This is because, the court explained, Congress intended to isolate substantial burdens, which are associated with strict scrutiny, from the independent Equal Terms provision.[219] The court noted that a plaintiff claiming a violation of RLUIPA's Equal Terms provision must show that "(1) it is a religious assembly or institution, (2) subject to a land use regulation which that (3) treats the religious assembly on less than equal terms with (4) a nonreligious assembly or institution (5) that causes no lesser harm to the interests the regulation seeks to advance."[220]

The court found that the government had treated Lighthouse on less than equal terms as a matter of law. While the new redevelopment plan might have passed muster, the ordinance did not. "The ordinance," the court asserted, "permitted a range of different uses in the Central Commercial District," and the city failed to show how a religious organization "would

214. *Id.*
215. *Id.*
216. *Id.* at 260.
217. *Id.*
218. *Id.* at 277.
219. *Id.* at 268–69.
220. *Id.* at 270.

cause greater harm to regulatory objectives" than a permitted secular assembly.[221] As such, the court granted summary judgment in favor of Lighthouse on its Equal Terms claim.[222]

Troubled by a perceived oversimplification of the concept of equality and the definition of assembly in the Eleventh Circuit and the enunciation of a "subjective and manipulable" test in the Third, the Seventh Circuit, in 2010, offered its own formulation for an Equal Terms standard in *River of Life Kingdom Ministries v. Village of Hazel Crest*.[223] River of Life, a small church, purchased a warehouse in a business district in the Village of Hazel Crest, Illinois, with the hope of obtaining a special exception for its proposed religious use.[224] The business district excluded "new noncommercial uses from the district, including not only churches but also community centers, schools and art galleries."[225] In other words, secular and religious nonprofit entities were both excluded from the business district. After being denied occupancy of the building, the church sued and filed a motion for preliminary injunction to use the property in the interim, which the district court denied.[226]

The Seventh Circuit, sitting en banc, affirmed the denial of the preliminary injunction after a long discussion of the appropriate test to apply to Equal Terms claims. After comparing the approaches of the Eleventh and Third Circuits, the court held that the focus of an Equal Terms case should be moved "from regulatory purpose to accepted zoning criteria."[227] The thinking was that this standard would give judges objective criteria to apply to cases, rather than forcing them to rely on speculation or explanations concerning malleable regulatory purposes. In this case, the business district in fact treated religious land use on the same terms as nonreligious, nonbusiness uses. If religious and secular land uses receive equal treatment "from the standpoint of an accepted zoning criterion, such as 'commercial district' or 'residential district' or 'industrial district,'" the court concluded, "that is

221. *Id.* at 272–73.
222. *Id.*
223. 611 F.3d 367, 370–71 (7th Cir. 2010) (en banc).
224. *Id.* at 368.
225. *Id.*
226. *Id.*
227. *Id.* at 371.

enough to rebut an Equal Terms claim and thus, in this case, to show that River of Life is unlikely to prevail in a full litigation."[228]

In reaching its decision, the court concluded that the case was "straightforward because, after the amendment to its zoning ordinance, *Hazel Crest* really was applying conventional criteria for commercial zoning in banning noncommercial land uses from a part of the village suitable for a commercial district because of proximity to the train station."[229] Under this framework, a jurisdiction prohibiting a certain religious use outright is justified when the secular counterpart to that use is also prohibited.[230]

One year later, the Ninth Circuit added an additional modification by acknowledging that jurisdictions may still justify treatment of a religious organization on less than equal terms so long as the disparate treatment is pursuant to a legitimate regulatory purpose. In *Centro Familiar Cristiano v. City of Yuma*,[231] a church had purchased a vacant foreclosed building. In order to hold services in the building, the church needed a conditional-use permit (CUP).[232] However, the owner of the building refused to wait to sell the building until the church acquired such a permit, so the church purchased the building knowing the permit might be denied.[233]

Owners of several neighboring properties expressed concern about issuing a conditional-use permit to the church, namely because state law proscribed new bars, nightclubs, or liquor stores from being located within 300 feet of a church.[234] The city also wanted a section of the Main Street area to serve as an entertainment district, and having a church in this district would prevent any bars, nightclubs, or liquor stores from operating in a major portion of the district.[235]

---

228. *Id.* at 372–73.
229. *Id.* at 373–74.
230. Eagle Cove Camp & Conf. Ctr. v. Town of Woodboro, 734 F.3d 673, 682–83 (7th Cir. 2013) (citing *River of Life* and holding that a county ordinance forbidding religious and secular camps in a secluded area does not violate equal terms).
231. 651 F.3d 1163 (9th Cir. 2011).
232. *Id.* at 1166.
233. *Id.*
234. *Id.*
235. *Id.*

If the church had been a secular organization, the city code would not have required it to obtain a CUP.[236] All nonreligious membership organizations—as well as other establishments, including auditoriums, museums, and even jails or prisons—did not need a conditional-use permit to operate in the Main Street area.[237] The district court initially determined that the city's differential treatment of churches did not violate RLUIPA.[238] However, two events that occurred while the appeal was pending changed the circumstances: the property was lost to foreclosure, and the state changed its ban on having liquor licenses within 300 feet of a church.[239]

On appeal, the Ninth Circuit addressed the four elements of the Equal Terms provision in RLUIPA: (1) there must be an imposition or implementation of a land use regulation (2) by a government (3) on a religious assembly or institution, and (4) the imposition must be "on less than equal terms with a nonreligious assembly or institution."[240] The court determined that the city's express mandate that religious organizations needed a conditional-use permit to operate in the Main Street district, while all other membership organizations did not need such a permit, demonstrated that the city clearly treated religious organizations on less than equal terms.[241]

The court further explained that once the church established the city's less-than-equal-terms treatment, RLUIPA shifted the burden to the city to demonstrate that it had a compelling government interest for such a discrepancy.[242] Like the Third Circuit, the Ninth Circuit declined to apply strict scrutiny but, significantly, decided that the city could still justify the less than equal treatment "on account of a legitimate regulatory purpose."[243] This approach shifts the burden away from the religious organization to proffer a similarly situated secular organization and onto the city to show that the treatment is not in effect unequal even when the letter of the law suggests otherwise.

236. *Id.* at 1166–67.
237. *Id.*
238. *Id.* at 1167.
239. *Id.*
240. *Id.* at 1170–71.
241. *Id.* at 1171.
242. *Id.*
243. The Lighthouse Institute for Evangelism, Inc. v. The City of Long Branch, New Jersey, 100 Fed. Appx. 70 3rd Cir. Ct. of Appeals (2004).

The city's justification, however, was unpersuasive for three reasons. First, the city code excludes religious organizations specifically rather than organizations that would impair obtaining liquor licenses. Second, the exception cannot be explained solely based on the liquor license restriction because it does not exclude only churches but all "religious organizations," even though only churches were able to cause the restriction on liquor licenses. Finally, the exclusion of educational services in the city code was not included in contemplation of the liquor license restriction, since only kindergarten through 12th-grade schools cause the restriction on liquor licenses. But the broadly stated educational services category disallowed numerous other educational institutions other than K–12 schools.[244]

Based on this reasoning, the court ultimately determined that the city code's requirement that religious assemblies, but not similarly situated secular groups, obtain a conditional-use permit violated RLUIPA's Equal Terms provision.[245]

Centro Familiar was also the first post-*Sossamon v. Texas*[246] decision in which a court recognized that monetary damages are available under the land use section of RLUIPA.[247]

b. Comparator Criteria

Despite some differences in methodology, courts have offered a variety of useful guidelines for advancing comparators in Equal Terms claims. For starters, many cases have stressed that though comparators need to be similar, they need not be exact in all respects. For instance, this principle was a significant deciding point in the Second Circuit's opinion in *Third Church of Christ Scientist of New York City v. City of New York*,[248] which emphasized the unimportance of technical differences between religious and secular organizations. Here the court was asked to define the parameters of the Equal Terms component of RLUIPA.[249] But after outlining the three prevailing tests, the court decided not to adopt any test but, rather, found

244. *Id.* at 1173–74.
245. *Id.* at 1175.
246. 563 U.S. 277, 131 S. Ct. 1651, 179 L. Ed. 2d 700 (2011).
247. *Centro Familiar*, 651 F.3d at 1168–69.
248. 626 F.3d 667 (2d Cir. 2010).
249. *Id.*

that the district court did not abuse its discretion in issuing a permanent injunction. The church, faced with a decision to close a historic building or seek alternative sources of funding to pay for the multimillion-dollar renovation of the site, entered into a contract with a private catering company to use the building for private catering events.[250] The city sought to close the use, and the church filed suit seeking a preliminary injunction under the Equal Terms provision of RLUIPA.[251] The district court granted the injunction, finding that the city allowed secular institutions in the church's neighborhood to conduct the same type of events.[252]

On appeal, the city urged dismissal of the injunction, claiming that the church and secular institutions were not similarly situated. Finding that the differences between the secular and religious uses were mere formalities and that the uses were similar for all functional intents and purposes, the appellate court affirmed the decision of the district court.[253] The court concluded that the church activities and other catering activities are similarity situated with regard to their legality under New York City law.[254]

When the unique nature of land use proposal makes finding a comparator unreasonable, the finding that a jurisdiction would otherwise permit land uses with a more severe land impact can function as a substitution. In *Bensalem Masjid Inc. v. Bensalem Township*,[255] Bensalem Masjid, an Islamic religious organization with a congregation mostly in Bensalem, Pennsylvania, worshipped in a rented fire hall because there was no mosque nearby. This created an arrangement conflicting with their religious beliefs in several important ways.[256]

In 2008, the plaintiff began an unsuccessful five-year search for suitable property in a nearby area zoned to permit religious institutions. In 2012, however, the plaintiff secured leases on three neighboring parcels spanning across three zoning districts, requiring a variance for a mosque.[257] Following

250. *Id.* at 668–69.
251. *Id.*
252. *Id.* at 669.
253. *Id.* at 671.
254. *Id.* at 672.
255. 2015 U.S. Dist. LEXIS 127364 (E.D. Pa. 2015).
256. *Id.* at *5.
257. *Id.* at *6.

the town's advice, the plaintiff applied for a variance instead of seeking to have the property rezoned. After five public hearings, the town zoning board denied the variance request—the first time ever for a religious institution. Alleging that it was the subject of harsher scrutiny, more stringent criteria and religious animus, the plaintiff filed suit under RLUIPA, the First and Fourteenth Amendments, and Pennsylvania state law.[258]

With respect to its Equal Terms claim, the plaintiff indicated that a variety of other permitted uses for the property in question would have significantly greater land impacts than the proposed mosque. Furthermore, the court indicated that Bensalem Township was "wrong in insisting plaintiff must identify an identical comparator," which in this case would be "a secular developer with three differently zoned lots."[259] In other words, the unexplained discrepancy in the land use impact was enough to justify technical differences between the proposed mosque and a rigidly similar comparator. This led the court to deny the township's motion to dismiss.

Though it may seem intuitive, the Second Circuit in *Chabad-Lubavitch v. Litchfield Historic District*[260] offered the important reminder that comparators should fall within the same regulatory scheme as the religious land use proposal. The Chabad Lubavitch of Litchfield County, a religious membership organization led by Rabbi Joseph Eisenbach, purchased property in the historic district of Litchfield, Connecticut, with an intent to expand the existing building for religious purposes. However, all buildings within the historic district were required to have alterations approved beforehand by the historic district commission.[261]

After two public hearings, the application was denied, with the commission's citing concerns primarily over the large size of the alteration and the extent to which it would disrupt the historic character of the area. The commission then granted some accommodations but ultimately declined to grant the Chabad a certificate of appropriateness. Subsequently, the Chabad

258. *Id.* at *7–8.
259. *Id.* at *14–15.
260. 768 F.3d 183 (2d Cir. 2014).
261. *Id.* at 187–88.

filed suit, alleging, among other things, RLUIPA violations under Substantial Burden, Equal Terms, and nondiscrimination.[262]

Pursuant to its Equal Terms claim, the Chabad pointed to one alleged comparator but failed to provide sufficient evidence to establish claim. The court found the comparator—the Wolcott Library, altered in 1965 from residential to institutional—to be inappropriate because it was approved by a different authority under a different regulatory code.[263] Additionally, though "minor differences" in regulatory schemes do not necessarily defeat such comparisons, the law at the time also prohibited consideration of relative size, whereas it currently requires the historic district commission to consider scale. The framework for administrative decision making, therefore, was simply too different to warrant allowing the comparator.[264]

Like entities subject to vastly different regulatory schemes, vastly different land uses, such as private residences, are also off limits as Equal Terms comparators. In *Roman Catholic Diocese of Rockville Centre v. Incorporated Village of Old Westbury*,[265] the Diocese of Rockville Centre, New York, a nonprofit religious corporation, submitted an environmental-assessment form in 1994 to the village of Old Westbury in order to develop a plot of land as a cemetery. The diocese became owner of the property in 1995 and submitted a development proposal to the village, which denied it. The village board of trustees also concluded that the cemetery did not constitute a religious use.[266]

In 1996, the diocese filed suit in state court. After a trial in 2000, the court found both that the cemetery was a religious use and that the matter should be remitted to the board of trustees with instructions to issue a special permit.[267] Shortly after, the board passed several comprehensive zoning amendments, including a Places of Worship (POW) law that permitted places of worship in residential districts subject to a series of conditions.[268] Then in 2004, the diocese filed for a special permit, to which the board responded

262. *Id.*
263. *Id.* at 196–97.
264. *Id.* at 197–98.
265. 2015 U.S. Dist. LEXIS 117808 (E.D.N.Y. 2015).
266. *Id.* at *8.
267. *Id.* at *10.
268. *Id.* at *14.

positively. But after years of complications surrounding compliance with largely environmental regulations,[269] the diocese filed suit again in 2009 under RLUIPA.[270] However, the board approved the cemetery in 2010 with various conditions and exceptions. Yet, because of disagreement on the restrictions, the litigation lived on.[271]

Interpreting the facts in the light most favorable to the diocese, as the nonmoving party, the court noted that the diocese had made a prima facie showing with respect to its substantial-burden claim to create genuine issues of material fact to avoid summary judgment. The diocese's Equal Terms argument, however, was doomed, as it could only point to land use authority decisions over 40 years old, similarly impermissible as the library in *Chabad-Lubavitch*, and a private residence. The court noted not only that the land impact would differ markedly between a private residence and a large cemetery but also that the diocese could not use a private residence as a comparator for the simple reason that it was not an assembly or institution within the plain meaning of either term.[272]

For broader guidance, a recent Equal Terms decision from the District Court for the Middle District of Florida outlines some of the most important factors a court considers in determining whether an entity is a similarly situated comparator. In *Church of Our Savior v. City of Jacksonville Beach*,[273] the Church of Our Savior in Jacksonville Beach, Florida, had grown dissatisfied with its venue rented for worship, citing overly limited storage space and a maximum capacity unsuitable for the growing church. It sought a new location that would be affordable, visible, and accessible.[274] The ideal property was zoned in an area that treated religious organizations as conditional uses subject to permit approval, even though secular uses such as playgrounds and recreational facilities were permitted as of right.[275]

The Church of Our Savior submitted a permit application twice. Both times they were rejected unanimously on grounds that resident testimony

269. *Id.* at *16–26.
270. *Id.* at *26–27.
271. *Id.*
272. *Id.* at *50–53.
273. 69 F. Supp. 3d 1299 (M.D. Fla. 2015).
274. *Id.* at 1304–05.
275. *Id.* at 1306.

voiced disapproval of the permit as inconsistent with the character of the location, that the proposal contradicted the city's comprehensive plan designating that institutional uses locate away from residential areas, and that the proposal would exceed maximum lot coverage requirements.[276] Consequently, the Church of Our Savior filed suit under RLUIPA. However, two days before trial, the city council amended the Land Development Code to place parks and other uses on the same footing as religious institutions in designating conditional uses.[277]

For its Equal Terms argument, the church presented two comparators. The first was a school board's receiving permission to improve a middle school, which constitutes an assembly or institution, on a 20-acre lot by replacing 60,000 square feet of land with 90,000 square feet of new construction without increasing enrollment. The structure was next to another school and was approved without any public objections, While the church wanted to use the new property for similar purposes, the court concluded that this comparator was "too dissimilar in size, intensity of use, location, fit with the surrounding neighborhood and public support."[278]

However, the church fared better with its second comparator, a recently approved conditional-use permit to expand a private school. The court found the school's 1.9-acre size to be similarly small compared with the church's 1.34 to 1.7 acres. For both properties, the immediate area was not completely low-density and residential but included public works and other similar facilities. Both also faced objections from nearby residents but also apparently received an approval recommendation from the Planning and Development Department. In sum, there were "substantial similarities" between the two with respect to "circumstances and the considerations at play in both situations."[279]

The city objected, claiming that the permit approval was not a similarly situated comparator because of its "remoteness in time."[280] While the court acknowledged that, in some cases, this could be an important distinction

276. *Id.* at 1307–10.
277. *Id.* at 1310–11.
278. *Id.* at 1321–22.
279. *Id.* at 1322–23.
280. *Id.* at 1323.

"considering the potential for the sensibilities of the community and the policies of the local government to change," it rejected the argument here both because the approval was recent and because it was the second major land use approval for the same school at the same location within the decade.[281] From this "preponderance of evidence," the court held that the city selectively enforced the Land Development Code and subjected the church to less than equal treatment in violation of RLUIPA's Equal Terms provision.[282]

c. Justifying Differential Treatment

Courts have identified certain land use regulatory aims under a state's police power that can legitimize differential treatment between religious organizations and secular comparators and thereby distinguish those entities in an Equal Terms analysis. Some of the most commonly referenced legitimate aims include controlling population density and traffic, limiting noise, and ensuring parking sufficiency.[283] But it is not always clear which regulatory aims pursuant to state police power are legitimate, let alone where and when. As the Supreme Court has acknowledged, the line separating "the legitimate from the illegitimate assumption of power is not capable of precise delimitation" at least because "[i]t varies with circumstances and conditions" within varying jurisdictions.[284]

For instance, some courts have held that the ability to generate tax revenue can suffice to differentiate a proposed comparator from a religious organization. In *Joan Dachs Bais Yaakov Elementary School–Yeshivas Tigeres Tzvi v. City of Evanston*,[285] a Jewish elementary school operated two facilities in Chicago but, since the 2000s, had been searching for a new property to replace a crowded facility. In 2006, it contracted to purchase property in Evanston, Illinois, in a zoning district that does not permit schools.[286] After the transaction closed in 2007, the school applied for a special-use permit as a religious institution, only to have it rejected because the zoning administrator determined that the school was more properly

281. *Id.*
282. *Id.* at 1323–24.
283. Vill. of Belle Terre v. Boraas, 416 U.S. 1, 18 (1974).
284. *Vill. of Euclid*, 272 U.S. at 367.
285. 2015 Ill. App. Unpub. LEXIS 421 (Ill. App. 1st 2015).
286. *Id.* at *2–3.

classified as a nonpermitted private educational institution.[287] The school then submitted an application for a unique-use permit in 2008, which was denied, and an attempt to change the zoning classification through a map amendment also failed.[288] Subsequently, the school filed suit under RLUIPA, and the trial court sided with Evanston.[289]

For its Equal Terms comparators, the school pointed to four approved applications for map amendments. The court arguendo took the comparators (a townhome, work-live condo, gas station, and shopping center) as assemblies, but the comparison still failed. Each comparator was a taxable use, and the school's proposed use would remove a large industrial parcel from property tax rolls.[290] "The generation of tax revenues," the court affirmed, "is a legitimate concern of land use regulation."[291] Circumstance here is important, considering that the presence of Northwestern University in Evanston took nearly half of the city's land off the tax rolls already, meaning that generating tax revenue was a significant concern for the jurisdiction.[292] Some concerns were also raised about the safety of children at the school, given the property's close proximity to an industrial labor area. "[T]he determination of the compatibility of land uses and their impact on public safety," the court continued, "is also a legitimate concern of land use regulation."[293]

Some courts have held that setting aside a commercial district, excluding churches, for purposes of generating revenue generally is a legitimate land use interest. This notion, the Seventh Circuit indicated, is buttressed by the acknowledgment that "commercial" is not synonymous with "secular," and therefore excluding noncommercial assemblies or institutions is not inherently less than equal treatment.[294] Courts that adopt this line of reasoning normally add the important qualification that an area designated to function as a commercial district must exclude all noncommercial and

287. *Id.* at *6–7.
288. *Id.* at *8–12.
289. *Id.* at *20.
290. *Id.* at *36–38.
291. *Id.* at *38.
292. *Id.* at *40.
293. *Id.* at *38.
294. *River of Life*, 611 F.3d at 372–73.

nontax-generating uses in the area—it cannot single out one variety of the sort, such as churches.

The Fifth Circuit made precisely this assertion in *Opulent Life Church v. City of Holly Springs*.[295] In this case, Opulent Life Church, a small Christian congregation, sought a larger meeting space in Holly Springs, Mississippi. In 2011, the church entered into a lease agreement to use new property as a church and soon after applied for a renovation permit and submitted a comprehensive building plan. However, the Holly Springs Planning Commission tabled the request because the church did not satisfy certain zoning ordinance requirements that apply only to churches. To use property as a church, owners were required, among other things, to get at least 60 percent approval from owners within a 1,300-foot radius and to obtain approval from Holly Springs' mayor and board of aldermen.

The church filed suit in 2012, but the district court denied a motion for preliminary injunction, which the church appealed. One day before oral argument, however, Holly Springs amended the ordinance, replacing the provisions that singled out churches with a categorical ban on religious institutions within the district. Holly Springs conceded that the now-repealed regulations violated the Equal Terms Clause. But even under the new ordinance, Holly Springs had to prove the validity of the ban. The city contended that it wished to designate the area as a commercial district, but the court was not swayed, since the city would still be allowing noncommercial and nontax-generating uses within the district. In turn, the court granted the church a preliminary injunction.

Although being subjected to diminished land use rights is not necessarily unequal treatment, being granted more expansive rights, perhaps counterintuitively, can be seen as less than equal. The Seventh Circuit made this claim in *Digrugilliers v. Consolidated City of Indianapolis*.[296] Toby Digrugilliers was pastor of the Baptist Church of the West Side, which was in a part of Indianapolis zoned a C-1 district,[297] making it a buffer between residential and commercial zones.[298] C-1 zones allowed for an extensive list

295. 697 F.3d 279 (5th Cir. 2012).
296. 506 F.3d 612 (7th Cir. 2007).
297. *Id.* at 614.
298. *Id.* at 614–15.

of uses, including assembly halls, day care centers, and auditoriums—but excluded religious institutions.[299] Because the church constituted a religious use, Digrugilliers would have had to either move his church or apply for a variance. He did neither and instead brought suit, alleging violation of the Equal Terms provision of RLUIPA. The district court denied Digrugilliers' request for a preliminary injunction on the grounds that the suit had negligible prospects of success, leading Digrugilliers to appeal.[300]

The central question on appeal was whether, by requiring the church to obtain a variance, the city treated the church on less than equal terms compared to a nonreligious institution.[301] The district judge thought not, because the zoning code defines religious use broadly to include residential uses, such as a rectory for the minister. Therefore, the judge reasoned, to allow the church to operate without a variance would give churches greater rights than secular uses.[302]

Judge Posner of the Seventh Circuit disagreed. The church's lease prohibits the structure from being used for residential purposes, and there was no indication that the church was being used as a residence. The city, he then reasoned, "may not, by defining religious use so expansively as to bestow on churches more rights than identical secular users of land have, justify excluding churches from the districts in which, were it not for those superadded rights, the exclusion would be discriminatory."[303] Though the city tried to argue that alternative sites were available to offset the alleged discrimination, Posner offered the important reminder that, unlike in substantial-burden claims, the existence of alternative sites is not relevant in establishing an Equal Terms violation.[304]

Using the same reasoning, Posner addressed the city's alternative explanation that permitting the use would create conflict with the Indiana law forbidding the selling of liquor within 200 feet of a church.[305] He found it

299. *Id.*
300. *Id.* at 615.
301. *Id.*
302. *Id.*
303. *Digrugilliers*, 506 F.3d at 615.
304. *Id.* at 616 (noting that the existence of alternative sites is only relevant to substantial burden calculus, and that "[i]f proof of substantial burden were an ingredient of the equal-terms provision, the provisions would be identical, which could not have been Congress's intent").
305. *Id.*

irrelevant that one law was created by the state and the other by the city, as both are part of the government of Indiana. "A state," Posner continued, "cannot be permitted to discriminate against a religious land use by a two-step process in which the state's discriminating in favor of religion becomes a predicate for one of the state's subordinate governmental units to discriminate against a religious organization in violation of federal law."[306] The case was reversed and remanded to consider the claim.

An important precept of Equal Terms lurks here. That is, it is not always clear that being subjected to different treatment equates to being subjected to less than equal treatment. The adjudication is more nuanced. For example, creating a historical district or designating a religious organization as a landmark might seem to amount to a form of discrimination when doing so attaches burdensome regulations on the selected entity. Indeed, a church advanced precisely this argument in *Roman Catholic Bishop of Springfield v. City of Springfield*,[307] when Springfield, Massachusetts, enacted an ordinance creating a single-parcel historic district encompassing the church's property.

Because of declining attendance and financial support, the Roman Catholic bishop of Springfield, Massachusetts, closed the Our Lady of Hope Church with the intention of merging with another parish. Under Roman Catholic canon law, closed churches must protect their religious ornamentation from casual and disrespectful treatment. This entails undergoing a process of deconsecrating, which mandates that the church either remove (protect or destroy) its symbols or protect them from "sordid" use.[308]

Many of the church's parishioners were unhappy with the merger, and many of them, along with other residents, began lobbying to have the church designated as a historic district—the first and at the time only single-parcel historic district in the city, though other historic districts existed. Under the Massachusetts Historic Districts Act, municipalities are empowered to designate areas as historic districts.[309] Buildings within a district may not be altered without permission from the state historical commission.

306. *Id.* at 617.
307. 724 F.3d 78 (1st Cir. 2013).
308. *Id.* at 84.
309. *Id.* at 85.

The lobbying was a success, and a historic district ordinance was passed and took effect in January 2010. But the church did not respond by attempting to proceed with deconsecrating or seek permission to alter the church's exterior. Rather, the church filed suit in Massachusetts Superior Court before the city removed the case to the U.S. District Court, where the court granted summary judgment to the city because the church's claims were not ripe.[310]

The First Circuit reversed the unripe finding[311] but, of greater relevance, also found that being singled out in this way does not necessarily mean that a religious organization is being subjected to less than equal treatment compared to secular organizations that are not required to comply with the associated restrictions. The church tried to compare itself to all other secular institutions in the city, but the court was unconvinced. Forming a historic district for a single property or designating that property as a landmark, however, is not by itself a form of discriminatory targeting, since preserving historic and aesthetic interests is a legitimate concern, and all properties within the jurisdiction would be subject to the same process guided by objective criteria within the same comprehensive plan.[312]

Subjective justifications for differential treatment, however, are highly suspect. In *Corporation of the Catholic Archbishop v. City of Seattle*,[313] Bishop Blanchet High School, a private Catholic institution in a residential single-family zone in north Seattle, wished to improve lighting for its athletic field by installing 70-foot poles. But the height limit under the city land use code for the zone was 30 feet, requiring the school to apply for a variance. The school submitted an application that initially was conditionally approved but later rejected after an appeal by nearby homeowners, as the city found that the school had not established the necessary first criterion of the existence of unusual conditions not created by property owners.[314]

Importantly, the city exempted public schools in residential zones from having to seek a variance for the same purpose, requiring only that the schools submit an engineer's report ensuring that the lighting impact will

310. *Id.* at 86–88.
311. *Id.* at 92.
312. *Id.* at 97–101.
313. 28 F. Supp. 3d 1163 (W.D. Wash. 2014).
314. *Id.* at 1165.

be minimal. And indeed, public schools within north Seattle residential zones took advantage of the exemption. After its variance rejection, Bishop Blanchet brought suit, arguing that the public schools' exemption violated the Equal Terms provision of RLUIPA.[315]

The court assessed whether two institutions (the private and public high schools), similarly situated for regulatory purposes, were given equal treatment under "accepted zoning criteria." Thus the question centered on whether any accepted zoning criteria could justify the exemption for public schools. The city maintained that the exemption could be justified because it was "fostering the provision of public facilities by governmental agencies."[316] But the court was unpersuaded because acceptable zoning criteria are understood to refer to objective determinations of whether a use should be permitted within a zone. The city's justification was subjective and bore no relation to zoning concerns expressed in the city code (e.g., light, tree cover, density, structure height).[317] Given that the public and private schools were similarly situated with generally the same zoning concerns, the city failed to demonstrate that the treatment was less than equal in violation of RLUIPA.[318]

3. Nondiscrimination Claims

Congress also adopted a provision in RLUIPA that protects religious entities from governments using land use regulations discriminatively. The so-called nondiscrimination provision states that "[n]o government shall impose or implement a land use regulation that discriminates against any assembly or institution on the basis of religion or religious denomination."[319] Nondiscrimination cases have not been abundantly litigated, in large part because of the difficulty in proving discrimination and the absence of established standards for the provision.

The provision, nonetheless, is generally linked with the Fourteenth Amendment's Equal Protection Clause and existing equal protection

315. *Id.* at 1166.
316. *Id.* at 1168.
317. *Id.* at 1168–69.
318. *Id.* at 1169–70.
319. 42 U.S.C. § 2000cc(b)(2).

jurisprudence.[320] Under this lens, nondiscrimination claims do not necessarily require proof of a similarly situated entity,[321] but the absence of evidence showing relevant discriminatory animus can seriously damage a nondiscrimination claim.[322] Not many courts have spent a considerable amount of time on nondiscrimination claims, but the Fourth Circuit helped illustrate some of these principles in *Bethel World Outreach Ministries v. Montgomery County Council*.[323] In Bethel, a Christian church with two locations in Maryland was still in dire need of additional space because of growing attendance.[324] Thus, the church bought a 119-acre parcel in Montgomery County on which it planned to build a larger facility.[325] However, the county denied the church's request for public water and sewer service, and the county later amended its zoning ordinance such that no institutions in rural areas would receive water or sewer service.[326] The church appealed the county's decision to the local state court and included claims that the county's denial violated RLUIPA's nondiscrimination provision, as well as other federal and state constitutional provisions.[327] The state court held for the county.[328]

Bethel eventually filed a federal suit alleging RLUIPA violations after the county had amended its zoning ordinances in a way that prohibited Bethel from building a smaller church.[329] After the district court found for the county, the Fourth Circuit affirmed the decision.[330] As to the nondiscrimination claim, the court held that the relevant zoning ordinance that the church challenged was neutral and generally applicable. Bethel maintained, however, that it had offered extensive evidence proving that the county

320. Church of Scientology v. City of Sandy Springs, 843 F. Supp. 2d 1328, 1370 (N.D. Ga. 2012).
321. Muslim Cmty. Ass'n of Ann Arbor & Vicinity v. Pittsfield Charter Twp., 947 F. Supp. 2d 752, 764 (E.D. Mich. 2013).
322. Irshad Learning Ctr. v. Cnty. of DuPage, 937 F. Supp. 2d 910, 939 (N.D. Ill. 2013).
323. 706 F.3d 548 (4th Cir. 2013).
324. *Id.* at 552.
325. *Id.*
326. *Id.* at 553.
327. *Id.*
328. *Id.*
329. *Id.* at 554.
330. *Id.*

adopted its ordinance out of discriminatory animus.[331] Evidence existed that some public officials and residents opposed the size of the proposed church, and the county ordinance at issue was amended after two churches had inquired into building in the pertinent district.[332] This, however, was not enough evidence to prevent the court from granting summary judgment for the county on the nondiscrimination claim. The church was unable to show that any discrimination was directed at religion itself or that the concern with size was pretextual.[333]

4. Exclusion Cases

Congress included an "exclusions" prong in RLUIPA that provides, in relevant part, that a local government "may not impose or implement a land use regulation that . . . totally excludes religious assemblies from a jurisdiction."[334] Like the statue's nondiscrimination provision, there has not been much litigation on this particular prong, though primarily because most governmental entities already recognized that they could not wholly exclude religious uses from their jurisdictions.

Still, when RLUIPA was enacted, some local governments maintained a provision in their zoning ordinances excluding religious uses, justifying it on the grounds that it maintained a tax base or preserved property values. Such was the case in *Elsinore Christian Center v. City of Lake Elsinore*[335] and *Vietnamese Buddhism Study Temple in America v. City of Garden Grove*.[336] In Elsinore, the California city denied a church's conditional-use permit and articulated three principal bases for its denial: (1) maintaining needed services provided by the site's current tenant (a discount food store and recycling center), (2) preventing a loss of property tax revenue by replacing a commercial tenant with a noncommercial user, and (3) the possible inadequacy of on-site parking for the church's proposed use and

331. *Id.* at 559.
332. *Id.*
333. *Id.* at 559–60.
334. 42 U.S.C. § 2000cc(b)(3)(A),(B).
335. 291 F. Supp. 2d 1083 (C.D. Cal. 2003) (holding that City's denial of church's application for a CUP violated RLUIPA), *rev'd on other grounds*, 197 F. App'x 718 (9th Cir. 2006) (holding RLUIPA constitutional).
336. 460 F. Supp. 2d 1165, 1174–75 (S.D. Cal. 2006).

potential adverse consequences on the parking needs of adjacent users.[337] The court found that "the maintenance of property tax revenue is a potentially pretextual basis for decision-making that appears to have been a specific target of RLUIPA."[338]

These claimed interests were also rejected in the *Vietnamese Buddhism Study Temple* case, where the land use and zoning ordinance in Garden Grove, California, permitted nonreligious assemblies to operate as a matter of right in zones where religious assemblies were completely forbidden.[339] One of these zones was the office professional zone where the temple's property was located.[340] The temple was forced to shut down and sought a preliminary injunction against Garden Grove to allow the congregation to assemble and practice its faith on the property.[341] The primary concerns raised in the city planning commission's denial of the temple's applications were increased traffic, increased on-street parking, and loss of revenue. The court found that "[t]hese three concerns simply do not justify facially unequal treatment between a church and a private club"[342] and concluded:

> [I]f a tax exempt nonprofit private organization decides to purchase property in the office professional zone, the city would suffer the same loss of revenue as it would if a religious association operated the property as a church. The city has not shown that a church or religious assembly would have a demonstrably different impact on the office professional zone than would a private club or lodge. This strongly suggests that the zoning ordinance impermissibly pursues Garden Grove's interests only against conduct motivated by religious belief.[343]

337. 291 F. Supp. 2d at 1083, 1085, *rev'd on other grounds*, 197 F. App'x 718 (9th Cir. 2006) (holding RLUIPA constitutional).

338. 291 F. Supp. 2d at 1093 (citing Report of the House Comm. on the Judiciary (H.R. REP. No. 106-219) (July 1, 1999), at text accompanying n.79 (cited in Hatch-Kennedy Statement, 146 CONG. REC. S7774, at S7775)).

339. 460 F. Supp. 2d at 1166.

340. *Id.*

341. *Id.*

342. *Id.* at 1174.

343. *Id.* at 1175.

In response to these decisions, many local governments have changed their zoning ordinances to either exclude all assembly uses or to allow religious assembly. This action also violates the Exclusions Clause, for the reason that once secular assemblies (such as private clubs, lodge halls, social and similar organizations, including assembly halls and even funeral homes) are permitted, religious assembly uses must be approved as well. "[B]ecause special uses, as such, are considered compatible with other uses in the zoning district in which they are included, it is generally held that an application for a special-use permit may not be denied on the ground that the use is not in harmony with the surrounding neighborhood."[344]

5. Unreasonable Limitations

The "unreasonable limitations" prong of RLUIPA provides that a governmental entity "may not impose or implement a land use regulation that . . . unreasonably limits religious assemblies, institutions or structures within a jurisdiction."[345] The text implies that government may reasonably limit religious organizations, and the provision was adopted not to assess restrictions on particular landowners but rather the regulations that unreasonably limit where religious entities may locate within a given jurisdiction. Otherwise, it would essentially duplicate the substantial-burden provision.[346] As with the nondiscrimination and exclusions prongs, few cases have interpreted the provision.

In *Chabad of Nova Inc. v. City of Cooper City*,[347] the Chabad alleged that Cooper City's zoning code constituted an unreasonable limitation on the ability of religious assemblies to purchase property within the city.[348]

344. City of Chi. Heights v. Living Word Outreach Full Gospel Church & Ministries Inc., 749 N.E.2d 916, 929 (Ill. 2001) (citing 3 K. Young, Anderson's American Law of Zoning § 21.13, at 743 (4th ed. 1996)). *See also* Sts. Constantine & Helen Greek Orthodox Church v. City of New Berlin, 396 F.3d 895, 900 (7th Cir. 2005) (RLUIPA protects against "the vulnerability of religious institutions—especially those that are not affiliated with the mainstream Protestant sects or the Roman Catholic Church—to subtle forms of discrimination when, as in the case of the grant or denial of zoning variances, a state delegates essentially standardless discretion to nonprofessionals operating without procedural safeguards).

345. 42 U.S.C. § 2000cc(b)(3)(B).

346. Church of Our Savior v. City of Jacksonville, 69 F. Supp. 3d 1299, 1324–25 (M.D. Fla. 2014).

347. 575 F. Supp. 2d 1280, 1289 (S.D. Fla. 2008).

348. *Id.* at 1290.

The city argued that approximately 85 percent of its property was currently zoned to permit religious assemblies and that 19 places of worship currently existed in the city.[349] However, under a city ordinance, the frontage specifications in the residential districts still required religious assemblies to aggregate an average of three to four properties.[350] Religious assemblies were therefore subject to approximately $500,000 to $1.4 million in additional costs to locate in the residential districts.[351] Further, Chabad provided evidence regarding the lack of available properties in the agricultural districts and the OP and P-1 districts, which religious assemblies were permitted to enter after October 2006 amendments to the ordinance.[352]

The district court found that "the only properties available to religious assemblies are in the residential districts, and at great expense. . . ." Further, the number of existing religious assemblies in the city was not evidence regarding the availability of reasonable opportunities for the entry of new religious assemblies under the current zoning ordinances. The court found that even after the October 2006 amendments, the city continued to provide inadequate opportunity for new religious assemblies to locate within the jurisdiction because the city imposed unreasonable restrictions on their purchase of property.[353] The court concluded that Chabad was therefore entitled to summary judgment with respect to its unreasonable-limitations claim.[354]

In sum, the case law interpreting the unreasonable-limitations provision of RLUIPA still needs to be flushed out. Its parameters will likely remain a reasonableness inquiry: what is reasonable must be determined in light of all the facts, including the actual availability of land and the economics of religious organizations.[355] And time will tell whether courts will incorporate this test as broadly acceptable.

349. *Id.* at 1291.
350. *Id.*
351. *Id.*
352. *Id.* at 1291.
353. *Id.* at 1292.
354. *Id.*
355. *Vision Church*, 468 F.3d at 978 (2006) (citing 146 CONG. REC. E1563 (daily ed. Sept. 22, 2000) (statement of Rep. Canady)).

C. Damages and Equitable Relief

RLUIPA's provision authorizing a cause of action states that "[a] person may assert a violation of this chapter as a claim or defense in a judicial proceeding and obtain appropriate relief against a government."[356] The statute broadly defines the term "government" to include the following:

i. A state, county, municipality or other governmental entity created under the authority of a state.
ii. Any branch, department, agency, instrumentality or official of an entity listed in clause (i). and
iii. Any other person acting under color of state law.[357]

While the phrase "appropriate relief" may seem simple enough, these two words have turned out to be more problematic than one would imagine. Following are some examples of the different forms of relief that courts have deemed "appropriate" under RLUIPA.

It is a familiar canon of statutory construction that "[i]n the absence of contrary indication, we assume that when a statute uses . . . a term [of art], Congress intended it to have its established meaning."[358] However, courts have had trouble agreeing on the established meaning of "appropriate relief" within the context of RLUIPA. As one court put it mildly, "There is a division of authority" on whether "appropriate relief" encompasses monetary damages.[359] The federal district courts are currently split: some courts conclude that RLUIPA does not encompass monetary damages, while others have found the opposite, concluding that the phrase "appropriate relief" is sufficiently broad to include some forms of monetary relief. Meanwhile, a third category of interpretation has developed in some district courts that have assumed that monetary relief is available without resolving the disputed definition of "appropriate relief."[360]

---

356. 42 U.S.C. § 2000cc-2(a) (2000).

357. *Id.* § 2000cc-5(4)(A).

358. *See, e.g.*, McDermott v. Wilander, 498 U.S. 337, 342 (1991).

359. Smith v. Allen, 502 F.3d 1255, 1270 (11th Cir. 2007) (quoting Madison v. Virginia, 474 F.3d 118, 130 (4th Cir. 2006)).

360. "No federal courts of appeal have ruled on whether RLUIPA allows damages against state officials sued in their individual capacities, and federal district courts are split on the

This current conflict among district courts regarding the availability of monetary damages stems from the issues inherently involved in claimants suing governmental officials in their individual capacities—a sphere that federal courts appear to be hesitant to let claimants near, let alone expand. Likewise, claims of punitive damages against municipalities under RLUIPA are questioned, given that the U.S. Supreme Court has concluded that punitive damages are not available against municipalities and officials sued in their official capacity in section 1983 cases.[361]

The term "appropriate relief" has a well-established meaning, summed up in the Supreme Court's seminal decision in *Franklin v. Gwinnett County Public Schools*.[362] There, the court defined "appropriate relief" under Title IX to include monetary damages,[363] based on the federal courts' traditional authority to fashion broad remedies for violations of federally guaranteed rights.[364] Guided by this tradition, the court in *Franklin* concluded that "[t]he general rule, therefore, is that absent clear direction to the contrary by Congress, the federal courts have the power to award any appropriate relief in a cognizable cause of action brought pursuant to a federal statute."[365]

In *Franklin*, the issue before the court was what types of remedies were available to a claimant in a private action for sex discrimination under Title IX of the Education Amendments of 1972. The Court tried to put to rest the argument that a damages award unduly expands the federal courts' power in violation of separation-of-powers principles, as such an argument

question." Bess v. Alameida, 2007 WL 2481682 (E.D. Cal. 2007); *compare* Shidler v. Moore, 409 F. Supp. 2d 1060, 1071 (N.D. Ind. 2006) (recognizing RLUIPA claim for damages), *and* Charles v. Verhagen, 220 F. Supp. 2d 937, 953 (W.D. Wis. 2002) (same), *and* Guru Nanak Sikh Soc'y of Yuba City v. Sutter, 326 F. Supp. 2d 1128, 1136 (E.D. Cal. 2003) ("'government' in RLUIPA includes officials, so actions are permitted against them at least in their official capacities"), *with* Boles v. Neet, 402 F. Supp. 2d 1237, 1241 (D. Colo. 2005) (damages are not available under RLUIPA).

361. City of Newport, R.I., v. Fact Concerts Inc., 453 U.S. 247 (1981).

362. 503 U.S. 60, 66 (1992).

363. *Id.* at 76.

364. *Id.* at 66.

365. *Id.* at 70–71; Sch. Comm. of Burlington, Mass., v. Dep't of Educ. of Mass., 471 U.S. 359, 369 (1996) (defining "appropriate" relief to include compensatory damages); Reich v. Cambridgeport Air Sys. Inc., 26 F.3d 1187, 1191 (1st Cir. 1994) (construing "all appropriate relief" to include monetary damages and other forms of relief).

"misconceives the difference between a cause of action and a remedy."[366] In further explanation, the Court noted:

> Unlike the finding of a cause of action, which authorizes a court to hear a case or controversy, the discretion to award appropriate relief involves no such increase in judicial power and, in fact, historically has been thought necessary to provide an important safeguard against legislative and executive abuses and to insure an independent judiciary. Moreover, selective adjudication of the sort advocated here would harm separation of powers by giving judges the power to render inutile causes of action authorized by Congress through a decision that no remedy is available.[367]

In its attempts to put to rest the theory that a court's ability to award appropriate relief does extend into the legislative and executive branches' powers, the decision in *Franklin* should have carried quite a punch among lower courts when analyzing RLUIPA by instructing that, absent any intent to the contrary reflected in a statute, the presumption should be in favor of all available relief, both injunctive and monetary. However, although this should have occurred in theory, such was not the case practically, as federal district courts still are in flux over what *Franklin* means for the future of RLUIPA's available relief.

In 2003, as redress for defendants' violation of RLUIPA, the church plaintiff in *Guru Nanak Sikh Society of Yuba City v. County of Sutter* sought declaratory, injunctive, and compensatory relief against the county for land use regulations that infringed upon the church's religious rights.[368] The county was trying to prevent the church from assembling at its property to worship. As the majority of courts agree, the court in *Guru Nanak* found it readily apparent that declaratory and injunctive relief are "appropriate relief" under RLUIPA, and, accordingly, the court declared the challenged

366. *Id.* at 73–74.
367. *Id.*
368. Guru Nanak Sikh Soc'y of Yuba City v. Cnty. of Sutter, 326 F. Supp. 2d 1140 (E.D. Cal. 2003).

land use decision as invalid and enjoined the county defendants from enforcing it.[369]

However, in deciding the church's rights to monetary relief, the district court in *Guru Nanak* allowed only a claim for nominal damages. The court did deny a claim for compensatory damages, but that claim was limited only to the land use permit application deposit of $1,938.93. The court did not find that such a modest cost actually added to the burden on the church's religious exercise (compensable on a "substantial burden" theory) or find that those costs were applied differentially (compensable on an "equal terms" theory) or unreasonably (compensable on an "unreasonableness" theory).[370] The Third Circuit also followed *Smith* in its interpretation of pursuing monetary claims against individuals in their individual capacities and decided that "government" in RLUIPA includes officials, so actions are permitted against them at least in their official capacities.[371]

Almost four years later, in *Lighthouse Institute for Evangelism Inc. v. City of Long Branch*,[372] the Third Circuit did not go into a lengthy discussion whether monetary damages were available to the church under RLUIPA but, rather, assumed so. The church sued the city for its zoning ordinance's placing religious organizations on less than equal terms with nonreligious assemblies. The city changed its zoning plan so injunctive relief no longer was available or necessary because where a regulation is challenged as invalid on its face, "if an amendment removes those features . . . being challenged by the claim, any claim for injunctive relief becomes moot as to those features."[373] Since the plan superseded the ordinance in all relevant respects, its enactment mooted Lighthouse's claims for injunctive relief based on the facial invalidity of the ordinance. However, the court noted that Lighthouse's claims for compensatory damages and attorney fees

369. *Id.* at 1162. (citing Elrod v. Burns, 427 U.S. 347, 373–74 (1976) ("The loss of First Amendment freedoms, for even minimal period of time, unquestionably constitutes irreparable injury."); Bell v. Hood, 327 U.S. 678, 684 (1946) ("[I]t is established practice for this Court to sustain the jurisdiction of federal courts to issue injunctions to protect rights safeguarded by the Constitution.")).

370. *Id.*

371. *Id.* at 1136.

372. 510 F.3d 253 (3d Cir. 2007).

373. *Id.* at 260 (citing Nextel W. Corp. v. Unity Twp., 282 F.3d 257, 262 (3d Cir. 2002)).

remained viable.[374] The Third Circuit thus allowed Lighthouse's claims only insofar as they were claims for compensatory damages and attorney fees.[375]

Because such a great conflict exists among federal district courts regarding the availability of nominal, punitive, and compensatory damages in an RLUIPA action, the only truly reliable reasoning can be found in Congress's legislative history when it enacted the controversial statute in 2000. Congress's use of the term of art "appropriate relief" in RLUIPA, enacted against the backdrop of *Franklin* and *Burlington*,[376] can only mean that Congress intended monetary damages to be one of the remedies available to successful RLUIPA plaintiffs. Indeed, it would be especially ironic if Congress's use of a term of art that underscores the breadth of available relief prompted the courts instead to narrow the scope of that relief.

Such a narrow interpretation of "appropriate relief" would be less appropriate in light of other statutory provisions of RLUIPA. Section 4(f) grants the United States authority to enforce the provisions of the act by "an action for injunction relief."[377] Congress knew how to limit available relief only to declaration and injunction and even did so in another part of the act, preferring instead broader language to describe the relief available to private plaintiffs.[378] Moreover, section 5(g) expressly calls for the construction of the act that is most protective of religious exercise.[379] And construing "appropriate relief" to encompass damages serves that purpose in various ways.

To pick just one example, the land use process—and the subsequent litigation process—often takes so long to complete that religious institutions face a high risk of either losing their leases or being forced to resell the properties at issue. This would moot injunctive relief and, if damages were

374. *Id.* (citing Donovan v. Punxsutawney Area Sch. Bd., 336 F.3d 211, 218 (3d Cir. 2003) (holding that although plaintiff's claim for declaratory and injunctive relief was moot, her "damages and attorney fees claims continue[d] to present a live controversy")).

375. *Id.* at 261.

376. Sch. Comm. of Burlington, Mass., v. Dep't of Educ. of Mass., 471 U.S. 359, 369 (1996) (defining "appropriate" relief to include compensatory damages).

377. 42 U.S.C. § 2000cc-2(f).

378. Agrawal v. Briley, 2006 WL 3523750 (N.D. Ill. Dec. 6, 2006) ("Had Congress intended in § 2000cc-2(a) to limit relief available to individuals to injunctive or declaratory relief, Congress could have used the same language it used in § 2000cc-2(f).").

379. 42 U.S.C. § 2000cc-3(g) ("This Act shall be construed in favor of a broad protection of religious exercise, to the maximum extent permitted by the terms of this Act and the Constitution.").

unavailable, the entire case. Thus, the absence of damages would create a perverse incentive for municipalities to drag out the conditional-use-permit and litigation process for as long as possible, with the hope that an appellant will eventually lose the land and with it the entire cause of action.

Although the use of a term of art that encompasses damages, particularly in the context of other reinforcing statutory provisions, provides sufficient clarity about Congress's intent to allow for damages, RLUIPA's legislative history provides additional confirmation. The detailed analysis of RLUIPA's provisions included in the Congressional Record states that the remedy provisions "track RFRA, creating a private cause of action for damages, injunction and declaratory judgment and creating a defense to liability and providing for attorneys' fees."[380] Legal analysis presented to both the House and Senate committees that passed RLUIPA confirms this construction: "Appropriate relief includes declaratory judgment, injunctions and damages."[381] Reading "appropriate relief" not to include damages would contravene this congressional intent. Thus, many courts have allowed RLUIPA damages claims with less detailed discussion, including in the land use context.[382]

Finally, the availability of damages is in keeping not only with RFRA but also with claims under 42 U.S.C. § 1983 for analogous constitutional violations.[383] Particularly in light of this broader context, RLUIPA should be read to provide the same remedies as available under section 1983, including

380. 146 Cong. Rec. E1563-01, 2000 WL 1369378 (Sept. 21, 2000) (emphasis added).

381. Emphasis added. *See also Religious Liberty Protection Act: Hearing on H.R. 1691 Before the Subcomm. on the Constitution of the H. Comm. on the Judiciary*, 106th Cong., 1st Sess., No. 62-491, at 219 (May 12, 1999); *Issues Relating to Religious Liberty Protection, and Focusing on the Constitutionality of a Religious Protection Measure: Hearing Before the S. Comm. on the Judiciary*, 106th Cong., 1st Sess., No. 106-689 (June 23 & Sept. 9, 1999) (statement of Prof. Douglas Laycock, University of Texas School of Law) [hereinafter Senate Hearing].

382. *See, e.g.*, Chase v. City of Portsmouth, 428 F. Supp. 2d 487 (E.D. Va. 2006); Maranatha High Sch. v. City of Sierra Madre, 2003 WL 25338413 (C.D. Cal. Mar. 12, 2003); *see also* Gainer v. Cooper, 2006 WL 2946061 (S.D. Ga. Oct. 13, 2006) (permitting First Amendment and RLUIPA claims for monetary damages to go forward), 2006 WL 3307146 (adopting magistrate's report); Ghashiyah v. Wis. Dep't of Corr., 2006 WL 2845701 (E.D. Wis. Sept. 29, 2006) (suggesting punitive damages are available under RLUIPA); Price v. Caruso, 451 F. Supp. 2d 889, 895 (E.D. Mich. 2006) (dismissing injunctive and declaratory claims as moot, but allowing damages claim under RLUIPA to go forward).

383. *See* Senate Hearing, *supra* note 380 ("This section should be read against a large body of federal law on remedies and immunities under other civil rights legislation.").

damages.[384] One reason that there simply is no terror effect based on the availability of damages along the lines of many opponents' speculations is that RLUIPA prisoner and land use plaintiffs can already obtain damages under section 1983 for conduct by prison and zoning officials that is similar if not exactly the same. RLUIPA largely restates, and to a limited extent expands, existing constitutional protections under the Free Exercise, Establishment, Free Speech, and Equal Protection Clauses of the First and Fourteenth Amendments.[385] Any suggestion that zoning officials will begin doling out unwarranted favors to religious institutions out of fear—simply because RLUIPA makes damages available for the small increment of zoning conduct that RLUIPA prohibits but the Constitution does not—is as implausible as it is unsupported and should be rejected.

In any event, such deterrence would not even threaten to violate the Establishment Clause. Even if the damages increment did somehow tend to deter zoning officials from treading as closely to the constitutional line in denying permits to assemble for worship and religious instruction, RLUIPA will have done its job under the Enforcement Clause, not failed in it under the Establishment Clause.[386] The Establishment Clause should not be read so aggressively that people and groups cannot benefit from the deterrence of Enforcement Clause legislation simply because they are religious or because the rights they assert involve religious exercise.[387]

---

384. *See Agrawal*, 2006 WL 3523750, at *11 (finding it "unlikely that Congress, in attempting to provide greater protection for religious freedom than was available under the First Amendment, would simultaneously subject regulations to stricter scrutiny but deny relief that had traditionally been available"). *See also* Jama v. INS, 343 F. Supp. 2d 338, 374–75 (D.N.J. 2004) (similar regarding RFRA).

385. *See* Freedom Baptist Church v. Twp. of Middletown, 204 F. Supp. 2d 857, 868–71 (E.D. Pa. 2002) (discussing parallel constitutional protections restated or approximated in various provisions of RLUIPA § 2). *See also* Bd. of Trs. of Univ. of Ala. v. Garrett, 531 U.S. 356, 365 (2001) ("Congress is not limited to mere legislative repetition of this Court's constitutional jurisprudence," but may also prohibit "a somewhat broader swath of conduct.").

386. *See* City of Boerne v. Flores, 521 U.S. 507, 518 (1997) ("Legislation which deters or remedies constitutional violations can fall within the sweep of Congress' enforcement power even if in the process it prohibits conduct which is not itself unconstitutional. . . .").

387. *See* Cutter v. Wilkinson, 544 U.S. 709, 724 (2005) (rejecting the proposition that "giving greater protection to religious rights than to other constitutionally protected rights" violates the Establishment Clause). *See also* Emp't Div., Dep't of Human Res. of Or. v. Smith, 494 U.S. 872, 877 (1990) ("The government may not . . . impose special disabilities on the basis of religious views or religious status. . . .").

Even if the availability of damages under RLUIPA would generate constitutional issues under the Establishment Clause—and it does not at all—courts must address (and reject) those constitutional issues, rather than simply avoid them.[388] Under *NLRB v. Catholic Bishop*,[389] when a court finds that a certain statutory interpretation would generate a constitutional issue, that does not end the analysis but instead calls for a second inquiry: whether Congress's intent nonetheless mandates the interpretation that generates the constitutional issue.[390]

Here, the answer to that question is yes. Congress has made clear that it intends for courts to construe RLUIPA "in favor of a broad protection of religious exercise, to the maximum extent permitted by the terms of this act and the Constitution," leaving no room for constitutional avoidance.[391] If the Constitution allows an interpretation that "favor[s] a broad protection of religious exercise," then the interpretation must be allowed, even if it might generate constitutional issues. Of course, if the interpretation results in a constitutional violation, then it is forbidden. But in light of section 5(g), Congress's intent is clear that nothing short of an actual constitutional violation can defeat a protective interpretation. Accordingly, if allowing damages did generate constitutional issues, courts should address rather than avoid those issues and reject them as meritless.

Nearly all courts agree that "appropriate relief" includes injunctive and declaratory relief. However, some courts initially disagreed as to whether RLUIPA allowed for monetary damages.[392]

388. Any suggestion that RLUIPA's land use provisions are unconstitutional should also be rejected, *see id.* at 4 n.7, as the Ninth Circuit has either rejected those challenges directly, or rejected challenges to the indistinguishable prisoner provisions of RLUIPA. Guru Nanak Sikh Soc'y of Yuba City v. Cnty. of Sutter, 456 F.3d 978 (9th Cir. 2006) (rejecting Enforcement Clause challenge to RLUIPA § 2(a)); Mayweathers v. Newland, 314 F.3d 1062 (9th Cir. 2002), *cert. denied*, 540 U.S. 815 (2003) (rejecting Spending and Establishment Clause, Tenth and Eleventh Amendment, and Separation-of-Powers challenges to RLUIPA § 3). *See also* Midrash Sephardi Inc. v. Town of Surfside, 366 F.3d 1214, 1227 (11th Cir. 2004) (rejecting constitutional challenge to RLUIPA § 2(b)).

389. 440 U.S. 490 (1979).

390. *See id.* at 504.

391. RLUIPA § 5(g).

392. *See, e.g.*, Smith v. Allen, 502 F.3d 1255, 1270 (11th Cir. 2007) (quoting Madison v. Va., 474 F.3d 118, 130 (4th Cir. 2006)).

In 2011, the U.S. Supreme Court addressed the availability of damages within the institutionalized-persons context of RLUIPA in *Sossamon v. Texas*.[393] Plaintiff Harvey Leroy Sossamon III, an inmate at a Texas state prison, had filed suit challenging the decision of a warden to refuse to allow cell-restricted inmates to attend religious services and to deny all inmates the use of the prison chapel for religious purposes.[394] Sossamon sought declaratory and injunctive relief as well as monetary damages under RLUIPA.[395] The federal district court granted summary judgment in favor of Texas, holding that Texas had sovereign immunity under the Eleventh Amendment and was not liable for damages. The Fifth Circuit affirmed.[396]

The question before the Supreme Court was whether an individual may sue a state or state official in his official capacity for damages for RLUIPA violations.[397] Writing for the majority, Justice Thomas argued that the broadly stated "appropriate remedies" provision of RLUIPA, without more specificity, does not subject states to prisoner claims for monetary damages.[398] The court ruled that in the context of RLUIPA's institutionalized-persons provision—not the land use provisions—the statute does not allow inmates to seek damages from the state because in accepting federal funding, states "do not consent to waive their sovereign immunity to private suits for money damages under RLUIPA."[399]

In dissent, Justice Sotomayor argued that the majority's interpretation that RLUIPA does not provide for a remedy of monetary damages "severely undermines the 'broad protection of religious exercise' Congress intended the statute to provide."[400] Justice Sotomayor supported this contention by citing statutes in which Congress made the effort to explicitly note that the terms "relief" or "appropriate relief" were meant to exclude damages.[401]

Although the court in *Sossamon* did not squarely address the issue of damages on the land use side of RLUIPA, the transcript of the oral argument

393. 131 S. Ct. 1651 (2011).
394. *Id.* at 1656.
395. *Id.*
396. *Id.* at 1656–57.
397. 42 U.S.C. § 2000cc (2000).
398. Sossamon v. Texas, 563 U.S. 277, 285-289, 131 S. Ct. 1651, 179 L. Ed. 2d 700 (2011).
399. *Id.* at 186.
400. *Id.* (citing 42 U.S.C. § 2000cc-3(g) (2000)).
401. *Id.* at 289.

shows that the justices were considering the implication of its decision in defining "appropriate relief" to the land use cases.[402] To date, there has been no definitive answer either way from the court.

However, a few weeks after the *Sossamon* decision, the Ninth Circuit of the U.S. Court of Appeals answered the question in *Centro Familiar Cristiano Buenas Nuevas v. City of Yuma* (2011).[403] The court concluded that the decision in *Sossamon* was limited in scope, as the Supreme Court found that prisoners could not recover monetary damages under RLUIPA because states did waive their sovereign immunity.[404] In other words, the court held that *Sossamon* is grounded on the line of Eleventh Amendment authority requiring "clear expression" to abrogate the sovereign immunity of states from damages claims.[405] As the Eleventh Amendment requirement does not apply to municipalities, the court held that the city of Yuma may be liable for monetary damages under RLUIPA, if plaintiffs prove a violation and damages.[406]

In *International Church of Foursquare Gospel v. City of San Leandro*,[407] the Northern District of California held that the church could recover monetary damages for the city's violations of RLUIPA's substantial-burden provision, but it dismissed the church's claim for purported lost contributions.[408] The church calculated into its damages total an amount ranging from $10,400,000 to $14,320,000, which apparently represented the "lost collection plate revenues from anticipated parishioners who did not materialize as new church members, calculated at a rate of $118 per person per month."[409] In dismissing the damages for lost contributions, the court found that the inquiry into whether the church could continue to grow at its normal rate absent the city's conduct was speculative. The church also

402. Transcript of Oral Argument at 14-15, Sossamon v. Texas, (No. 08-1438), http://www.supremecourt.gov/oral_arguments/argument_transcripts/08-1438.pdf.
403. 651 F.3 1163, 1168–69 (9th Cir. 2011).
404. *Id.*
405. *Id.*
406. *Id.*
407. Case No. C 07-3605, 2012 U.S. Dist. LEXIS 117347 (N.D. Cal. Aug. 20, 2012).
408. 634 F.3d 1037 (9th Cir. 2011).
409. International Church of Foursquare Gospel v. City of San Leandro, California, 651 F. 3rd 1168.

was unable to show any relationship between the city's actions and its claimed lost contributions.[410]

In addition, the court rejected the city's argument that an award of damages for an RLUIPA violation constituted unjust enrichment. The court noted that RLUIPA's allowance for "appropriate relief" for a violation has been interpreted by the Ninth Circuit to include monetary damages.[411] Based on this interpretation, awarding damages for RLUIPA violations does not violate the Establishment Clause as a preference for religion over nonreligion.[412]

Therefore, although the RLUIPA provision does not expressly state that monetary damages are available, it also does not preclude them. Accordingly, it is logical, especially in light of RLUIPA's statutory language and some courts' interpretations of the language, that a plaintiff may proceed on his or her RLUIPA claims for monetary damages against defendants in both their official and individual capacities.

D. Recovery of Attorney Fees and Cost in Religious Land Use Cases

Under 42 U.S.C. § 1988(b),[413] courts are able to award reasonable attorney fees to the prevailing party in an action that seeks to protect the plaintiff's civil rights. The statute specifically states that successful plaintiffs in a Religious Land Use and Institutionalized Persons Act (RLUIPA) case are entitled to recover their attorney fees from liable defendants.[414]

In *Northern Cheyenne Tribe v. Jackson*,[415] the Eighth Circuit interpreted the meaning of "prevailing party" under section 1988 in a case involving RLUIPA claims. The plaintiffs—several Native American tribes—sought an injunction against the U.S. Department of Housing and Urban Development to stop HUD from disbursing funds to South Dakota to build a shooting range near spiritually significant Native American land.[416] The district court granted plaintiffs a preliminary injunction, and the project

410. *Id.* at *10.

411. *Id.* at *11.

412. *Id.*

413. "In any action or proceeding to enforce [RLUIPA,] the court, in its discretion, may allow the prevailing party . . . a reasonable attorney's fee as part of the costs. . . ."

414. 42 U.S.C. 1988.

415. 433 F.3d 1083 (8th Cir. 2006).

416. *Id.* at 1084.

was later abandoned and defendants moved to dismiss based on the claims being moot.[417] Plaintiffs agreed on the mootness issue but further argued that they were entitled to attorney fees under section 1988.[418] The district court denied the request for attorney fees, finding that the plaintiffs were not considered "prevailing parties" under the statute.[419]

On appeal, the Eighth Circuit agreed with the district court's ruling. The appellate court noted that the district court merely determined whether plaintiffs were likely to succeed on the merits. However, the interim grant of injunctive relief merely "preserved the status quo until [the court] could resolve the merits of the tribes' claims."[420] The court also noted that the plaintiffs had received their desired result based on HUD's regulatory action, which was entirely unrelated to the merits of plaintiffs' RLUIPA claims. As such, the court deemed it inappropriate to award the plaintiff's attorney fees when defendant's voluntary action created the result.[421]

In a case before the Northern District of Illinois, *Power of Praise Worship Center Church v. Village of Dixmoor*,[422] the court addressed the calculation of attorney fees pursuant to 42 U.S.C. § 1988 in a case involving RLUIPA. The court entered a permanent injunction against the village to enjoin the government from preventing the church from using leased property that allegedly violated the village's zoning ordinance.[423] The church was thus the "prevailing party" under section 1988 for purposes of attorney fees.[424] The court explained that the appropriate method by which to calculate attorney fees is the lodestar method, "which is calculated by multiplying a reasonable hourly rate by the number of hours reasonably expended."[425]

Pursuant to the lodestar method, the court awarded the church $46,438 in attorney fees.[426] The award was warranted, the court held, because the church's lawyers had to perform "extensive research into the village's zoning

417. *Id.* at 1084–85.
418. *Id.* at 1085.
419. *Id.*
420. *Id.* at 1086.
421. *Id.*
422. No. 10 C 5436, 2011 WL 1157550 (N.D. Ill. Mar. 29, 2011).
423. *Id.* at *1.
424. *Id.*
425. *Id.* (quoting Gastineau v. Wright, 592 F.3d 747, 748–49 (7th Cir. 2010)).
426. *Id.* at *2.

codes, investigate the history between the church and the village, draft a comprehensive complaint, draft and prepare to orally argue the temporary restraining order motion, negotiate a permanent injunction, attend multiple court hearings and reasonably calculate damages."[427]

As discussed earlier, the Ninth Circuit decided in *Centro Familiar* that federal courts could award monetary damages against municipalities under RLUIPA.[428] The court cited RLUIPA's language, which allows a successful plaintiff to "obtain appropriate relief against a government"[429] and which also includes states and municipalities in its definition of "government."[430] The Ninth Circuit also distinguished the case from *Sossamon*, in which the Supreme Court held that states could not be held liable under RLUIPA for monetary damages because there is no "clear expression" of their abrogation of sovereign immunity from claims for damages.[431]

Centro Familiar, in contrast, involved a municipality, not a state. The Eleventh Amendment's requirement of a "clear expression" in order to abrogate sovereign immunity does not apply to municipalities.[432] Since the Eleventh Amendment's requirement did not apply to the city of Yuma, the court determined that the city could be liable for monetary damages under RLUIPA, and it remanded so the district court could appropriately determine Centro Familiar's damages.[433]

Under 42 U.S.C. § 1988(b), "the court, in its discretion, may allow the prevailing party" in an RLUIPA action to recover "a reasonable attorney's fee as part of the costs." In recognition of Congress's intent in enacting 42 U.S.C. § 1988, the Supreme Court has held that a prevailing plaintiff "should ordinarily recover an attorney's fee unless special circumstances would render such an award unjust."[434] Although the statutes make an award of attorney fees "discretionary," it is an abuse of discretion to deny attorney

---

427. *Id.*

428. Centro Familiar Cristiano Buenas Nuevas v. City of Yuma, 651 F.3d 1163, 1168–69 (9th Cir. 2011).

429. *Id.* at 1168 (quoting 42 U.S.C. § 2000cc-2(1)).

430. 42 U.S.C. § 2000cc-5(4).

431. *Centro Familiar*, 651 F.3d at 1168–69.

432. *Id.* at 1169 (citing Alaska v. EEOC, 564 F.3d 1062, 1066 (9th Cir. 2009)).

433. *Id.* at 1169, 1175.

434. Hensley v. Eckerhart, 461 U.S. 424, 429 (1983) (internal quotation marks omitted).

fees to a prevailing plaintiff in a successful suit for violation of civil rights.[435] Since the "purpose of § 1988 is to ensure 'effective access to the judicial process' for persons with civil rights grievances," a prevailing party should "recover attorney's fees unless special circumstances would render such an award unjust."[436]

In addition, the prevailing party in a Fair Housing Act (FHA) action is allowed, at the court's discretion, a reasonable attorney fee under 42 U.S.C. § 3613(c)(2). The Fifth Circuit interprets the meaning of "prevailing party" under the FHA the same as under 42 U.S.C. § 1988 because the FHA specifically provides that the term "prevailing party" as used in section 3613(c)(2) has the same meaning as the term in section 1988.[437] If a lawsuit itself causes the legal relationship between the parties to change—for example, by a settlement—then the plaintiff is the "prevailing party" for purposes of the attorney fees issue under section 3613(c)(2) of the FHA.[438]

In determining whether a plaintiff is a "prevailing party" within the meaning of section 1988, "the touchstone of the prevailing-party inquiry must be the material alteration of the legal relationship of the parties."[439] A material alteration requires that "[t]he plaintiff . . . obtain an enforceable judgment against the defendant from whom fees are sought or comparable relief through a consent decree or settlement."[440] According to the Fifth Circuit, to be considered "prevailing," the party must "have succeeded on any significant issue of litigation which achieves some of the benefit the parties sought in bringing the suit."[441]

In *Riley v. City of Jackson*, the Fifth Circuit overturned a lower court decision that refused to grant attorney fees under section 1988 to successful civil rights plaintiffs.[442] The parties agreed to a settlement on the merits of the case in favor of the plaintiffs and in which the plaintiffs were explicitly

435. Dean v. Riser, 240 F.3d 505, 508 (5th Cir. 2001) ("[A] prevailing plaintiff ordinarily is to be awarded attorney's fees in all but special circumstances.").

436. *Hensley*, 461 U.S. at 429.

437. *See also* Lopez v. City of Dallas, 328 F. App'x 944, 945 (5th Cir. 2009).

438. *See* Energy Mgmt. Corp v. City of Shreveport, 467 F.3d 471, 482 (5th Cir. 2006).

439. Farrar v. Hobby, 506 U.S. 103, 111 (1992) (internal citations omitted).

440. *Id.* (emphasis added).

441. E.E.O.C. v. ClearLake Dodge, 60 F.3d 1146, 1153 n.9 (5th Cir. 1995).

442. 99 F.3d 757 (5th Cir. 1996).

considered "prevailing parties" under section 1988.[443] The Fifth Circuit explained that because the lawyers assisted the plaintiffs in obtaining their primary objective—injunctive relief—the plaintiffs' success was not a mere "technical victory" meriting no award of attorney fees.[444] In summary, attorney fees and costs are available for a successful claimant under RLUIPA.

II. State Religious Freedom Act Claims

In addition to the federal RFRA, since 1993, 21 states have enacted their own version of the invalidated law that spurred enactment of RLUIPA.[445] The *Smith* decision itself recognized that state legislators may provide greater protection for religious liberty than is provided by the U.S. Constitution. Moreover, as long as a state RFRA is worded so that it is clear that the legislature is creating a new right and not merely telling the courts how to interpret the state constitution, there will be no violation of the separation of powers mandated by most state constitutions. At times, the claim is made that state RFRAs violate the federal Establishment Clause because they have the purpose and effect of advancing religion. In a similar context, the U.S. Supreme Court has never accepted such arguments. Moreover, the justices ignore that the compelling-interest test was applied to protecting religious liberty half a century before 1990, yet the Supreme Court never ruled that this was a violation of the Establishment Clause.

As of this writing, there have been no significant land use decisions based on state RFRAs. Nonetheless, these laws are intended to echo the federal RFRA but are not necessarily identical to the federal law. Arkansas and

443. *Id.* at 759.

444. *Id.*

445. RFRAs have become law in the following states: Alabama, ALA. CONST. art. 1, § 3.01; Arizona, ARIZ. REV. STAT. § 41-1493.01; Arkansas, 2015 SB 975, enacted Apr. 2, 2015; Connecticut, CONN. GEN. STAT. § 52-571b; Florida, FLA. STAT. §§ 761.01, *et. seq*.; Idaho, IDAHO CODE § 73-402; Illinois, ILL. REC. STAT. ch. 775, § 35/1; Indiana, 2015 SB 101, enacted Mar. 26, 2015, 2015 SB 50, enacted Apr. 2, 2015; Kansas, KAN. STAT. § 60-5301; Kentucky, KY. REV. STAT. § 446.350; Louisiana, LA. REV. STAT. § 13:5231; Mississippi, MISS. CODE § 11-61-1; Missouri, MO. REV. STAT. § 1.302; New Mexico, N.M. STAT. § 28-22-1; Oklahoma, OKLA. STAT. tit. 51, § 251; Pennsylvania, PA. STAT. tit. 71, § 2403; Rhode Island, R.I. GEN. LAWS, § 42-80.1-1; South Carolina, S.C. CODE, § 1-32-10; Tennessee, TENN. CODE § 4-1-407; Texas, TEX. CIV. PRAC. & REMEDIES CODE § 110.001; Virginia, VA. CODE § 57-2.02.

Indiana are the most recent states to enact an RFRA, doing so in 2015. These laws have responsibly given religious people and institutions protection from an increasingly intrusive government bureaucracy. Despite the dire prediction of critics, these acts have not given rise to a flood of lawsuits, protected child abusers, exempted churches from all zoning laws, or negated other civil rights.

State RFRAs are a response to the significant loss of federal protections of religious liberty over the past 15 years. They are passed by state legislatures to restore the standard that has historically protected religious freedom—a standard known as the "compelling state interest" test. This standard requires that any state action that substantially burdens the religious freedom of any person be justified by showing that the state act is the least restrictive means of protecting a "compelling state interest." Such interests would include the protection of life, liberty, property, and health of others, as well as similarly strong community interests. The test requires the state to show that it has no less restrictive means of protecting its interests that avoids a conflict with religious exercise. It is clear that the compelling-interest standard that RFRAs institute has a stellar history of nearly half a century of fairly protecting the religious freedom of individuals and institutions. A state RFRA does not establish an unknown and uncertain standard but, rather, restores a known and effective legal protection.

States RFRAs are still needed because federal law no longer provides the protection for religious liberty that it once did. Some states, such as Michigan, have inadequate religious-freedom protection in light of state court decisions.[446] Therefore, an RFRA is needed in states like Michigan. And because relief from religious discrimination need not be found solely in the courts but also through the legislature, the author has proposed an RFRA for his home state of Michigan and encourages others to push for a similar law among the respective states that have not yet done so.

446. Greater Way Temple v. City of Jackson, 478 Mich. 373 (2007).

III. Fair Housing Act Claims

In addition to looking at federal and state constitutional provisions, a religious entity may also wish to consider the Fair Housing Act (FHA) to determine whether a cause of action exists. This is particularly true if the ministry of the church, temple, or mosque is a homeless shelter or drug and alcohol rehabilitation facility.

The Fair Housing Act[447] provides that it is unlawful:

- To make unavailable or deny a dwelling to any person because of race, color, religion, sex, familial status, or national origin.
- To discriminate against any person in the provision of services or facilities in connection therewith, because of race, color, religion, sex, familial status, or national origin.[448]

As defined under the statute, discrimination includes "a refusal to make reasonable accommodations in rules, policies, practices or services when such accommodations may be necessary to afford such person equal opportunity to use and enjoy a dwelling."[449]

In 1988, Congress amended the FHA and expanded coverage of the statutory scheme to those with handicaps, including people who have "a physical or mental impairment which substantially limits one or more of such person's major life activities, a record of having such impairment or being regarded as having such an impairment."[450] Congress had defined "handicapped persons" as including those "individuals who have recovered from" an addiction or "are participating in a treatment program or self-help group such as Narcotics Anonymous. . . . Depriving such individuals housing or evicting them would constitute irrational discrimination that may seriously jeopardize their continued recovery."[451]

447. Douglas E. Miller, *The Fair Housing Act, Oxford House, and the Limits of Local Control over the Regulation of Group Homes for Recovering Addicts*, 36(4) Wm. & Mary L. Rev. 1467, 1493.

448. 42 U.S.C. § 3604(a)(b).

449. *Id.* § 3604(f)(3)(B).

450. *Id.* § 3602(h).

451. H.R. Rep. No. 711, reprinted in 1988 U.S.C.C.A.N. at 2183; 42 U.S.C. § 3602(k).

Federal courts have subsequently read the 1988 amendment to apply to drug and alcohol recovery houses.[452] The House Judiciary Committee has made clear that the FHA was intended to apply to zoning decisions: "The committee intends that the prohibition against discrimination against those with handicaps apply to zoning decisions and practices."[453] The remedies provided for successfully bringing suit pursuant to the FHA include actual and punitive damages, injunctive relief, and reasonable attorney fees and costs.[454] There is a two-year statute of limitations to bring such claims.[455]

Under the FHA, there are three theories of housing discrimination. First, there are FHA claims alleging discriminatory intent on the part of those city officials who decide whether the requested permit will be granted.[456] Notably, a broad interpretation exists of what constitutes discriminatory intent under the FHA. Courts have found discriminatory intent when a zoning decision is reversed at the behest of neighbors, as well as intent based on the public comments from city officials or even residents at city meetings.[457] Discriminatory intent is also present when the government selectively enforces provisions of its zoning ordinance, particularly when it is done so to appease complaining neighbors.[458]

Second, there is a discriminatory impact theory FHA claim, which involves the application of a facially neutral ordinance that, while uniformly

---

452. United States v. S. Mgmt. Corp., 955 F.2d 914, 918 n.1 (4th Cir. 1992) (affirming injunction against apartment complex that refused to rent apartments to recovering drug addicts, holding that recovering drug addicts were considered handicapped under the FHA based on the attitudes society has against those who are in such recovery); Tsombanidis v. City of W. Haven, 180 F. Supp. 2d 262, 283 (C.D. Conn. 2001) ("There is no dispute in this case that the John Doe plaintiffs, as non-abusing, recovering alcoholics and drug addicts are members of a protected class under the FHA."); United States v. S. Mgmt. Corp., 955 F.2d 914, 921 (4th Cir. 1992) ("Individuals who have been perceived as being a drug user or an addict are covered under the definition of handicap if they can demonstrate that they are being regarded as having an impairment and that they are not currently using an illegal drug.").

453. H.R. REP. No. 711, reprinted in 1988 U.S.C.C.A.N. at 2185.

454. 42 U.S.C. § 3613.

455. *Id.*

456. Oxford House Inc. v. Town of Babylon, 819 F. Supp. 1179, 1184–85 (E.D.N.Y. 1993).

457. *Id.* at 1184; Oxford House-Evergreen v. City of Plainfield, 769 F. Supp. 1329, 1342–43 (D.N.J. 1991) (discriminatory intent found after zoning officer reversed determination to grant requested permit based on citizen complaints at city council meeting against issuing the permit.).

458. *Id.*; Oxford House Inc. v. Town of Babylon, 819 F. Supp. 1179, 1184–85 (E.D.N.Y. 1993).

applied, has a discriminatory impact on a protected class.[459] Although the legitimacy of disparate-impact theory under the FHA was not always clear, the Supreme Court recently affirmed that such claims are cognizable in *Texas Department of Housing and Community Affairs v. Inclusive Communities Project Inc.*[460] In doing so, the court acknowledged that the FHA plays an important role in "uncovering discriminatory intent" by "permit[ting] plaintiffs to counteract unconscious prejudices and disguised animus that escape easy classification as disparate treatment."[461] A party alleging a discriminatory impact need not show intentional discrimination.[462] The party challenging the ordinance first must show a discriminatory impact on the protected class based on statistical evidence that the practice in question has created the adverse effect.[463]

If government can show that the disparate-impact claim is not caused by government policy, the claim fails.[464] But if a sufficient showing is made, the burden is on the government to show that the impact is necessary to meet a legitimate state interest.[465] If the government satisfies that burden, the plaintiff must show that the defendant's reason is a pretext or that there is an alternative practice to achieve the government interest in a way that does not result in the discriminatory impact.[466] Restrictive family definitions in zoning ordinances, for example, commonly impose a disparate burden on group recovery homes.[467]

---

459. Simms v. First Gibraltar Bank, 83 F.3d 1546, 1555 (5th Cir. 1996) (holding that "a violation of the FHA may be established not only by proof of discriminatory intent, but also by a showing of significant discriminatory effect"); Horizon House Developmental Servs. Inc. v. Twp. of Upper Southampton, 804 F. Supp. 683 (E.D. Pa. 1992).

460. 576 U.S. 519 (2015).

461. *Id.* slip op. at 17.

462. Munoz v. Orr, 200 F.3d 291, 299 (5th Cir. 2000).

463. Homebuilders Ass'n of Miss. Inc. v. City of Brandon, 640 F. Supp. 2d 835, 841 (S.D. Miss. 2009) (citation omitted).

464. *Inclusive Communities*, slip op. at 19–20 ("[A] disparate-impact claim that relies on a statistical disparity must fail if the plaintiff cannot point to a defendant's policy or policies causing that disparity.").

465. *Id.*

466. *Id.*

467. Moore v. City of E. Cleveland, 431 U.S. 494 (1977); Oxford House Inc. v. City of Albany, 819 F. Supp. 1168, 1176 (N.D.N.Y. 1993) (holding that restricting the number of unrelated people in a home to three created a disparate impact on group recovery home).

The third and final category is a reasonable-accommodation claim, which at least one commentator has said is the strongest of the three FHA claims.[468] While the FHA is thought to afford equal rights to those highlighted protected classes, the reasonable-accommodation claim is thought to grant those in the protected classes a preferred status in land use decisions.[469] Under such a claim, "a violation occurs when the disabled resident is first denied a reasonable accommodation, irrespective of the remedies granted in subsequent proceedings."[470] In other words, a denial from the government for the requested reasonable accommodation can be actual or constructive, "as an intermediate delay has the same effect as an outright denial."[471] In *Groome Resources*, an application had been completed and submitted but had been pending without review for more than four months, and there was no indication that any decision was forthcoming.[472] That was enough to find the matter ripe, according to the Fifth Circuit, which noted that housing discrimination causes a uniquely harmful and immediate injury that makes such matters ripe.[473]

In *U.S. v. Jackson*,[474] the federal government won enforcement of a consent decree requiring the city of Jackson, Mississippi, to permit Christians in Action (CIA) to operate a home for disabled or otherwise disadvantaged children in a residential neighborhood, pursuant to the reasonable-accommodation claim that CIA brought under the FHA.[475] The United States and the city of Jackson had originally entered into a consent decree in 1997 based on the city's alleged violation of the reasonable-accommodation provision of the FHA with respect to a land use applicant that sought to operate a group home for Alzheimer's patients.[476]

In the enforcement action, the federal government alleged that the city breached the agreement in 2000 when the city council twice voted to deny

468. 42 U.S.C. § 3604(f)(3)(B).
469. *Id.*
470. Groome Res., Ltd. v. Parish of Jefferson, 234 F.3d 192, 199 (5th Cir. 2000) (quoting Bryant Woods Inn Inc. v. Howard Cnty., Md., 124 F.3d 597, 602 (4th Cir. 1997)).
471. *Id.*
472. *Id.*
473. *Id.* at 200.
474. 318 F. Supp. 2d 395 (S.D. Miss. 2002).
475. *Id.* at 397.
476. The remedy was affirmed in *United States v. City of Jackson*, 359 F.3d 727 (5th Cir. 2004).

the nonprofit CIA a use permit under the city's zoning ordinance to establish a "group home for the handicapped" in a subdivision.[477] In sending out the Notice of Hearing, the city stated that granting the use permit would not change the zoning classification.[478] The planning board held an evidentiary hearing in June 2000, at which time a number of neighbors expressed concerns that granting the permit would rezone the area, more businesses would follow, and CIA would alter the character of the surrounding subdivision.[479] Despite reminders that the permit would not rezone the area and that CIA's presence would not hurt property values, the city's planning board voted to recommend denial of the use permit. Working off the record from the planning board, the city council voted unanimously to deny the use permit.[480]

Upon hearing of the denial, the federal government brought a motion for civil contempt seeking enforcement of the consent decree, and the court evaluated the merits of CIA's FHA reasonable-accommodations claim.[481] First, the court evaluated whether the accommodation CIA sought from the city was in fact reasonable.[482] A requested accommodation is reasonable under the FHA unless "it imposes an undue financial and administrative burden on the defendant," or the accommodation "requires a fundamental alteration in the nature of the program at issue, which in this case is the City's zoning scheme."[483] In the case of the use permit CIA had requested, the court found no undue financial or administrative burden on the city to follow its administrative process to grant the permit.[484] The city already had an administrative process in place for evaluating such requests, so the city suffered no increased cost or administrative burden.[485]

Additionally, the issuance of the use permit would not have fundamentally altered the city's zoning scheme or changed the character of the surrounding area.[486] The court noted seven reasons for this conclusion: (1) the CIA

477. 318 F. Supp. 2d at 397.
478. *Id.* at 402.
479. *Id.* at 403–04.
480. *Id.* at 405–06.
481. *Id.*
482. *Id.* at 412.
483. *Id.*
484. *Id.*
485. *Id.*
486. *Id.*

home would have been consistent with the single-family residential use; (2) group homes, even if they are for-profit businesses, are sometimes the only available options for people with disabilities to live in residential communities; (3) the use permit would not lead to rezoning or otherwise change the character of the neighborhood, as neighbors had feared; (4) generalized concerns of neighbors about safety were speculative; (5) granting CIA the use permit would create the same impact as that or other residential uses permitted in the same district, as there was no proof that CIA's presence would diminish property values; (6) the "NIMBY" complaints of neighbors were insufficient to deny the use permit; and (7) CIA's application met all six factors the city looked at when determining whether to approve a use permit.[487]

After determining that the accommodation was reasonable, the court took the second step in the reasonable-accommodation process and looked at "whether the accommodation being sought 'may be necessary' to allow disabled persons 'equal opportunity to use and enjoy a dwelling.'"[488] The court began by noting that the FHA "gives handicapped persons the right to live in the residence of their choice. This right extends to all areas in a city, including single-family neighborhoods."[489] Thus, the city could not simply state that it would permit CIA to remain in its current location even though CIA had already stated that it needed to expand and wanted to do so at the site where it had sought the use permit. "Restricting CIA to that location, based on a desire to accede the insular preferences of residents of Brookhollow Place without any legitimate reason, denies persons with disabilities 'equal opportunity' to live in the housing of their choice."[490] It was not enough that the city would have permitted CIA to operate and expand in other sections of the city.

The court additionally noted that it had previously held that "the concept of 'necessity' under the amended FHA includes the concept that the desired accommodation affirmatively enhance the quality of life of a person with a disability by ameliorating the effects of that disability."[491] Shelters for

487. *Id.* at 412–15.
488. *Id.* at 412.
489. *Id.* at 415.
490. *Id.* at 416.
491. *Id.* at 416–17.

children, including some who were recovering from addictions, "provide a beneficial living environment for abused and neglected children."[492] The accommodation was also necessary because a critical need for such housing existed in the city.[493]

In *Oxford House Inc. v. City of Baton Rouge* (2013),[494] Oxford House alleged that the city of Baton Rouge, Louisiana, violated the FHA by "using and enforcing discriminatory zoning ordinances to exclude Oxford House from operating in an area zoned for single-family use."[495] Two Oxford Houses were the subject of the litigation after they had received letters from the city stating that the homes violated the city's zoning ordinance because more than two unrelated people lived in the homes.[496] Oxford House replied with a request for a reasonable accommodation because the residents in the homes were the "functional equivalent" of a family.[497] At the city's request, Oxford House formally sought the reasonable accommodation but was denied, and its subsequent request for reconsideration was never ruled upon.[498]

In evaluating the claims, the court applied the Eleventh Circuit Court of Appeals method in examining whether the city had issued a refusal, the requested accommodation was reasonable, and the accommodation was necessary.[499] The court quickly found that the city had refused the accommodation request, even if a formal response to the request for reconsideration had been submitted.[500] As to reasonableness, the court found that the city suffered no undue burden, primarily because the city failed to raise the argument.[501] The court then found that the accommodation would not alter the zoning scheme, as the complaints of neighbors about increased traffic and simply not wanting a "halfway house" in their neighborhood did not alter the zoning scheme.[502]

492. *Id.* at 417.
493. *Id.*
494. 2013 U.S. Dist. LEXIS 38002 (M.D. La. Mar. 18, 2013).
495. *Id.* at *2.
496. *Id.* at *4.
497. *Id.*
498. *Id.* at *5–6.
499. *Id.* at *16.
500. *Id.* at *18–20.
501. *Id.* at *22.
502. *Id.* at *22–23.

As to the "necessity" prong, the court found that the reasonable accommodation was necessary for people with disabilities to have an equal opportunity to live where they desire because before moving into the home, the residents' "prospects for recovery were bleak, and the residents were unable to function. However, after moving into Oxford House, the residents are able to care for themselves, hold employment and pay bills. The residents all stated that the supportive structure of Oxford House has enabled them to turn their lives around."[503]

Therefore, with all three prongs satisfied, the court found that the city of Baton Rouge had violated the FHA by denying the reasonable-accommodation request of the Oxford Houses.

Additionally, the court found that the city had violated the disparate-treatment provision of the FHA.[504] To show intentional discrimination, Oxford House had to show that "a motivating factor behind the city's refusal to classify [Oxford House] as a single-family household was the residents' status as recovering drug addicts and alcoholics."[505] The court held that the first part of the ordinance at issue that put additional and onerous safety and permit requirements on homes for the developmentally disabled violated the FHA.[506] In particular, it was impermissible under the FHA for an Oxford House to have to take additional steps for a reasonable accommodation simply because its homes were not staffed 24 hours a day.[507] The court also found discriminatory intent in part based on the fact that the city knew it was violating the FHA, based on its knowledge that the Oxford House residents were handicapped as defined under the FHA.[508]

In summary, the addition of an FHA claim may be beneficial to a religious land use if the ministry has programs covered by the act.

503. *Id.* at *25–26.
504. *Id.* at *33–34, *43–44.
505. *Id.* at *30 (citation omitted).
506. *Id.* at *34 (citing Marbruna Inc. v. City of Stow, 974 F.2d 43, 46–47 (6th Cir. 1992)).
507. *Id.* at *35.
508. *Id.* at *43–44.

Chapter 4

Religious Land Use and Zoning: Constitutional Claims

I. The Free Exercise Clause

The Free Exercise Clause[1] to the First Amendment of the U.S. Constitution provides that "Congress shall make no law respecting an establishment of religion, or prohibiting the free exercise thereof."[2] This protection, the first freedom of the Bill of Rights, was based on the desire of the Founding Fathers to protect the religious diversity of the people who risked their lives to come to America and to practice their religion as they deemed fit.[3] They hoped that by protecting the freedom to worship, they would eliminate the religious conflicts that had been present in Europe for centuries.[4]

The First Amendment, in its entirety, provides that "Congress shall make no law respecting an establishment of religion, or prohibiting the free exercise thereof; or abridging the freedom of speech, or of the press; or the right of the people peaceably to assemble, and to petition the government for a redress of grievances."[5] The provision, known more commonly as the Free

1. This review touches upon the history of the Free Exercise Clause as it relates to land use and zoning. A more thorough review of the Free Exercise Clause can be found in Professor Michael McConnell's excellent article, *The Origins and Historical Understanding of the Free Exercise of Religion*, 103 Harv. L. Rev. 1409 (1990).

2. U.S. Const. amend. I.

3. See Steven Waldman, Founding Faith: How Our Founding Fathers Forged a Radical New Approach to Religious Liberty (2008).

4. *Id.*

5. U.S. Const. amend. I.

Exercise Clause, has long been interpreted by the U.S. Supreme Court as guaranteeing "freedom for religious organizations, an independence from secular control or manipulation."[6] Indeed, much of the nation's founding history can be fairly characterized as an "escape" from excessive governmental control of religion.[7] Accordingly, the clause demonstrates the high regard this country has for religious exercise.

This high regard for religious freedom also carries over into land use and zoning. Religious entities are often subjected to unequal treatment compared to their secular counterparts with respect to municipalities' land use and zoning decisions.

This unequal treatment may arise for a variety of reasons. Perhaps the municipality prefers a secular entity to occupy a certain property rather than a religious organization in order to obtain property tax revenue, since the Supreme Court has long held that houses of worship are exempt from paying property taxes.[8] Or a municipality's actions may be more blatant and based on an actual discriminatory animus against the religious institution.

Whatever the case, it has always been a top priority in this country to ensure that religious institutions are given the opportunity to freely exercise their beliefs without impermissible governmental interference.

In the cases that followed the adoption of the Free Exercise Clause, the courts were asked whether individuals or groups who had sincerely held religious beliefs were exempt from governmental regulations based on those beliefs. The issue first arose in 1878 when the government pursued a polygamy case.[9] In *Reynolds v. United States*,[10] the Supreme Court was faced with balancing a federal law enacted in 1862 that prohibited polygamy with the religious practices of the Church of Jesus Christ of Latter-day Saints, which adopted the practice as a sincerely held religious belief.[11] A unanimous court upheld governmental restrictions over religious practices,

6. Kedroff v. Saint Nicholas Cathedral of Russian Orthodox Church of N. Am., 344 U.S. 94, 116 (1952) (citing Watson v. Jones, 80 U.S. 679 (1872)).

7. Hosanna-Tabor Evangelical Lutheran Church & School v. Equal Employment Opportunity Comm'n, 132 S. Ct. 694, 702 (2012).

8. *See* Walz v. Tax Comm'n of City of N.Y., 397 U.S. 664 (1970).

9. Reynolds v. United States, 98 U.S. 145 (1878).

10. *Id.*

11. *Id.*

concluding that "[l]aws are made for the government of actions, and while they cannot interfere with mere religious beliefs, they may [interfere] with practices."[12] The effect of this decision was to give the federal government extremely broad authority to regulate and invariably interfere with the religious behavior of any individual or group.[13]

Sixty years later, the Supreme Court incorporated the First Amendment Free Exercise Clause and applied it to the states in *Cantwell v. Connecticut*.[14] In this case, the high court reversed a state court criminal conviction of Cantwell, who incited a disturbance by playing an anti-Catholic record.[15] While the decision focused more on the free speech element than the Free Exercise Clause, the court reaffirmed the Reynolds principle when concluding that the Free Exercise Clause "embrace[s] two concepts: freedom to believe and freedom to act. The first is absolute but, in the nature of things, the second cannot be. Conduct remains subject to regulation for the protection of society."[16]

The *Reynolds* and *Cantwell* decisions remained the basis of Free Exercise Clause jurisprudence until 1963, when the Supreme Court decided *Sherbert v. Verner*.[17] Adele Sherbert was a Seventh-Day Adventist who observed Saturday as the Sabbath (holy) day. Her employer removed her from her job when she refused to work on Saturdays, and the state of South Carolina rejected her unemployment claim, concluding that she refused to accept "suitable work when offered."[18] The Supreme Court found that the state's unemployment policy directly conflicted with her religious beliefs, forcing her to choose between her religion and unemployment benefits.[19] Having determined that she was faced with a "substantial burden," the court examined whether the state had a "compelling state interest" to justify burdening her religious beliefs.[20] Finding no evidence of a compelling state interest, the court ordered the payment of unemployment benefits and observed that "it

12. *Id.* at 166.
13. *Id.* at 165–67.
14. 310 U.S. 296, 300–03 (1940).
15. *Id.*
16. *Id.* at 303–04.
17. 374 U.S. 398 (1963).
18. *Id.* at 401.
19. *Id.*
20. *Id.* at 405.

is basic that no showing merely of a rational relationship to some colorable state interest would suffice; in this highly sensitive constitutional area, '[o]nly the gravest abuses, endangering paramount interest, give occasion for permissible limitation."[21]

The *Sherbert* decision marked a turning point in the balancing of the free exercise of religion with governmental regulation to public health, safety, and other societal interests. It removed the *Reynolds* and *Cantwell* principles and instead applied a strict scrutiny test to governmental conduct that affected the religious beliefs of individuals and groups.[22]

A decade later, the Court reaffirmed the strict scrutiny analysis to a facially neutral state law in *Wisconsin v. Yoder*.[23] In *Yoder*, the state of Wisconsin required all children to attend school until the age of 16. The state criminally prosecuted Amish parents who did not send their children to high school. Applying the strict scrutiny test from *Sherbert*, the Court held that requiring the Amish children to attend high school would seriously burden their Free Exercise rights and that the state's interest in educating Amish children was less than compelling because the alternative—education within the Amish communities—adequately achieved the two primary goals of compulsory education: preparing children for adult life and protecting them from child labor exploitation.[24]

Everything changed, however, in 1990 with the Supreme Court's Free Exercise opinion in *Employment Division v. Smith*.[25] That case involved two individuals who were fired from their employment at a drug rehabilitation center after ingesting peyote, a hallucinogen, at a religious ceremony for their Native American church.[26] Oregon had a criminal law that labeled peyote a "controlled substance" and provided a blanket prohibition on using the drug in the state.[27] After they were fired, the individuals sought unemployment benefits from the state. The Oregon employment division denied the requests, finding the individuals ineligible based on their firings

21. *Id.* at 406.
22. *Id.*
23. 406 U.S. 205 (1972).
24. *Id.* at 211.
25. 494 U.S. 872 (1990).
26. *Id.* at 882.
27. *Id.*

for work-related misconduct.[28] The individuals claimed that the state's conduct violated the Free Exercise Clause, but the court disagreed.[29] In its opinion, the high court explained that when a particular religious activity is burdened by the mere incidental effect of a valid, generally applicable law, the First Amendment is not offended.[30] Specifically, the court explained:

> We have never held that an individual's religious beliefs excuse him from compliance with an otherwise valid law prohibiting conduct that the State is free to regulate. On the contrary[,] "[c]onscientious scruples have not . . . relieved the individual from obedience to a general law not aimed at the promotion or restriction of religious beliefs. The mere possession of religious convictions which contradict the relevant concerns of a political society does not relieve the citizen from the discharge of political responsibilities."[31]

Since the Oregon criminal law did not attempt to regulate the individuals' religious beliefs, the court deemed it a "neutral law of general applicability."[32] Therefore, the employment division's decision to dismiss the individuals' unemployment compensation claims was entirely consistent with the Free Exercise Clause, and the First Amendment did not require religious exemptions from generally applicable laws that incidentally burden religious conduct.[33]

Soon after the *Smith* case was decided, the Supreme Court expanded its holding in *Church of the Lukumi Babalu Aye Inc. v. City of Hialeah*.[34] In some ways, the Church of Lukumi tempered the austerity of *Smith* by carving a path to relief under the Free Exercise Clause for when government impermissibly targets and thereby unduly restrains a particular religious activity.

28. *Id.* at 883.
29. *Id.* at 884–85.
30. *Id.* at 885.
31. *Id.* at 885–86 (citing Minersville Sch. Dist. Bd. of Educ. v. Gobitis, 310 U.S. 586, 594–95 (1940)).
32. *Id.* at 886.
33. *Id.* at 890.
34. 508 U.S. 520 (1993).

The case involved a Santeria congregation that attempted to establish a church in Hialeah, Florida. Santeria, which translates to "the way of the saints," originated with slaves who traveled from Africa to Cuba, thereby infusing their traditional African religious beliefs with various aspects of Roman Catholicism, including the iconography of Catholic saints and the Catholic sacraments.[35] Other important aspects of the Santeria faith include animal sacrifice and fulfillment of one's religious destiny through a personal relationship with the orishas, which are spirits to which Santeria followers express their devotion.[36]

When the church leased property within Hialeah, the city council held an emergency session at which it passed a resolution acknowledging residents' concerns over religious practices they deemed "inconsistent with public morals, peace or safety." The council announced that the city was committed to prohibiting these types of practices[37] and also announced several ordinances pertaining to animal cruelty and the sacrificing and slaughtering of animals.[38]

In response to the new ordinances, the church filed suit, alleging that the city violated its rights under the Free Exercise Clause of the First Amendment.[39] The district court found no violations of the Free Exercise Clause, instead determining that the ordinances were meant to end animal sacrifice in the city, not to exclude the church.[40] The Eleventh Circuit affirmed, but the Supreme Court reversed and found for the church.[41]

In its ruling, the Court found that the main purpose of the ordinances was to suppress the chief aspect of Santeria rituals. Further, the Court determined that many of the ordinances, when considered together, solely addressed the religious exercise of Santeria members.[42]

For example, one of the ordinances pertaining to animal sacrifices made exceptions for practically all killings except those done for religious

35. *Id.* at 524.
36. *Id.*
37. *Id.* at 526.
38. *See id.* at 527.
39. *Id.*
40. *Id.* at 528–29.
41. *Id.* at 530.
42. *Id.* at 534–35.

sacrifice.[43] Also, an ordinance prohibited keeping animals with the intent of slaughtering them for food. Again, however, the ordinance provided numerous exemptions, including one for kosher slaughter.[44] The kosher exemption especially made it clear to the court that the ordinance was specifically targeting Santeria sacrifices.[45]

Another ordinance prohibited the unnecessary killing of an animal but provided exemptions for "hunting, slaughter of animals for food, eradication of insects and pests, and euthanasia as necessary."[46] These broad exemptions further supported the Court's notion that the city devalued religious reasons for animal slaughter by deeming them less important than secular reasons, and the city's devaluation constituted discrimination against the church in violation of the Free Exercise Clause.[47]

When the "purpose" of a law is to suppress religious exercise, as in *Church of Lukumi*, the law will be subject to the same "strict scrutiny" standard of RFRA and RLUIPA and "will survive strict scrutiny only in rare cases."[48] The framework the court set forth for subjecting a claim to this standard is first "[t]o determine the object of a law," beginning "with its text."[49]

But just because a law is neutral and generally applicable on its face, that does not mean it is not discriminatory or intended to restrict religious exercise.[50] Free Exercise Clause jurisprudence is more nuanced, since the clause both "forbids subtle departures from neutrality"[51] and "covert suppression of particular religious beliefs."[52] Courts, therefore, are permitted to consider

> . . . direct and circumstantial evidence . . . includ[ing], among other things, the historical background of the decision under challenge, the specific series of events leading to the enactment or official policy in

43. *Id.* at 535–36.
44. *Id.* at 536.
45. *Id.*
46. *Id.* at 537.
47. *Id.* at 537–38.
48. *Id.* at 546.
49. *Id.* at 533.
50. *Id.* (affirming that "[f]acial neutrality is not determinative").
51. *Id.* (quoting Gillette v. United States, 401 U.S. 437, 452 (1971)).
52. *Id.* (quoting Bowen v. Roy, 476 U.S. 693, 703 (1986)).

question and the legislative or administrative history, including contemporaneous statements made by members of the decision-making body.[53]

In sum, courts will closely scrutinize a law challenged under the Free Exercise Clause regardless of its surface neutrality "if the object . . . is to infringe upon or restrict practice because of [an organization's] religious motivation."[54]

A. Hybrid Free Exercise Claims

One alternative to a pure Free Exercise claim is the "hybrid" claim. That is, a violation of a plaintiff's Free Exercise rights in conjunction with other constitutional rights. The use of "hybrid" in this context comes from the Supreme Court's decision in *Smith*, in which Justice Scalia noted that the only cases in which the Court had struck down neutral and generally applicable laws involved Free Exercise claims in conjunction with some other constitutional claim.[55] In explaining why the facts of *Smith* did not warrant a heightened level of review, the Court indicated that government action imposing burdens on Free Exercise and other constitutional rights might be subject to a more searching level of review than the rational-basis test when litigants can successfully assert such a hybrid claim.[56] Justice Scalia's dicta has become known as endorsing a "hybrid rights" claim, in effect creating an exception to the rule in *Smith* and *Lukumi* that only laws that are not neutral or generally applicable can be strictly scrutinized.

Lower courts have downplayed the application of hybrid rights claims despite a discordant willingness to entertain them. The Sixth Circuit initially rejected the notion of hybrid rights as illogical.[57] More recently, however,

---

53. *Id.* at 540 (noting that this analysis overlaps with assessing claims pursuant to the Fourteenth Amendment Equal Protection Clause and citing *Arlington Heights v. Metro. Hous. Dev. Corp.*, 429 U.S. 252, 266 (1977)).

54. *Id.* at 533.

55. *Smith*, 494 U.S. at 881 (citations omitted)

56. *Id. See also* City of Boerne v. Flores, 521 U.S. 507, 513–14 (1997).

57. Kissinger v. Bd. of Trustees of Ohio State Univ., 5 F.3d 177, 180 (6th Cir. 1993) ("We do not see how a state regulation would violate the Free Exercise Clause if it implicates other constitutional rights but would not violate the Free Exercise Clause if it did not implicate other constitutional rights. . . . Such an outcome is completely illogical; therefore, at least until the

that circuit declined to apply the compelling-interest test under a hybrid rights theory not because such a theory is untenable but because the plaintiff failed to establish a Free Exercise violation.[58]

The Ninth Circuit has taken a different approach. In *American Family Ass'n v. City and County of San Francisco*,[59] the court dismissed the plaintiffs' Free Exercise claim involving the city's and county's formal disapproval of an advertising campaign that espoused the view that homosexuality is a sin. Notwithstanding the absence of a colorable Free Exercise claim, the court nevertheless proceeded to analyze whether strict scrutiny should apply to the case under the hybrid rights approach. Only upon determining that plaintiffs failed to allege a colorable free speech and viewpoint discrimination claim did the court dismiss the hybrid claim as well.[60]

The Tenth Circuit has taken an approach similar to the Ninth's in not requiring a Free Exercise violation to entertain a hybrid claim. In *Swanson By and Through Swanson v. Guthrie Independent School District No. I-L*,[61] the court first considered whether plaintiffs had a viable Free Exercise claim regarding the district's refusal to allow their home-schooled child to attend school part time. Upon determining that plaintiffs did not have a colorable Free Exercise claim, the court proceeded to consider whether plaintiffs' parental rights claim warranted strict scrutiny under a hybrid rights theory. The court concluded that because plaintiffs did not make a colorable showing of a recognized and specific constitutional right, the hybrid rights claim must be dismissed.[62]

A federal Free Exercise claim in RLUIPA litigation can seem redundant when furthered alongside a substantial-burden argument, given that the latter would seem to cover the same concerns and offer the same if not better protection from government from those concerns. But hybrid claims are

---

Supreme Court holds that legal standards under the Free Exercise Clause vary depending on whether other constitutional rights are implicated, we will not use a stricter legal standard than that used in Smith to evaluate generally applicable, exception-less state regulations under the Free Exercise Clause.").

58. Prater v. City of Burnside, 289 F.3d 417, 430 (6th Cir. 2002) ("Absent a violation of the Free Exercise Clause, the Church's hybrid-rights theory necessarily fails.").

59. 277 F.3d 1114 (9th Cir. 2002).

60. *Id.* at 1123–25.

61. 135 F.3d 694, 700 (10th Cir. 1998).

62. *Id.*

one important facet of Free Exercise jurisprudence that can distinguish constitutional claims from their statutory cousin in RLUIPA. As Justice Scalia himself noted in *Smith*, the Supreme Court has found that the First Amendment can bar application of a neutral, generally applicable law when a Free Exercise claim is advanced "in conjunction with other constitution protections, such as freedom of speech."[63] Litigants should thus consider how their constitutional rights aside from religious exercise might be implicated and interwoven in a given case. Freedom of speech is a striking starting point.

II. Free Speech Claims

Another clause in the First Amendment provides that Congress cannot pass a law "abridging the freedom of speech" of citizens of the United States.[64] Free speech can be implicated in a very wide range of cases because communication is so inextricably tied to almost all that we do. Again, while the Free Speech Clause may seem straightforward enough, federal courts are constantly addressing issues that have arisen in relation to the nuances of the provision.

First Amendment liberties under the Free Speech Clause are broader than the act of speaking itself. "[S]peech" is not to be construed literally. The clause encompasses communication broadly, including the nonverbal or symbolic, as well as the right to "receive information and ideas."[65] The Supreme Court does not agree with "the view that an apparently limitless variety of conduct can be labeled 'speech' whenever the person engaging in the conduct intends thereby to express an idea."[66] Yet it still acknowledges that conduct "sufficiently imbued with elements of communication" is subject to First Amendment protection.[67]

The level of scrutiny a court will apply to a regulation that impedes speech depends on two key considerations: the forum of the speech and

63. *Smith*, 494 U.S. at 881.
64. U.S. CONST. amend. I.
65. Kleindienst v. Mandel, 408 U.S. 753, 762 (1972).
66. United States v. O'Brien, 391 U.S. 367, 376 (1968).
67. Spence v. Washington, 418 U.S. 405, 409 (1974).

whether the regulation is neutral. Different environments afford different levels of protection to the speaker, depending largely on a historical expectation to be able to engage in expressive activity at a particular location. Such forums cascade on a spectrum from public to nonpublic. Speech in a traditional public forum, such as a public park, is afforded the most First Amendment protection. Government may regulate speech with reasonable restrictions specifying the "time, place and manner" that one may engage in speech. But if its restrictions discriminate on the basis of the content of speech, that law will be subject to strict scrutiny. Where government creates limited public forums, such as public meeting rooms, it may impose reasonable limitations on who may use the forum, but content discrimination is still subject to strict scrutiny. In a nonpublic forum, such as a jail, government may, by reasonable regulation, make content-based curtailments of speech. However, in no forum may the government restrict speech because of the opinion expressed about particular content.

As noted, court interpretations of the Free Speech Clause have shifted over the years. A review of a few recent cases will help illustrate some of the jurisprudential issues that judges continue to grapple with in the area. The Supreme Court addressed the issue of freedom of speech in relation to picketing soldiers' funerals in the 2011 case of *Snyder v. Phelps*.[68] Plaintiff, the father of a deceased military service member, brought suit against the Westboro Baptist Church for various torts, including intentional infliction of emotional distress, based on the church's picketing the funeral of the plaintiff's son.[69] The church frequently picketed military funerals in an attempt to spread its message that God was punishing the United States for its sins, particularly for its tolerance of homosexuality.[70] In this instance, the church informed authorities in advance that it planned to picket the funeral, and the picketing occurred on a designated piece of public land.[71] Church members did not attend the funeral, enter the church property where the funeral was held, or incite any violence involving its protests.[72]

68. 131 S. Ct. 1207 (2011).
69. *Id.* at 1214.
70. *Id.* at 1213.
71. *Id.*
72. *Id.*

The district court found the church liable for several million dollars in damages, but the Fourth Circuit reversed based on the conclusion that the First Amendment protected the church's statements.[73] The Supreme Court agreed with the Fourth Circuit that the First Amendment shielded the church from tort liability based on its picketing of the funeral of the plaintiff's son.[74]

The crux of the case was whether the content of the church's speech concerned matters of public or private concern, as the First Amendment heavily protects speech on matters of public concern.[75] Here, the Supreme Court determined that the speech conveyed on the church's picketing signs related to public issues, namely "the political and moral conduct of the United States and its citizens, the fate of the nation, homosexuality in the military and scandals involving the Catholic clergy[.]"[76] This overreaching theme of public speech was not affected by a few of the signs targeting a specific individual.[77] Also, the inappropriateness or controversy surrounding the church's statement was wholly irrelevant to a determination of whether the statement concerned a public matter.[78]

Additionally, the fact that the church chose to picket a high-profile military funeral to increase publicity for its cause and that its speech may have been especially hurtful did not justify affording the speech less constitutional protection.[79] The court further determined that the church lawfully conducted its protest on public grounds, which qualified as a traditional public forum that is properly used as a means to engage in public debate and assembly.[80] Thus, based on the fact that the church's protest occurred in a public space and discussed matters of public concern, the church's speech received special protection under the First Amendment.[81] This special protection thus negated any potential tort liability and damages against the church.[82]

---

73. *Id.* at 1214.
74. *Id.*
75. *Id.* at 1215.
76. *Id.* at 1217.
77. *Id.*
78. *Id.* at 1216.
79. *Id.* at 1217.
80. *Id.* at 1218.
81. *Id.* at 1219.
82. *Id.*

The court specifically mentioned the narrowness of its holding and further emphasized the power of speech, and it noted that the United States has chosen "to protect even hurtful speech on public issues to ensure that we do not stifle public debate."[83] While this decision to protect hurtful speech may sometimes appear to produce unjust results, the court explained that it cannot decide to punish a speaker based on its reaction to the hurt that speech may cause.[84]

More recently, the Supreme Court resolved a free-speech dispute over a municipality's sign use regulation that placed stricter regulations on religious signs than others with different content. In *Reed v. Town of Gilbert*,[85] Gilbert, Arizona, adopted a comprehensive code to regulate the public display of signs. The sign code prohibits the display of outdoor signs in the town without a permit, with 23 exemptions.[86] Signs subject to the most stringent regulations, however, are those directing the public to a nonprofit group's meeting. These are significantly limited with respect to size, the number of which that can be placed on a property at one time and display time. Clyde Reed, the pastor of Good News Community Church in Gilbert, used temporary signs to inform the public about the shifting locations for his church's worship services. Gilbert's sign code compliance manager soon took notice and began citing the church for violations. Reed tried to seek an accommodation but was denied, prompting him to file suit under the First and Fourteenth Amendments.[87]

The court found the sign code "content based on its face" and that it should therefore be subject to strict scrutiny.[88] Since other categories of displays such as political signs would invoke different regulatory restrictions solely because of differing communicative content, signs are viewed differently under the law because of their messages. It did not matter that Gilbert may not have adopted the code out of disagreement with a message or out of a regulatory concern unrelated to the content of the sign. In

83. *Id.*
84. *Id.*
85. 135 S. Ct. 2218 (2015).
86. *Id.* at 2224.
87. *Id.* at 2224–26.
88. *Id.* at 2227.

the Court's view, "an innocuous justification cannot transform a facially content-based law into one that is content-neutral."[89]

Gilbert proffered two compelling interests to justify the differential sign-code treatment: "preserving the town's aesthetic appeal and traffic safety." For the sake of argument, the Court treated these as compelling but found them "hopelessly underinclusive."[90] First, Gilbert could not claim that the regulations were necessary to beautify the town when it placed severe restrictions on one type of sign while allowing an unlimited number of others to be placed all over town, creating the same problem. Second, Gilbert did not provide evidence that placing these restrictions on directional signs is necessary to eliminate traffic safety threats. Problematically, it seemed that types of displays that could theoretically pose a greater distractive threat because of their ideological content were given more leeway than displays that would pose less, such as those merely providing directions.[91]

Highlighting the complexities of Free Speech Clause analysis, the majority opinion was accompanied by three separate concurrences. While Justice Alito wrote to ease concerns that the ruling would cripple a government's ability to regulate signs,[92] Justices Breyer[93] and Kagan[94] wrote to express concern that the court too liberally applied strict scrutiny, which could lead to unintended consequences. These disputes illustrate how the court is constantly monitoring and tweaking its approach to free-speech cases and demonstrate that doctrine in this area is still perhaps as much in development as ever.

All of this begs the question: Is land use intertwined with religion a form of speech guarded by the First Amendment? In most cases, courts have answered negatively,[95] though they will often acknowledge that land use

89. *Id.* at 2227–28.
90. *Id.* at 2231.
91. *Id.* at 2231–32.
92. *Id.* at 2233–34 (Alito, J., concurring).
93. *Id.* at 2234–36 (Breyer, J., concurring).
94. *Id.* at 2236–39 (Kagan, J., concurring).
95. *See, e.g.*, San Jose Christian Coll. v. City of Morgan Hill, 360 F.3d 1024, 1032 (9th Cir. 2004) (finding that renovating a religious institution is not protected by the Free Speech Clause); Messiah Baptist Church v. Cty. of Jefferson, 859 F.2d 820, 825–26 (10th Cir. 1988) (finding that a building permit denial is not an abridgement of speech protected by the First Amendment).

regulations can at least implicate the Free Speech Clause.[96] Land use might also be thought of as something that facilitates speech, but the Supreme Court has held that something that "can be used as a vehicle for communication" does not necessarily command First Amendment protection.[97] Again, many courts will acknowledge that religious exercise often has an expressive component, but they tend to concentrate their analysis of religious land use arguments in the Free Exercise Clause domain.[98] However, the land use context poses a unique claim to religious freedom of expression.

While acknowledging their necessity in creating opportunities to engage in expressive conduct, courts have a long-held suspicion of permit and licensing requirements in the realm of free speech. And, of course, permit and licensing requirements are very much the lifeblood of land use. Suspicion is aroused because these requirements confer authority on public officials to grant permission for expressive activity to take place before it ever can take place. In making these decisions, officials are not permitted to consider the substance of the ideas in the expressive activity, and this principle of content neutrality seems simple enough.

Nevertheless, a jurisdiction may grant an excessive amount of discretion to the official in this process, allowing him to deny a permit and consequently suppress speech on pretextual grounds. For example, the Supreme Court in *Lakewood v. Plain Dealer Publishing Co.*[99] invalidated an ordinance on First Amendment grounds because it granted unfettered discretion to a mayor to determine which newspapers would be available for sale on public property. The arrangement allowed government to pick and choose favored speakers based on the content of their speech, a notion that stands against "the time-tested knowledge that in the area of free

96. *See, e.g.*, Cornerstone Bible Church v. City of Hastings, 948 F.2d 464, 468–69 (8th Cir. 1991) (holding that zoning ordinances placing "determinative weight on the fact that the proposed use is a church" in a land use assessment implicated the Free Speech Clause); Tree of Life Christian v. City of Upper Arlington, 16 F. Supp. 3d 883, 904 (S.D. Ohio 2014) (finding that a zoning ordinance "restrict[ing] the location of a religious use . . . implicat[es] the Free Speech Clause).

97. City Council of L.A. v. Taxpayers for Vincent, 466 U.S. 789, 814 (1984).

98. Tenafly Eruv Ass'n Inc. v. Borough of Tenafly, 309 F.3d 144, 163 (3d Cir. 2002) (noting that "courts consistently analyze the constitutionality of zoning regulations" implicating religious land use under the Free Exercise Clause).

99. 468 U.S. 750 (1989).

expression, a licensing statute placing unbridled discretion in the hands of a government official or agency constitutes a prior restraint and may result in censorship."[100]

When the ability to engage in expressive conduct hinges on government approval, the possibility of unconstitutional prior restraint becomes a legitimate concern. Some laws punish speakers for engaging in certain forms of speech after the fact. Others, however, pull the rug from underneath the speaker and prevent expressive conduct from ever taking place. The latter constitutes prior restraint, which is subject to strict scrutiny and is usually unconstitutional.

Courts view zoning ordinances that merely regulate where speech may occur with a lower level of scrutiny, and these limitations are more commonly upheld as falling within a category of "time, place and manner" regulations, even though they may have an incidental effect on expressive conduct.[101] But, according to Supreme Court precedent, a lack of "adequate standards to guide [an] official's decision" may suffice for a finding of prior restraint.[102] Despite a judicial reluctance in many cases to entertain religious land use claims in the free speech context, the Supreme Court has affirmed that "religious worship and discussion . . . are forms of speech . . . protected by the First Amendment."[103] The Court has also acknowledged that "one is not to have the exercise of his liberty of expression in appropriate places abridged on the plea that it may be exercised in some other place."[104] Denial of a religious land use on the whim of zoning administrators accompanied by an explanation that a religious organization can relocate elsewhere, therefore, can raise serious questions of Free Speech Clause constitutionality.

The Eastern District of Pennsylvania made such a finding when it addressed whether a Hindu group's desire to construct a temple on a parcel of land it owned qualified as "expressive conduct" for purposes of the

100. *Id.* at 757 (citing Shuttlesworth v. Birmingham, 394 U.S. 147, 151 (1969); Cox v. Louisiana, 379 U.S. 536 (1965); Staub v. City of Baxley, 355 U.S. 313, 321–22 (1958); Kunz v. New York, 340 U.S. 290, 294 (1951); Niemotko v. Maryland, 340 U.S. 268 (1951); Saia v. New York, 334 U.S. 558 (1948)).

101. Renton v. Playtime Theatres Inc., 475 U.S. 41, 46 (1986).

102. Thomas v. Chicago Park Dist., 534 U.S. 316, 323 (2002).

103. Widmar v. Vincent, 454 U.S. 263, 269 (1981).

104. Schneider v. State, 308 U.S. 147, 163 (1939).

First Amendment. In *Adhi Parasakthi Charitable, Medical, Educational, and Cultural Society v. Township of West Pikeland*,[105] a case litigated by the author, the plaintiff sought to build a Hindu temple on a plot of land it bought outside Philadelphia, in line with the wishes of its spiritual leader.[106] The land was bought with a restrictive covenant allowing development on only a portion of the property.[107] Adhi Parasakthi sought conditional-use approval to build a 26,000-square-foot temple and a 9,100-square-foot auxiliary building. While granting approval, the township's ruling effectively amounted to a denial since the construction was confined to 5,000 square feet.[108]

After the township granted approval, Adhi Parasakthi brought suit with claims of violation of RLUIPA; the First Amendment's Free Speech, Free Exercise, and Free Assembly Clauses; and the Fourteenth Amendment's Equal Protection and Due Process Clauses.[109] The court granted summary judgment to Adhi Parasakthi on its free speech and free assembly claims, finding that its desire to build a temple for worship constituted expressive conduct protected by the First Amendment.[110]

Initially, the court noted that "in the absence of evidence supporting a contrary conclusion," the Free Speech Clause of the First Amendment as "expressive conduct" does not protect building a house of worship.[111] Here, Adhi Parasakthi did not provide any evidence demonstrating that building its temple should be considered speech.[112] However, the court did find that plaintiff's intended use of the premises for worshiping and conducting religious festivals qualified as expressive speech and deserved First Amendment protection.[113] The township unconstitutionally regulated Adhi Parasakthi's expressive speech through its zoning ordinance, which the court deemed too vague and found that it granted the zoning board overly broad discretion

105. 721 F. Supp. 2d 361 (E.D. Pa. 2010).
106. *Id.* at 369.
107. *Id.*
108. *Id.* at 371.
109. *Id.* at 371–72.
110. *Id.* at 372.
111. *Id.* at 373–74.
112. *Id.* at 374.
113. *Id.*

to decide whether to allow an expressive religious use of land.[114] This discretion thus constituted a prior restraint on religious speech, in violation of the First Amendment.[115]

The court reserved any determination of damages on the free speech and free assembly claims until the end of trial. The case was settled on January 3, 2011, with the township's (1) giving Adhi Parasakthi the use of land to build a temple, (2) paying the attorney fees of the temple and (3) enacting a new constitutional land use ordinance. Nonetheless, it demonstrates that courts are willing to entertain certain free speech claims within the sphere of religious land use.

However, when government itself is the speaker, it is under no obligation to remain neutral with its own expressive conduct under the "government speech" doctrine. For instance, in *Pleasant Grove City v. Summum*, the Supreme Court held that a city's decision to allow certain private monuments to be permanently located in a public park, while rejecting other private monuments, was a valid expression of governmental speech and did not unconstitutionally interfere with the First Amendment's guarantee of free speech.[116]

Pleasant Grove involved a city park that contained 11 permanent displays, all of which were privately donated. One of the displays was a Ten Commandments monument.[117] Summum is a religious organization based in Salt Lake City that wanted to donate a monument containing "the Seven Aphorisms of SUMMUM" to be erected in the city park.[118] The city denied Summum's request to construct the monument.[119] In response, Summum filed suit and asserted that the city violated its free speech rights by rejecting its proposed monument but allowing the Ten Commandments monument to be built.[120] Summum also argued that because the city park constituted

114. *Id.* at 377.
115. *Id.*
116. 555 U.S. 460 (2009).
117. *Id.* at 464–65.
118. *Id.* at 465.
119. *Id.*
120. *Id.* at 466.

a public forum, the city needed to demonstrate a compelling interest in not constructing the Seven Aphorisms monument.[121]

The Supreme Court unanimously disagreed, finding that the placement of permanent monuments on public property falls under the category of government speech, and therefore the city's rejection was not subject to strict scrutiny.[122] The Free Speech Clause "restricts government regulation of private speech but not government speech, [meaning that] whether [the government was] engaging in their own expressive conduct or providing a forum for private speech determines which precedents govern here."[123] The court noted that privately donated monuments, like government-funded monuments, seem to speak on behalf of the property owner (here, the city government).[124] The court also emphasized that the city never actively sought private donors to construct monuments in the park. Rather, the city had "effectively controlled" the messages delivered through the monuments in the park by having final authority to approve the monuments that got built and only constructed monuments that presented a message the city wanted to convey to the park's visitors.[125]

While the court noted that Summum had a "legitimate" concern that the city's favoring of certain private speakers might amount to viewpoint-based discrimination, it further reasoned that Summum's proposal to create a formal process by which a municipality would consider the message of a proposed monument would impose too onerous a requirement on municipalities.[126] The Court also rejected Summum's comparison of permanent monuments in a public park and speeches and demonstrations that occur on public property. Unlike demonstrations, where "[s]peakers, no matter how long-winded, eventually come to the end of their remarks, . . . monuments . . . endure."[127] Based on this distinction, the court held that the city engaged in government speech by accepting only certain privately donated

121. *Id.*
122. *Id.* at 470.
123. *Id.*
124. *Id.* at 470–71.
125. *Id.* at 472–73.
126. *Id.* at 473.
127. *Id.* at 479.

monuments, and the city's decision was outside the regulation of the Free Speech Clause.[128]

III. Free Association/Assembly Claims

The First Amendment affirms that "Congress shall make no law . . . abridging . . . the right of the people peaceably to assemble and to petition the Government for a redress of grievances."[129] Freedom to assemble has stood as a palladium of liberty for social groups and movements of all kinds, both popular and unpopular, in the nation's history.[130] The text of the Petition and Assembly Clauses presents a degree of ambiguity, and it was not always clear whether it protected a single right that conjoined assembling for the purpose of petitioning or whether it distinguished those activities as separate rights. In fact, in an early interpretation, the Court limited these protections even further than simply restricting the federal government by claiming that they extended only to assembly connected with petitioning the government and not merely assembly itself.[131]

However, the line separating petition from assembly rights blurred. It proved difficult to detach articulations of freedom of speech or other First Amendment liberties from notions of assembly because the ability to assemble in many cases allows the full potential of those liberties to be actualized. Worship, for example, would in many cases be impossible unless people are permitted to peaceably assemble.

The Supreme Court came to recognize the connection and acknowledged that "[t]he right of peaceable assembly is a right cognate to . . . free speech."[132] It further found assembly rights "fundamental" and incorporated them to apply against state governments through the Due Process Clause of the Fourteenth Amendment.[133] In subsequent years, the Court also held that assembly rights were not limited solely to activity involving "religious

128. *Id.* at 480.
129. U.S. Const. amend. I.
130. United States v. Cruikshank, 92 U.S. 542 (1876).
131. Presser v. Illinois, 116 U.S. 252 (1886).
132. De Jonge v. Oregon, 299 U.S. 353, 364 (1937).
133. *Id.*

or political" causes.[134] It seemed, therefore, that the right "peaceably to assemble" inscribed in the First Amendment would be sufficient as a stand-alone right to confer associational protections of various sorts.

One of the few landmark free assembly cases was *Edwards v. South Carolina*.[135] In this case, a number of African American students met early in the morning at a Columbia, South Carolina, church and then proceeded to walk in groups of about 15 to the grounds of the South Carolina State House.[136] The purpose of the event was to peacefully protest South Carolina laws that discriminated against African Americans.[137] Law enforcement knew of the planned demonstration and was already present when the protesters arrived. The officers informed the protesters that they had the right to conduct their demonstration so long as they were peaceful.[138] After those gathered sang patriotic and religious songs for more than 15 minutes, they were arrested and eventually convicted in state court for breaching the peace, even though there had been no impact on pedestrians or traffic.[139]

The Supreme Court, in a direct and clear decision, threw out the convictions:

> The state courts have held that the petitioners' conduct constituted breach of the peace under state law, and we may accept their decision as binding upon us to that extent. But it nevertheless remains our duty in a case such as this to make an independent examination of the whole record. And it is clear to us that in arresting, convicting and punishing the petitioners under the circumstances disclosed by this record, South Carolina infringed the petitioners' constitutionally protected rights of free speech, free assembly and freedom to petition for redress of their grievances.[140]

---

134. Thomas v. Collins, 323 U.S. 516, 531 (1945).
135. 372 U.S. 229 (1963).
136. *Id.* at 230.
137. *Id.*
138. *Id.*
139. *Id.* at 233–34.
140. *Id.* at 235.

Though thereby already broad and ripe to be invoked independent of other First Amendment clauses, the right to peaceably assemble spun off in a new direction, primarily because of strong court-perceived ties between freedom of speech and assembly rights. A judicially crafted "freedom of association" would effectively overtake freedom of assembly, and claims under the former would come to be analyzed in a free speech lens, often without any reference to the Petition and Assembly clauses.[141]

While the First Amendment makes no explicit mention of a right to freedom of association, courts view it as a natural derivation of the amendment's guarantees of liberty, again particularly that of free speech. Freedom of association can therefore be understood as protecting individual activity that would otherwise be protected by the First Amendment but in circumstances where collective individuals engage in said activity. The distinction between assembly and association is not of critical importance, however, as both courts and litigants often employ them interchangeably in like claims.[142] But a litigant may find more support for a claim in the freedom of association channel of case law because it is more developed than its assembly counterpart.

Courts recognize a freedom of association in two senses. First, in protecting "a fundamental element of personal liberty," the right encompasses

> . . . choices to enter into and maintain certain intimate human relationships . . . against undue intrusion by the state because of the role of such relationships in safeguarding the individual freedom that is central to our constitutional scheme.[143]

Second, as already indicated, the Supreme Court has recognized that freedom of association covers a right

141. John Inazu, *The Forgotten Freedom of Assembly*, 84 Tul. L. Rev. 565, 606–11 (2010) (examining "the rise of association and the end of assembly").

142. *See, e.g.*, San Jose Christian College v. City of Morgan Hill, 360 F.3d 1024, 1033 (9th Cir. 2004) (assessing a "freedom of assembly" claim in terms of whether the "right to free association was abridged"); MAUM Meditation House of Truth v. Lake Cnty., 55 Supp. 3d 1081, 1090 (N.D. Ill. 2014) (discussing a freedom of association claim in terms of how a regulation impacts church "assembly").

143. Roberts v. United States Jaycees, 468 U.S. 609, 617–18 (1984).

> to associate for the purpose of engaging in those activities protected by the First Amendment . . . [because] [t]he Constitution guarantees freedom of association of this kind as an indispensable means of preserving other individual liberties.[144]

The framework for claims pursuant to freedom of association is hence not entirely unfamiliar because of that right's First Amendment roots. It is worth noting, though, that courts do acknowledge that freedom of association claims may overlap between the above two categories, as regulations placing certain restrictions on organizational activity can implicate associational rights in a variety of ways. In any event, according to the Supreme Court, laws having "the effect of curtailing the freedom to associate [are] subject to the closest scrutiny."[145]

However, a law will not be subject to this level of scrutiny unless its interference with associational rights is, at minimum, "direct and substantial" or "significant."[146] Like with free speech claims, courts assessing free association arguments will commonly look to whether a regulation burdening an ability to associate is content-based, which triggers the highest level of scrutiny. Pretextual enforcement can be one of the most important factors for a religious organization to look for in the land use context because—as noted in the section discussing RLUIPA substantial-burden jurisprudence and elsewhere—pretextual justifications can often lurk behind seemingly innocuous justifications for zoning decisions. The Supreme Court has also held that pretextual justification for an unfavorable zoning decision amounts to a content-based restriction,[147] putting a heavy and perhaps insurmountable burden on government to justify the regulation.[148] By contrast, regulations

144. *Id.* at 618.

145. NAACP v. Alabama ex rel. Patterson, 357 U.S. 449, 460–61 (1958).

146. Lyng v. Int'l Union, 485 U.S. 360, 366–67 (1988).

147. *Renton*, 475 U.S. at 48, 54.

148. Many commentators have remarked that it is almost unfathomable for a land use regulation to survive an invocation of strict scrutiny. *See, e.g.*, Robert Tuttle, *How Firm a Foundation? Protecting Religious Land Uses After Boerne*, 68 Geo. Wash. L. Rev. 861, 919 (2000) (noting that "few of the governmental interests at stake in land use regulation should be termed compelling").

that are neutral and generally applicable will be subject to less scrutiny and will normally be upheld.[149]

A regulation curtailing religious land uses might be seen as less directly implicating associational rights than Free Exercise concerns. But it probably also implicates associational rights more directly than freedom of speech because the inability to meet at a common location can flatly amount to the inability to associate. Courts have therefore acknowledged that completely denying a particular religious land use within a jurisdiction does raise legitimate freedom of association questions.[150]

Free association or assembly claims under the First Amendment can be brought in unison with RLUIPA claims. For example, a substantial-burden claim based on the deprivation of a permit necessary to build and occupy a church can be accompanied by a free assembly claim. In most instances, the First Amendment claim can be viewed as almost a backstop if the RLUIPA claims fail. And again, courts finding that a RLUIPA violation has occurred have forgone addressing free assembly and other First Amendment claims.[151]

IV. Redress of Grievance Clause; Retaliation

The very last clause of the First Amendment is one that is often overlooked: "Congress shall make no law respecting an establishment of religion, or prohibiting the free exercise thereof; or abridging the freedom of speech, or of the press; or the right of the people peaceably to assemble, and to petition the government for a redress of grievances" (emphasis added).

149. Civil Liberties for Urban Believers v. City of Chi., 342 F.3d 752, 765 (7th Cir. 2003) (finding an "incidental[]" regulation of speech and association content neutral and justified by "legitimate practical considerations as the promotion of harmonious and efficient land use").

150. Congregation Rabbinical Coll. of Tartikov Inc. v. Vill. of Pomona, 2015 U.S. Dist. LEXIS 132714, at *166–67 (S.D.N.Y. 2015) (holding that regulations effectively foreclosing the construction of a rabbinical college created a burden sufficient to state a free association claim).

151. Covenant Christian Ministries Inc. v. City of Marietta, 2008 U.S. Dist. LEXIS 54304 (N.D. Ga. Mar. 31, 2008) ("Having found that the November 10, 2004 ordinance violates the equal terms provision of RLUIPA and that Covenant is accordingly entitled to judgment as a matter of law on this claim, the Court does not reach the constitutional issues raised by Covenant.").

Claims arising out of the Redress of Grievances Clause are commonly known as First Amendment retaliation cases. These types of cases should also be considered in the land use context. To succeed on this claim, a plaintiff must demonstrate that (1) he or she was engaged in a constitutionally protected activity; (2) the defendant's adverse conduct caused the plaintiff to suffer an injury that would likely stop an ordinary person from continuing to engage in that activity; and (3) the adverse action was motivated, at least in part, in response to a plaintiff's exercising his or her constitutional rights.[152] A First Amendment retaliation claim often arises when a person speaks in opposition to a city's or township's decisions at a public meeting and in response the city or township takes action to "get back" at that person for the criticisms voiced at the meeting. A similar retaliation claim might arise when a religious organization verbally or otherwise contests the decision of the local government agency on a requested permit.

In a case decided by the Sixth Circuit, the court addressed a First Amendment retaliation claim brought by a citizen against a township and its supervisor. In *Fritz v. Charter Township of Comstock*,[153] the plaintiff worked out of her home office as an independent Farm Bureau Insurance agent.[154] Fritz applied for a special-use permit to operate the home office, and the permit was issued in October 2005.[155] While her permit application was pending, Fritz attended several township meetings. At various meetings, the township supervisor apparently expressed his frustration with Fritz's monitoring the meetings and tried to intimidate her from coming to future meetings.[156]

Soon after the permit was issued to Fritz, township residents and officials purportedly made false statements about Fritz, and in response she complained to the township supervisor.[157] The supervisor apparently spoke with Fritz's Farm Bureau supervisors three times about her conduct at the township meetings and her general reputation within the community.[158] In

152. Bloch v. Ribar, 156 F.3d 673, 678 (6th Cir. 1998).
153. 592 F. 3d 718 (6th Cir., 2010).
154. *Id.* at 720.
155. *Id.*
156. *Id.*
157. *Id.*
158. *Id.* at 720–21.

addition, a township planning commissioner called the Farm Bureau supervisors to express his displeasure with Fritz's bringing a lawyer to a Planning Commission meeting.[159]

In response to these calls, Fritz's employer discussed changing her behavior within the community and eventually terminated Fritz's relationship with Farm Bureau based on her "controversial community relations with [her] neighbors and with the local governmental unit."[160] After her termination, Fritz filed suit, alleging that the township unlawfully retaliated against her for publicly exercising her First Amendment rights at the township meetings, as well as various state tort violations.[161] The district court dismissed the First Amendment retaliation claim and declined to hear the state law claims after it dismissed the federal claim. Fritz appealed the district court's decision regarding the retaliation claim.[162]

On appeal, the Sixth Circuit determined that Fritz's complaint sufficiently stated a claim for First Amendment retaliation. To do so, she had to demonstrate two elements: that the township acted under color of law and that the township's conduct deprived her of rights secured under federal law.[163] First, the lower court did not dispute whether the township supervisor acted under color of law. With respect to whether the township's conduct constituted retaliation based on a prior exercise of her First Amendment rights, the court noted three factors Fritz must demonstrate:

- The plaintiff engaged in constitutionally protected conduct,
- An adverse action was taken against the plaintiff that would deter a person of ordinary firmness from continuing to engage in that conduct, and
- The adverse action was motivated at least in part by the plaintiff's protected conduct.[164]

159. *Id.* at 721.
160. *Id.*
161. *Id.*
162. *Id.* at 722.
163. *Id.* (citing Bloch v. Ribar, 156 F.3d 673, 677 (6th Cir. 1998)).
164. *Id.* at 723.

Here, the township did not contest that Fritz engaged in public comment at township meetings and that the First Amendment protected that such actions.[165] In addressing the "adverse action" the township took against Fritz, the court noted that Fritz sufficiently pled a "set of facts" that could entitle her to relief, and the specifics of the conversations between the township supervisor and Fritz's supervisors at Farm Bureau could be discovered through depositions.[166] Also, the facts could demonstrate that the supervisor's statements were specifically targeted toward Fritz's economic livelihood.[167] Further, Fritz had demonstrated that the township's denial of her zoning and sign variances were motivated in part by her protected conduct at the township meetings.[168]

Thus, based on these findings, the Sixth Circuit reversed the district court's grant of summary judgment in favor of the township with respect to the First Amendment retaliation claim, and it remanded the matter for further proceedings.[169]

V. Equal Protection Claims

The Equal Protection Clause of the Fourteenth Amendment provides that "[n]o state shall make or enforce any law which shall . . . deny to any person within its jurisdiction the equal protection of the laws."[170] Ratified in the years after the Civil War, the Equal Protection Clause had generally not been understood to restrain discriminatory state and local legal classifications aside from those pertaining to race and national origin. While suspect classifications would be subject to strict scrutiny, others would have only to satisfy a very low bar of a "reasonableness" standard.

Today, however, courts understand equal protection more broadly as a "direction that all persons similarly situated should be treated alike."[171] The

165. *Id.*
166. *Id.* at 725.
167. *Id.* at 728.
168. *Id.* at 729.
169. *Id.*
170. U.S. CONST. amend. XIV.
171. Cleburne v. Cleburne Living Center Inc., 473 U.S. 432, 439 (1985).

Supreme Court reached that understanding as it broadened the application of strict scrutiny under the Equal Protection Clause, most notably in the mid-20th century. It now applies to classifications that discriminate against "suspect" classes, which can include politically powerless, unpopular or historically marginalized groups. The court further extended strict scrutiny to classifications that burdened particular "fundamental" rights or interests. For purposes of equal protection, religious exercise has been recognized as both "fundamental"[172] and "an inherently suspect distinction."[173] Courts thus apply strict scrutiny to laws that make classifications based on religion.

Not all laws discriminate by their letter, rendering important the distinction between as-applied and facial challenges. A facial challenge claims that a law on its face violates the Equal Protection Clause. For example, a litigant may facially challenge a zoning ordinance specifically excluding churches altogether from a business district. In contrast, an as-applied challenge addresses the application of law, implying that government effectively made an improper classification by means of enforcement. An example could be a zoning board's denial of an application for a religious land use permit after having recently approved a similar secular land use. It is generally more difficult to prevail on a facial challenge because, under the Supreme Court's standards, "the challenger must establish that no set of circumstances exists under which the act would be valid."[174] In contradistinction, an as-applied challenge need only show that a particular application of law alone is unconstitutional.

The requirement to make a showing of discriminatory purpose is another essential ingredient for many forms of facial Equal Protection claims. Again, a neutral law may simply have no rational connection to a legitimate government interest and fail the reasonableness test. But for a court to apply strict scrutiny to a neutral law, it must be convinced that government intended for the law to have a discriminatory effect or be applied discriminatorily. This is a high bar, though the Supreme Court does not require plaintiffs to

172. Johnson v. Robison, 415 U.S. 361, 375 n.14 (1974).

173. New Orleans v. Dukes, 427 U.S. 297, 303 (1976).

174. U.S. v. Salerno, 481 U.S. 739, 745 (1987). In practice, however, courts have not always required that there be absolutely no constitutional applications. *See* Michael Dorf, *Facial Challenges to State and Federal Statutes*, 46 Stan. L. Rev. 235, 236 (1994).

show that the discrimination was the "sole" motivating factor behind the law.[175] As discussed in the section on Free Exercise claims, courts will look for alleged discriminatory purpose in Equal Protection and Free Exercise claims within the same broad array of relevant "direct and circumstantial evidence."[176] Plaintiffs will then have to make a sufficient showing that discriminatory animus was afoot.

Overlap delineated between Free Exercise and Equal Protection jurisprudence may make a claim pursuant to the Equal Protection Clause seem superfluous. In many cases, it would be, which in part explains why religious-discrimination claims often exclude Equal Protection arguments. But, it is feasible that a court could find an Equal Protection violation while simultaneously dismissing a Free Exercise claim. As discussed, discriminatory targeting will trigger strict scrutiny, and the absence of a showing of discrimination will subject a law to rational-basis review. But treating one religious group differently from another can raise issues unique to Equal Protection. Where a religious-exercise claim may fail because a plaintiff cannot demonstrate intentional discrimination, an Equal Protection claim may succeed if one religious group is treated less favorably than a similarly situated religious group without reasonable justification for the differential treatment, thereby failing even rational-basis review.[177]

In other words, a claim under the Free Exercise Clause alone may neither sufficiently highlight the irrationality of certain disparate treatment nor require government to address it.[178] This situation is not necessarily unlikely to arise in the land use context, given that administrators must assess many different religious requests and may be unable to approve them all, even if

175. Vill. of Arlington Heights v. Metro. Hous. Dev. Corp., 429 U.S. 252, 265–66 (1977).

176. Church of the Lukumi Babalu Aye, Inc. v. City of Hialeah, Florida. 508 U.S. 520, 546, 113 S. Ct. 2217, 124 L. Ed 2d 472 (1993).

177. Government treating certain religious groups more favorably than others as such may also run afoul of the Establishment Clause, which "prohibits government from abandoning secular purposes . . . to favor the adherents of any sect or religious organization." Gillette v. United States, 401 U.S. 437, 450 (1971).

178. Equal-protection claims can pose unique constitutional questions because they turn not on whether there is a rational basis for a particular government action but on whether "there is a rational relationship between the disparity of treatment and some legitimate government purpose." Heller v. Doe, 509 U.S. 312, 320 (1993) (citing Nordlinger v. Hahn, 505 U.S. 1, 11 (1992)) (emphasis added).

some could be construed as similarly situated.[179] It would also not be caught by RLUIPA's equal-terms dragnet, thought to be the statutory counterpart to equal protection, because that provision extends only to unequal treatment compared to "a nonreligious assembly or institution."[180]

The Supreme Court has established the following standards for determining the validity of state legislation such as zoning ordinances or other land use regulations that it would apply under the Equal Protection Clause:

> Unless a classification trammels fundamental personal rights or is drawn upon inherently suspect classifications such as race, religion or alienage, our decisions presume the constitutionality of the statutory discriminations and require only that the classifications challenged be rationally related to a legitimate state interest.[181]

If the legislative classification harms such a suspect class, then courts may uphold the classification only if it is "precisely tailored to serve a compelling governmental interest."[182] Absent an invidious or gender-based classification, according to the Supreme Court, "The general rule is that legislation is presumed to be valid and will be sustained if the classification drawn by the statute is rationally related to a legitimate state interest."[183] Further, interpreting this jurisprudence in the context of an Equal Protection challenge to municipal land use decisions, some circuit courts have explained:

> Absent a fundamental right or a suspect class, to demonstrate a viable Equal Protection claim in the land use context, the plaintiff must demonstrate "governmental action wholly impossible to relate to legitimate governmental objectives."[184]

179. See FRANK S. RAVITCH, BORIS I. BITTKER & SCOTT IDLEMAN, RELIGION AND THE STATE IN AMERICAN LAW 309 (2015) (making parallel argument in prison context).

180. 42 U.S.C. § 2000cc(b)(1) (emphasis added).

181. City of New Orleans v. Dukes, 427 U.S. 297, 303, 49 L. Ed. 2d 511, 96 S. Ct. 2513 (1976).

182. Sklar v. Byrne, 727 F.2d 633, 636 (7th Cir. 1984) (quoting Plyler v. Doe, 457 U.S. 202, 216–17, 72 L. Ed. 2d 786, 102 S. Ct. 2382 & n.14, 457 U.S. 202 (1982)).

183. *Cleburne*, 473 U.S. at 440 (citations omitted).

184. Forseth v. Village of Sussex, 199 F.3d 363, 370–71 (7th Cir. 2000), citing Esmail v. Macrane, 53 F.3d 176, 180 (7th Cir. 1995) and Olech v. Village of Willowbrook, 160 F.3d

Relatively recently, the Supreme Court recognized in *Olech v. Village of Willowbrook* that "an Equal Protection claim can in some circumstances be sustained even if the plaintiff has not alleged class-based discrimination but instead claims that she has been irrationally singled out as a so-called 'class of one.'"[185] To succeed on his class-of-one claim, a landowner must demonstrate that land use authorities (1) intentionally (2) treated the property owner differently from other similarly situated property owners, (3) without a rational basis.[186] Although the property owner must show that the authorities' decision was intentional, he need not show that they were motivated by subjective ill will.[187]

The "class of one" claims are rarely successful. In order to prevail, the claimant needs to allege and prove facts nearly identical to the *Olech* case to get past summary judgment and to trial. Thus, in light of the Supreme Court's relatively recent endorsement of class-of-one Equal Protection claims, being singled out in this way for unfavorable treatment within a classification can be a powerful argument to include in RLUIPA litigation. In *Olech*, the Court announced that plaintiffs can succeed on Equal Protection claims as a result of arbitrary disparate treatment compared to a similarly situated party.[188] Traditionally, under the Equal Protection Clause, courts had been concerned only with discrimination against a party resulting from that party's having a particular characteristic of a larger group.

To put it differently, a "classification" had to be made. So it was unsurprising when eight years later the Court backtracked in *Engquist v. Oregon Department of Agriculture*, suggesting that class-of-one claims may be inappropriate in cases where government has been granted discretionary decision-making authority because questioning differential treatment would seem to undermine discretionary power. Such a holding may have precluded

386, 387–88 (7th Cir. 1998), *aff'd*, 528 U.S. 562 (2000) (explaining that the Equal Protection Clause can be invoked by an individual who can prove that action taken by the state was a spiteful effort to "get" him) (additional citation omitted).

185. Engquist v. Or. Dep't of Agric., 553 U.S. 591, 601 (2008) (citing Vill. of Willowbrook v. Olech, 528 U.S. 562, 564 (2000) (per curiam)).

186. *Willowbrook*, 528 U.S. at 564; North Pacifica LLC v. City of Pacifica, 526 F.3d 478, 486 (9th Cir. 2008).

187. *Willowbrook*, 528 U.S. at 565 (rejecting the interpretation that a plaintiff must allege that the governmental action was the result of subjective ill will in a class-of-one claim).

188. 528 U.S. 562, 564–65.

the possibility of advancing class-of-one claims in a broad range of land use cases. However, the court appeared to qualify its line of reasoning by noting that such a principle "applies most clearly in the employment context."[189]

Lower courts have split on the reach of *Engquist*,[190] but some have still gone on to find class-of-one Equal Protection violations in religious land use cases. A notable example is *Fortress Bible v. Feiner*, in which the Second Circuit found that a town used environmental review processes and other zoning concerns as a pretext to block construction of a church.[191] Among other arguments, the plaintiff brought an Equal Protection class-of-one claim. The town attempted to argue that *Engquist* barred claims of injury resulting from discretionary activity and should therefore bar the claim in the current land use context. But the Second Circuit read *Engquist* not to restrict "all" such claims. Further, in the case at bar, the evidence indicated "a disparity in treatment that [could not] fairly be attributed to discretion."[192] Since the religious organization in *Fortress Bible* was able to point to another similarly situated religious organization posing parallel zoning concerns that the town had accommodated, the court found adequate basis for a class-of-one Equal Protection claim.[193]

Yet it is important to keep in mind that even if a land use regulation is presumptively valid in a court's eyes, there still must be some legitimate rationale behind the law. Even with these odds in its favor, a jurisdiction, such as the defendant in *Fry v. City of Hayward*,[194] will not see its zoning ordinances upheld when challenged in court under the Equal Protection Clause absent a legitimate explanation for how the law may disparately affect individuals. In *Fry*, a landowner held property that had traditionally been used as a golf course but had in recent years gone unused.[195] The owner wished to change the property designation from open space to

189. 128 S. Ct. 2146, 2154 (2008).

190. For instance, the Sixth Circuit limited *Engquist* to the employment context in *Franks v. Rubitschun*, 312 F. App'x 764, 766 n.3 (6th Cir. 2009) while the Eleventh Circuit applied *Engquist* to bar class of one claims outside the employment context in *Douglas Asphalt Co. v. Qore Inc.*, 541 F.3d 1269, 1274 (11th Cir. 2008).

191. 694 F.3d 208 (2d. Cir. 2012).

192. *Id.* at 222.

193. *Id.* at 222–24.

194. 701 F. Supp. 179 (N.D. Cal. 1988).

195. *Id.* at 180.

residential. But while an application for that change was pending, voters approved a referendum retaining the open-space designation and requiring voter approval before any subsequent changes could be made. As a result, the city denied the application.[196]

A lawsuit ensued as the landowner advanced a facial Equal Protection argument, among other claims.[197] Since the law did not create a suspect classification or implicate fundamental rights, the court applied rational-basis review. The city offered two justifications. First, it claimed that direct legislation is a legitimate way to accomplish land use goals. Unimpressed, the court offered the reminder that a referendum does not render a law immune from constitutional challenge.[198] In the other holster, the city contended that open-space legislation is a legitimate government interest. To its detriment, however, it failed to address how singling out the particular plot of land was rationally related to this interest. In the court's view, this amounted to imposition of "a special burden" that was unwarranted by the record before the court. Hence the law could not pass the rational-basis test.

Equal Protection claims are rarely successful in the context of land use and zoning. Therefore, great care must be taken at the outset to determine if the claim should be brought, and, if so, how it is to be pled and proven.

VI. Due Process Claims

On a fundamental level, due process is a command that government respect the legal rights of individuals. The U.S. Constitution contains two due process guarantees, in both the Fifth and Fourteenth Amendments. While the Fifth's imposes limitations on the federal government, the Fourteenth's ensures within the same section as the Equal Protection Clause that "[n]o state shall make or enforce any law which shall . . . deprive any person of life, liberty or property without due process of law."[199] In the Supreme Court's view, due process and equal protection are both "concepts . . .

196. *Id.*
197. *Id.* at 181.
198. *Id.* at 182.
199. U.S. CONST. amend. XIV.

stemming from our American ideal of fairness."[200] Though the Court recognizes that they are "not mutually exclusive," they nonetheless are not necessarily "interchangeable phrases."[201]

In a sense, equal protection arising from due process is a byproduct of the provision's focus on ensuring the nonarbitrary administration of justice for all. Yet, perhaps the most significant application of the Due Process Clause has been incorporating most provisions of the Bill of Rights, which initially only limited actions of the federal government, and applying them against state governments through the Fourteenth Amendment.

Due process claims come in two primary forms, the first of which is procedural. That government shall not deprive one of "life, liberty or property" without "due process" intimates a procedural concern. In this vein, the clause ensures that the government provide procedural protections appropriately proportionate to the degree of the life, liberty, or property interests at stake. Individualized assessments, such as those made by zoning administrators, can give rise to procedural due process questions because these assessments must conform to adequate procedural standards.

It is nonetheless important to remember that this constitutional protection does not necessarily mean that government may not deprive you of rights. Rather, it simply provides that you be afforded due process of law before your rights can be deprived. In accord with the Due Process Clause, moreover, individuals only have this interest in fair legal proceedings when government action threatens to deprive them of one of these three interests.[202] One can thus glean the three-step analysis all courts take for procedural due process claims:

1. Has there been a deprivation?
2. Does the deprivation implicate life, liberty, or property?
3. What procedures should be required?[203]

200. Bolling v. Sharpe, 347 U.S. 497, 499 (1954).
201. *Id.*
202. *See, e.g.*, Anselmo v. Cnty. of Shasta, 873 F. Supp. 2d 1247, 1255 (E.D. Cal. 2012) (noting that the "Due Process Clause does not guarantee individuals the right to a pre-deprivation hearing").
203. Erwin Chemerinsky, *Procedural Due Process Claims*, 16 Touro L. Rev. 871 (1999).

Whether government has an adequate justification for depriving someone of life, liberty, or property gives rise to the second and substantive form of due process. The doctrine of substantive due process is designed to curtail government from unreasonably interfering with important human interests. These interests are broad but limited, and only those that courts deem "fundamental" will be subject to strict scrutiny when impinged upon. Rights considered "fundamental" under due process analysis are typically those that in the court's view are either "of the very essence of a scheme of ordered liberty"[204] or "deeply rooted in this nation's history and tradition."[205] All other rights prompt courts to analyze law merely under rational-basis review.

Courts understand the most common applications of substantive due process as follows:

1. Application of one of the rights enumerated in the federal Constitution, such as the First Amendment, to a state.
2. Application of a right unenumerated in the federal Constitution to a state, such as the right to live together as a family.
3. An action of state or local government that "shocks the conscience" of the federal court.
4. The right not to be subject to "arbitrary or capricious" action by a state either by legislative or administrative action.[206]

Historically, significant shifts have occurred in substantive due process standards of review. Currently, the Supreme Court has narrowed fundamental rights for substantive due process claims down to concerns central to autonomy and various privacy interests, though broadly understood, which one commentator has labeled the sphere of "sex-marriage-childbearing-childrearing."[207] Yet there was a time in the nation's history when courts rampantly invoked the Due Process Clause to invalidate a broad range of economic regulations as an unreasonable application of state police

204. Palko v. Connecticut, 302 U.S. 319, 325 (1937).

205. Moore v. East Cleveland, 431 U.S. 494, 503 (1977).

206. Pearson v. City of Grand Blanc, 961 F.2d 1211, 1216–17 (6th Cir. 1992) (emphasis in original) (citations omitted).

207. John H. Ely, *The Supreme Court, 1977 Term, Foreword: On Discovering Fundamental Values*, 92 Harv. L. Rev. 5, 11 n.40 (1978).

power.[208] In stark contrast, today, similar sorts of economic regulations enacted pursuant to state police power, such as zoning regulations, are not only subject to rational-basis review but also perhaps even a watered-down version of the standard. Indeed, courts will begin their rational-basis review with a strong presumption of the constitutionality of a police power regulation.[209]

Furthermore, in searching for a reasonable explanation for the regulation, courts are not limited to reasons that litigants provide. Instead, they are free to hypothesize about what a legislature "might have concluded" when legislating[210] and can uphold a law under a justification never raised in the lawsuit.[211] And, in some cases still, courts may effectively abandon any level of scrutiny by refusing to entertain "vague contours" of due process.[212]

To succeed on both procedural and substantive due process claims, the property owner must first demonstrate that he was deprived of a constitutionally protected liberty or property interest.[213] In some instances, a person can have a constitutionally protected property interest in a government benefit, such as a license or permit.[214] To have a property interest in a government benefit, one must have something greater than an "abstract need,"

---

208. During the so-called Lochner era (1897–1937) federal courts under a now discredited concept of due process invalidated regulations perceived to be unduly infringing on economic liberties. However, as Justice Douglas explained, "[t]he day is gone when [the Supreme] Court uses the Due Process Clause of the 14th Amendment to strike down state laws, regulatory of business and industrial conditions, because they may be unwise, improvident, or out of harmony with a particular school of thought." Williamson v. Lee Optical Co., 348 U.S. 483, 488 (1955).

209. Usery v. Turner Elkhorn Mining Co., 428 U.S. 1, 15 (1976) ("It is by now well established that legislative Acts adjusting the burdens and benefits of economic life come to the Court with a presumption of constitutionality . . .").

210. Courts are not guided by formal distinctions between legislative, adjudicative or otherwise administrative government action. It is the character of the action that matters for due process purposes. *See* Bi-Metallic Inv. Co. v. State Bd. of Equalization, 239 U.S. 441 (1915) (implicitly recognizing this principle).

211. *Williamson*, 348 U.S. at 487.

212. Ferguson v. Skrupa, 372 U.S. 726, 731 (1963) (reasoning that a state legislature was "free to decide for itself" that debt adjustment regulation was necessary and that justificatory "arguments are properly addressed to the legislature, not to [the court]").

213. *See* Shanks v. Dressel, 540 F.3d 1082, 1087 (9th Cir. 2008) (substantive due process); Foss v. Nat'l Marine Fisheries Serv., 161 F.3d 584, 588 (9th Cir. 1998) (procedural due process).

214. Bd. of Regents v. Roth, 408 U.S. 564, 577 (1972); *see also* Groten v. California, 251 F.3d 844, 850 (9th Cir. 2001) (holding that plaintiff had a protected property right to a temporary appraiser's license).

"desire," or "unilateral expectation" of it.[215] There must be "a legitimate claim of entitlement to it."[216] But there is state law component to property interest analysis beyond these constitutional considerations. Property interests must "stem from an independent source such as state law—rules or understandings that secure certain benefits and that support claims of entitlement to those benefits."[217]

A number of factors can contribute to establishing a legitimate claim of entitlement. For instance, one can be established when state law "imposes significant limitations on the discretion of the decision-maker."[218] Such an arrangement would seem to suggest that only arbitrary administrative behavior could account for an unfavorable ruling. Most courts have therefore held that such an entitlement to a government permit exists when a state law or regulation requires that the permit be issued if certain requirements are satisfied and the application had satisfied them.[219] Others, meanwhile, have been unconvinced by this line of reasoning.[220]

In any event, the Supreme Court, in *Perry v. Sindermann*, recognized the existence of constitutionally protected property interests where a governmental body employs policies and practices that create a legitimate claim of entitlement to a government benefit.[221] The plaintiff in *Perry*, a nontenured junior faculty member at a state university, argued that he had a protected property interest in his job in light of his employer's "de facto tenure program" for which he qualified.[222] The court sided with *Perry*, explaining that

215. *Roth*, 408 U.S. at 577.

216. *Id.* (emphasis added).

217. *Id.*

218. Braswell v. Shoreline Fire Dep't, 622 F.3d 1099, 1102 (9th Cir. 2010) (internal quotation marks and alterations omitted).

219. *See, e.g.*, *Groten*, 251 F.3d at 850 (holding that a protected property right to a license existed where both federal and state law entitled the applicant to a license whenever certain statutory requirements were met); Bateson v. Geisse, 857 F.2d 1300, 1303 (9th Cir. 1988) (holding that a builder had a property interest in a building permit where city regulations provided that once an applicant met certain requirements, a permit must be issued).

220. *See, e.g.*, Muslim Cmty. Ass'n v. Pittsfield Charter Twp., 94 F. Supp. 2d 752, 763 (E.D. Mich. 2013) ("Even if Plaintiff is correct that the Michigan statute requires approval of a request if it is in compliance with the standards stated in the township's zoning ordinance–a proposition of which the Court is not convinced—the determination of whether the request is in compliance with those standards is a purely discretionary decision left to the local zoning authority.") (emphasis added).

221. 408 U.S. 593 (1972).

222. *Id.* at 600.

> a person's interest in a benefit is a "property" interest for due process purposes if there are such rules or mutually explicit understandings that support his claim of entitlement to the benefit and that he may invoke at a hearing.[223]

That holding underscored the principle that legitimate claims of entitlements need not exist formalistically by right and was rendered in the wake of an important related development in due process jurisprudence.

Before the 1970s, most courts thought of government benefits as privileges instead of property rights. Under this theory, being denied a government benefit would not create a property interest because privileges were revocable. But between 1970 and 1972, the Supreme Court underwent what some commentators have termed a "due process revolution" as the court redefined property interests to include government benefits.[224] The Supreme Court made the initial turn in *Goldberg v. Kelly*, holding that welfare payments were not "mere charity" but a property right to be protected against arbitrary government interference.[225] That decision set the stage for *Perry* and other cases to conduct a more holistic review of factors that contribute to establishing property interests. One such case from the Ninth Circuit, *Orloff v. Cleland*, further defined the standard that a reasonable expectation to continue enjoying a particular benefit can create a property interest:

> Despite the apparent expiration date of [the plaintiff's employment] contract, there may have arisen an understanding of continued employment based on prior treatment of [the plaintiff] or other . . . employees sufficient to constitute a de facto property interest.[226]

However, a person's belief of entitlement to a government benefit, no matter how sincerely or reasonably held, does not necessarily create a property right if government is not actually required by law to confer said benefit.

223. *Id.* at 602.
224. E. Thomas Sullivan & Toni M. Massaro, The Arc of Due Process in American Constitutional Law 43 (2013).
225. Goldberg v. Kelly, 397 U.S. 254, 265 (1970).
226. 708 F.2d 372, 377 (1983).

For example, if law dictates that a government agency make welfare payments, the government cannot deny that one who qualifies for the benefit has no claim to the benefit. However, if, say, a zoning administrator granted a particular land use permit request in the past on a discretionary basis, it is not clear that the landowner will be entitled to a renewal of that permit at a later date, even if the administrator in the past has been generally willing to grant renewals. The Supreme Court has explained that "[a] constitutional entitlement cannot be created—as if by estoppel—merely because a wholly and expressly discretionary state privilege has been granted generously in the past."[227] Circuit courts have gone on to hold so in a variety of contexts.[228]

As noted earlier, the Fourteenth Amendment's Due Process Clause says no state may "deprive any person of life, liberty or property without due process of law." The procedural component of the Due Process Clause ensures a fair adjudicatory process before a person is deprived of life, liberty, or property.[229] Not every denial of a fair hearing for which a remedy may be available under state law implicates constitutional due process.[230] "The requirements of procedural due process apply only to the deprivation of interests encompassed by the 14th Amendment's protection of liberty and property."[231] The range of interests protected by procedural due process is limited.[232]

Claims of procedural due process can be established out of the similar sorts of arbitrary administrative behavior seen in litigation pursuant to statutory or other constitutional claims. But an important point to keep in mind is that courts may entertain procedural due process claims under

---

227. Conn. Bd. of Pardons v. Dumschat, 452 U.S. 458, 465 (1981); Leis v. Flynt, 439 U.S. 438, 443 (1979) (concluding that no property right to appear pro hac vice in Ohio court existed because the plaintiff's counsel did not demonstrate "the requisite mutual understanding that they would be permitted to [appear pro hac vice].").

228. *See, e.g.*, Cassidy v. Hawaii, 915 F.2d 528, 531 (9th Cir. 1990) (rejecting the argument that because the government body "generally renews permits [and] this custom created an understanding that would justify a legal entitlement"); Punikaia v. Clark, 720 F.2d 564, 570 (9th Cir. 1983) (holding that a state's continuous operation of a nursing home was not the type of "custom" or "regularity of performance" that would create a legitimate entitlement (internal quotation marks omitted)).

229. Mullane v. Central Hanover Tr. Co., 339 U.S. 306, 313 (1950).

230. Clark v. City of Hermosa Beach, 48 Cal. App. 4th 1152, 1178 (1996).

231. *Roth*, 408 U.S. at 569.

232. *Id.* at 570.

easier-to-satisfy threshold requirements. *Nasierowski Brothers Investment Company v. City of Sterling Heights*,[233] a procedural due process case from the Sixth Circuit, well-illustrates such a path to relief in the land use context.

In *Nasierowski Bros.*, a developer purchased real estate in Sterling Heights, Michigan, intending to create a retail and warehouse facility, contingent on a favorable opinion from the city that the development would be permitted under current regulations. The city responded affirmatively, and the developer purchased the property and applied for site plan approval.[234] On review, the city conditioned approval on the developer's making certain improvements that the developer thought were unnecessary, leading him to apply for a variance.

At the variance hearing, a councilman, who happened to live near the parcel, expressed personal opposition to the proposal. The councilman wanted the land rezoned as a residential zone even though that area already had been developed commercially. The councilman declined to recuse himself at the developer's request, and the council voted to deny the variance.[235] During this time, the city Planning Commission adopted a new citywide master-zoning plan that would not hinder the developer's land use plans. However, the aforementioned councilman motioned to selectively rezone the parcel to prohibit the intended development while exempting nearby nonconforming uses. The motion passed, and the city denied the preliminary site plan approval, prompting the developer to file suit under the Due Process Clause.[236]

The city tried to argue that the developer did not first pursue an administrative appeal and that the claim was unripe for failure to exhaust nonjudicial remedies. Final decisions, the court responded, are not required for procedural due process claims. In its explanation, the court reasoned that if a claimed injury results from "the infirmity of the process, neither a final

233. 949 F.2d 890 (6th Cir. 1991).
234. *Id.* at 891.
235. *Id.* at 892.
236. *Id.* at 893.

judgment nor exhaustion [of administrative remedies] is required."[237] Thus the allegedly infirm process is an injury in itself.[238]

In this case, the last-minute redesignation was not a Planning Commission recommendation and was never submitted to public scrutiny, which is required under state law. The developer was not given notice before the change, and the court was troubled by the councilman's "legally questionable conduct and problematic, self-interested political maneuvering" that stripped the developer of site plan approval.[239] While a regulation that negatively but evenly affects many people does not necessarily give rise to due process requirements, the developer was singled out "for obviously personal reasons," and the councilman provided "no policy reasons" in "arbitrarily reclassify[ing]" the parcel.[240] This impact on an individual confers a right to notice and a hearing, equating to a procedural due process violation in the case at bar.[241]

The court then needed to look to state law to determine whether the developer had a property interest in the original zoning classification. In Michigan, a property interest in a zoning classification can be established if the landowner took significant steps toward land development.[242] These steps have to be taken in reliance on zoning stipulations as they existed, where a rezoning would be a substantial detriment to the pursued land use.[243] In this case, the developer clearly took important action to pursue the proposed development; he conditioned the original purchase on a favorable zoning opinion and would not have purchased the parcel without that opinion. He further spent considerable money in planning and petitioning the city for approval. Therefore, the court concluded, he should have been granted an injunction against the new zoning ordinance.[244]

237. *Id.* at 894 (quoting Hammond v. Baldwin, 866 F.2d 172, 176 (6th Cir. 1989) (citing Williamson Cnty. Reg'l Planning Comm'n v. Hamilton Bank, 473 U.S. 172, 194 (1985)) (emphasis added).

238. *Id.* at 894.

239. *Id.*

240. *Id.* at 896.

241. *Id.*

242. *Id.* at 897 (citing City of Lansing v. Dawley, 247 Mich. 394 (1929)).

243. *Id.*

244. *Id.* at 897–98.

The Due Process Clause of the U.S. Constitution guarantees more than fair process. Its substantive component prohibits certain government actions regardless of the fairness of the procedures used:

> Since the time of our early explanations of due process, [courts] have understood the core of the concept to be protection against arbitrary action. . . . [The Supreme Court has] emphasized time and again that the touchstone of due process is protection of the individual against arbitrary action of government, whether the fault lies in a denial of fundamental procedural fairness or in the exercise of power without any reasonable justification in the service of a legitimate governmental objective.[245]

Thus, a claim of substantive due process is based on the exercise of power without reasonable justification. Where government action does not deprive a plaintiff of a particular constitutional guarantee, that action will be upheld against a substantive due process challenge if it is rationally related to a legitimate state interest.[246] In equipoise, a zoning ordinance is unconstitutional as violative of substantive due process under rational-basis review if it is arbitrary, capricious, or not rationally related to a legitimate public purpose.[247]

This constitutional protection applies in the context of zoning. In a basic sense, the Sixth Circuit has explained, "[C]itizens have a substantive due process right not to be subjected to arbitrary or irrational zoning decisions."[248] Zoning ordinances have long been subject to constitutional challenge. These challenges come in the now familiar facial and as-applied varieties.

In *Village of Euclid v. Ambler Realty Co.*, the Supreme Court held that zoning ordinances "must find their justification in some aspect of the police

245. Cnty. of Sacramento v. Lewis, 523 U.S. 833, 845–46 (1998) (internal quotations and citations omitted) (emphasis added).

246. Valot v. Southeast Local Sch. Dist. Bd. of Educ., 107 F.3d 1220, 1228 (6th Cir. 1997), *cert. denied*, 522 U.S. 861 (1997).

247. WMX Technologies Inc. v. Gasconade Cnty., Mo., 105 F.3d 1195, 1198–99 (8th Cir. 1997).

248. Pearson v. City of Grand Blanc, 961 F.2d 1211, 1217 (6th Cir. 1992).

power, asserted for the public welfare."[249] Thus, a zoning ordinance is the product of legislative action; and before it can be declared unconstitutional under the Due Process Clause, a court must find that the provisions are clearly arbitrary and unreasonable, having no substantial relationship to the public health, safety, morals, or general welfare.[250]

To lay this out more simply for claims of substantive due process in land use litigation, courts typically require plaintiffs to show that:

1. A constitutionally protected property or liberty exists.
2. The constitutionally protected interest has been deprived through arbitrary and capricious action.[251]

Courts often do not give interests outside the fundamental rights purview much consideration. Such was the case in *EJS Properties LLC v. City of Toledo*.[252] In that case, the court painted an instructive picture of due process interests as they pertain to expectations of discretionary decision making in land use, the nuances of establishing property and liberty interests, and the somewhat rarer argument that government action may "shock the conscience" in violation of due process.

EJS Properties, a developer, wanted to build a charter school in a commercial zone in Toledo, Ohio. It entered into both an agreement to purchase a parcel contingent on obtaining a zoning change and a lease agreement with a charter school without such conditions.[253] At a lunch between the region's city council representative and executives of the Pilkington Corp., which owned the property, the representative allegedly requested that the executives donate a sum of money to a local community center. The Pilkington executives declined, and though it was unclear whether this request was intended as a quid pro quo, it was undisputed that the request was made.[254]

249. 272 U.S. 365, 387 (1926).
250. *Id.* at 395.
251. Braun v. Ann Arbor Charter Twp., 519 F.3d 564, 573 (6th Cir.), *cert. denied*, 555 U.S. 1062 (2008).
252. 698 F.3d 845 (6th Cir. 2012).
253. *Id.* at 851.
254. *Id.* at 852.

EJS began developing the site and obtained an early-start building permit. However, the city council eventually voted against EJS's rezoning request after the representative allegedly rallied several council members to reject the measure.[255] EJS did not appeal the denial, but two months later, the Toledo Public Schools initiated and won an eminent-domain dispute with Pilkington over the parcel, successfully rezoned it, and constructed a middle school on the property.[256] EJS then filed suit against both the city and the representative, citing a deprivation of substantive due process alongside other concerns.[257] The district court nevertheless dismissed the due process claim because it found that EJS lacked a liberty or property interest.[258]

On appeal, EJS claimed to have property interests in a "previously approved" rezoning ordinance, relevant contracts, and its early-start building permit.[259] Property interests may arise from existing zoning classifications,[260] but the court duly noted that the zoning ordinance in this case was never actually "previously approved" by the city council.[261] From there, EJS was unable to show that the city council lacked discretion to deny the land use as the council's authority was, in the court's view, of a "categorically discretionary nature."[262] Even if the city council acted with illicit motives, that would not change the discretionary nature of the zoning authority, and "[t]he law is clear that a party cannot have a property interest in a discretionary benefit, even if that discretion had never been exercised previously."[263]

Contract rights are property rights under Ohio law, making interests created by contracts property interests.[264] Here, however, the purchase agreement clearly indicated that EJS had no claim of interest in the property before closing.[265] The validity of the contract was also atypically contingent

255. *Id.* at 852–53.
256. *Id.* at 853–54.
257. *Id.* at 854.
258. *Id.* at 855.
259. *Id.* at 856.
260. *Id.* at 856 (citing *Nasierowski Bros.*, 949 F.2d at 897).
261. *Id.*
262. *Id.*
263. *Id.* at 857 (citing Mich. Envtl. Res. Assocs. Inc. v. Cnty. of Macomb, No. 87-2029 1989 WL 54116, at *4 (6th Cir. 1989)).
264. *Id.* at 857.
265. *Id.* at 857–58.

on EJS's ability to acquire title to the land it sought to lease. The contract thus could not be enforced and EJS had no interest at stake.[266]

EJS further claimed that it had liberty interests both in government decisions free from corruption and in the pursuit of business contracts without unlawful interference.[267] Contracting is a recognized liberty interest,[268] but EJS did not claim that it was deprived of "the general right to enter into contracts."[269] EJS was instead more concerned with unlawful interference "in the form of extortion and bribery."[270] But this interest, in the court's view, does "not stand for the proposition that the right to enter into contracts free from interference includes the right to be free from government interference with the occurrence of a wholly discretionary condition."[271] The court then further reasoned that because "a distinction must be drawn between the quality of the process owed a protected interest and the interest itself," no standalone liberty interest exists in having government make a discretionary decision free from corruption.[272]

Lastly, EJS claimed, in a variation of its liberty interest argument concerning corruption, that the zoning practices in this case "shock the conscience" in violation of due process. Still, conscience-shocking claims, including when made in the land use context, require a showing that a liberty or property interest was deprived.[273] Even if EJS did not need to establish that it had a protectable interest at stake, the court concluded that the representative's action in this case, though "unfortunate," did not shock the court's conscience "the way that pumping a detainee's stomach does."[274] In short, shocking the conscience is such a difficult claim to establish that even a showing of government corruption does not suffice.

266. *Id.* at 858–59.

267. *Id.* at 859.

268. *Id.* at 859 (citing Washington v. Glucksberg, 521 U.S. 702, 760 (1997)).

269. *Id.* at 860 (citations omitted).

270. *Id.*

271. *Id.* The court further claimed that "EJS's claim sounds more in torn law than in a violation of a liberty interest." *Id.* at 859–60.

272. *Id.* at 860.

273. *Id.* at 862 ("[P]rior precedent makes clear that in the context of a discretionary zoning decision, government action will not shock the conscience unless the arbitrary and capricious action touches on a protectable interest.").

274. *Id.*

In the context of land use and zoning cases, substantive due process claims are rarely successful. A great deal of care and thought is needed prior to raising this type of claim.

VII. State Constitutional Claims

Every state has a constitutional provision protecting the individual rights of those seeking to freely worship, restricting state and local governments from limiting those rights.[275] Most are much more detailed than the First Amendment, and many states' constitutional provisions dealing with religion developed over time, largely in response to specific conflicts.[276] In many instances, the state provisions also reveal a different perspective on the relationship between church and state than is found in the First Amendment's Free Exercise Clause.[277] Most scholars agree that the state constitutional free-exercise provisions served as important models in the drafting and consideration of the Free Exercise Clause.[278]

After the U.S. Supreme Court released its decision in *Employment Division v. Smith*,[279] many commentators concluded that a claimant in a Free Exercise claim look to each individual state constitutional free-exercise clause for relief. They agree that "[a]t the moment plaintiffs have a far better chance of success with the state constitutions than with the federal."[280]

275. *See generally* Jennifer Friesen, Chapter 4: Freedom of Religion, in State Constitutional Law: Litigating Individual Rights, Claims and Defenses (4th ed. 2006).

276. *Id.*

277. Paul Benjamin Linton, *Religious Freedom Claims and Defenses Under State Constitutions*, 7 U. St. Thomas J. L. & Pub. Pol'y 103; *see also* Linda S. Wendtland, *Beyond the Establishment Clause: Enforcing Separation of Church and State Through State Constitutional Provisions*, 71 Va. L. Rev. 625, 631–34, 638 (1985) (noting that the state religion clauses are more specific and detailed and can be described in five categories that produce different degrees of state activism).

278. *See* Donald S. Lutz, *The States and the U.S. Bill of Rights*, 16 S. Ill. U. L. J. 251, 253–54 (1992): An examination of the state bills of rights written between 1776 and 1787 shows that Madison effectively extracted the least common denominator from them as the basis for his proposed list of amendments, excepting those rights which might reduce the power of the national government. Almost every one of the 26 rights in the U.S. Bill of Rights could be found in two or three state documents, and most of them in five or more. *Id.* at 258.

279. 494 U.S. 872 (1990).

280. Douglas Laycock, *Summary and Synthesis: The Crisis in Religious Liberty*, 60 Geo. Wash. L. Rev. 841, 854 (1992).

Because courts treat religious-exercise rights in the federal and many state constitutions consubstantially, they further concluded that "[s]ome state courts will do no better than the federal courts, but some will do much better."[281]

In turn, state constitutional religion clauses may be interpreted to be more protective than the U.S. Supreme Court's interpretations of the First Amendment.[282] The Michigan Supreme Court made this observation in *People v. Dejonge*.[283] At issue was the constitutionality of a state law that required parents who conduct home schooling for their children to provide instructors certified by the state. The Michigan court held that the teacher certification requirement was an unconstitutional violation of the Free Exercise Clause of the First Amendment as applied to families whose religious convictions prohibit the use of certified instructors. In reaching this conclusion, the court noted the difference in interpreting the Michigan constitutional provision concerning the free exercise of religion compared to its federal counterpart:

> We are not unaware of the criticism generated in reaction to Smith, which held that the First Amendment does not bar the "application of a neutral, generally applicable law to religiously motivated" conduct unless the Free Exercise Clause is in "conjunction with other constitutional protections. . . ." Nevertheless, this court must follow the interpretation of the Free Exercise Clause in the prevailing opinions of the United States Supreme Court, "even though we may be in accord with the dissenting opinions in those cases." On the other

281. *Id.*

282. *See* Nicholas P. Miller & Nathan Sheers, *Religious Free Exercise Under State Constitutions*, 34 J. Church & St. 303 (1991) (examining the impact of Smith on the states' Free Exercise clauses and the subsequent level of scrutiny given to religious freedom cases among the states); Angela C. Carmella, *State Constitutional Protection of Religious Exercise: An Emerging Post-Smith Jurisprudence*, 1993 B.Y.U. L. Rev. 275 (1993); Stuart G. Parsell, Note, *Revitalization of the Free Exercise of Religion Under State Constitutions: A Response to Employment Division v. Smith*, 68 Notre Dame L. Rev. 747 (1993) (noting that in the aftermath of Smith states have begun to consistently provide greater state protection for religious liberty); Stanley H. Friedelbaum, *Free Exercise in the States: Belief, Conduct and Judicial Benchmarks*, 63 Alb. L. Rev. 1059 (2000) (exploring the development of the distinctions between state religion clauses and the First Amendment).

283. 442 Mich. 266, 501 N.W.2d 127 (1993).

> hand, we may certainly interpret the Michigan Constitution as affording additional protection to the free exercise of religion. However, because the ruling of Smith commands that strict scrutiny be applied in the case at issue, we do not undertake to determine at this time the extent of the Michigan Constitution's protection of the free exercise of religion generally. We do hold, however, that the Michigan Constitution mandates that strict scrutiny as articulated in this opinion be applied in the instant case. Our Michigan Constitution also contains a Free Exercise Clause.[284]

With varied results, Michigan courts have always applied strict scrutiny to state regulation of religious freedom.[285] Despite the textual and historical differences in state constitutional religion clauses and the First Amendment, many state courts interpret their constitutional provisions in the same manner as the federal counterpart.[286] Others, however, see their constitutional provisions as weaker. The New Jersey Supreme Court, for example, observed that the state constitution's protection of freedom of religion is "less pervasive, literally, than the federal provision."[287]

State constitutional provisions are important claims to assert in a complaint. However, since the *Smith* decision, the author is not aware of any significant land use cases granting or limiting rights to religious institutions in states based on their own constitutional free-exercise clauses. Perhaps this will be the new ground of litigation in the future.

---

284. *Id.* at 442 n.27 (citations omitted).

285. *See, e.g.*, Porth v. Roman Catholic Diocese, 209 Mich. App. 630, 532 N.W.2d 195 (1995); Sheridan Road Baptist Church v. Dep't of Ed., 426 Mich. 462; 396 N.W.2d 373 (1986), *cert. denied* 481 U.S. 1050 (1987); Dep't of Social Services v Emmanuel Baptist Preschool, 434 Mich. 380; 455 N.W.2d 1 (1990); Fisher v. Fisher, 118 Mich. App. 227, 231–32; 324 N.W.2d 582 (1982); McLeod v. Providence Christian Sch., 160 Mich. App. 333; 408 N.W.2d 146 (1987).

286. *See generally* Robert F. Williams, *State Courts Adopting Federal Constitutional Doctrine: Case-by-Case Adoptionism or Prospective Lockstepping?*, 46 WM. & MARY L. REV. 1499, 1504–10 (2005), https://scholarship.law.wm.edu/wmlr/vol46/iss4/12.

287. Resnick v. E. Brunswick Bd. of Educ., 389 A.2d 944, 952 (N.J. 1978).

VIII. Religious Uses Add Value to a Community

One other note of consequence. Social scientist have studied the question of whether religious uses add value to a local community. And social scientists have been researching the impact of religious institutions on communities in their role as a connector of people and have confirmed that when they work together, religious institutions and community leaders do indeed strengthen society.

Research shows that religious organizations provide jobs for the community and support a variety of local businesses.[288] They bring in individuals from surrounding areas to the community where the church is located, and these individuals provide economic support to local establishments.

Much like strong school systems, many families and individuals consider the presence of local religious organizations when deciding about moving to communities and purchasing property.[289] This, in turn, helps support local businesses and contributes to community growth, job creation, and overall economic vitality. Beyond these economic benefits, churches are the social services infrastructure for communities and provide significant economic value. Churches help communities complete vitally important social projects for which the government would need to provide funds if churches did not provide such support.

In a detailed study of churches in Philadelphia, the researchers found that if it were not for the impressive collective effort of some 2,100 religious congregations, life in Philadelphia would be extremely harsh.[290] The study assigned monetary values to 49 categories, ranging from hosting weddings to building enhancement to teaching children social responsibility. Those categories were then used by researchers to calculate the annual economic contributions that 12 religious congregations in the Philadelphia area made on the communities they serve. The study determined that each congregation provided an average of $476,663.24 per year in economic contributions

288. Ram A. Cnaan, Tuomi Forrest, Joseph Carlsmith, & Kelsey Karsh, *If You Do Not Count It, It Does Not Count: A Pilot Study of Valuing Urban Congregations*, J. MGMT., SPIRITUALITY & RELIGION (2013).

289. *Id.*

290. *Id.*

to the community. Additionally, it found, religious affiliation and religious behavior increased community volunteering as well as intra-church volunteering. The study also found that religious entities contributed volunteers to three organizations on average, though some churches provided dozens of volunteers to different projects.

Because it can be difficult to quantify the exact value of the volunteering and community-building benefits that churches provide to communities, these scholars referred to the replacement value of volunteering. The replacement value was calculated by adding monetary donations and in-kind support, staff and congregant volunteer hours, utilities, and the value of space. In the Philadelphia study, scholars valued community services at $115,009 per congregation and $230,018,400 for all the congregations in the city.

This is much greater than the taxable value of the land.

Further, studies indicate that churches actually increase property values. In one relevant study, the researchers found "that neighborhood churches are amenities that enhance property values [for] at least one-half mile. . . ."[291]

IX. Justiciability and Religious Land Use

Often a case involving the Religious Land Use and Institutionalized Persons Act (RLUIPA), and cases involving the related claims, can be dismissed on justiciability grounds before a court can even begin to evaluate the merits. Justiciability concerns, such as whether a claim is ripe or moot or whether a party has standing to bring suit, all must be resolved before the court can address the merits of a particular case.

This requirement is not unique to religious land use litigation, but special attention must be given to it within this area of law. As can be seen in the various case studies discussed, courts have ordinarily held that federal legal claims will not be ripe for adjudication until a religious organization has been denied a permit. In most instances, a full denial includes an

291. Thomas M. Carroll et al., *Living Next to Godliness: Residential Property Values and Churches*, 12 J. Real Est. Fin. & Econ. 319, 328 (1996).

organization's submitting the appropriate application, receiving a final decision from the appropriate body, and oftentimes appealing that decision to the local government's appellate body or seeking variance relief.

A. Standing

In passing RLUIPA, Congress provided that the "standing to assert a claim or defense under the statute shall be governed by the general rules of standing under Article III of the Constitution"[292] and by these rules alone.[293] In brief, standing involves an evaluation of whether a claimant can have its cause of action addressed in federal court.[294] Rules governing the standing doctrine are derived from the first clause of Article III, confining judicial power to "[c]ases" and "[c]ontroversies."[295] From this provision, courts have established a "case or controversy" requirement that prevents court consideration of constitutional issues unless incident to an actual, ongoing case or controversy in law. This requirement ensures that plaintiffs have a legitimate stake in litigation and in doing so restricts courts from unduly interfering with the activities of coequal branches of government. At present, constitutional requirements of standing applicable to every federal court litigant are as follows:

> First, the plaintiff must have suffered an "injury in fact"—an invasion of a legally protected interest that is (a) concrete and particularized and (b) "actual or imminent, not 'conjectural' or 'hypothetical.'" Second, there must be a causal connection between the injury and the conduct complained of—the injury has to be "fairly trace[able] to the challenged action of the defendant and not . . . th[e] result [of] the independent action of some third party not before the court." Third,

292. 42 U.S.C. § 2000cc-2(a).

293. *See, e.g.*, Andon LLC v. City of Newport News, 63 F. Supp. 3d 630, 636 (E.D. Va. 2014) (finding that "there is no requirement that a plaintiff be engaged in religious exercise to bring a RLUIPA claim" and that "[r]ecognizing an additional limitation for standing . . . would contradict one of the clearly stated purposes of the statute—to broadly protect religious exercise under RLUIPA").

294. Nat'l Org. for Marriage v. McKee, 649 F.3d 34, 46 (1st Cir. 2011) (citing U.S. CONST. art. III, § 2).

295. U.S. CONST. art. III, § 2, cl. 1.

it must be "likely," as opposed to merely "speculative," that the injury will be "redressed by a favorable decision."[296]

As a general rule, the rules of "standing" preclude one party from litigating the claims of another.[297] In *Cassidy v. City of Brewer*,[298] a Maine district court illustrated this point nicely. In this case, Dana Cassidy, an owner of a commercial building in Brewer, Maine, saw his property rezoned as a convenience business district, which did not allow churches as a permitted use. However, Cassidy leased part of the building to The Rock Church of Greater Bangor Inc. to use for worship.[299] As the congregation started to outgrow the space, it submitted a commercial building permit to the city for an expansion in 2012 but was denied because it amounted to an expansion of a nonconforming use. The church subsequently decided to terminate its tenancy and relocate. In turn, Cassidy filed suit under RLUIPA, alleging that the city caused him economic injury by violating the federal rights of a tenant.[300]

The court applied the ordinary third-party standing rules to the claim.[301] While Cassidy successfully identified a personal economic injury, the action did not have any prospect of remediating anyone's religious exercise rights because the church already had departed from the controversy and there was not another religious institution lined up to fill the space.[302] Thus, even though Cassidy's injury may be remedied, that relief would not address the

---

296. Ariz. Christian Sch. Tuition Org. v. Winn, 131 S. Ct. 1436, 1442 (2011) (quoting Lujan v. Defenders of Wildlife, 504 U.S. 555, 560–61 (1992)); Dixon v. Town of Coats, 2010 U.S. Dist. LEXIS 56740 (E.D. N.C. 2010); Knows His Gun v. Montana, 866 F. Supp. 2d 1235 (D. Mont. 2012); Cassidy v. City of Brewer, 2012 U.S. Dist. LEXIS 165723 (D. Me. 2012); Andon LLC v. City of Newport News, 63 F. Supp. 3d 630 (E.D. Va. 2014); Congregation Rabbinical Coll. of Tartikov Inc. v. Vill. of Pomona, 2015 U.S. Dist. LEXIS 132714 (S.D.N.Y. 2015).

297. Allen v. Wright, 468 U.S. 737, 751 (1984) (The additional prudential limitations on standing, including "the general prohibition on a litigant's raising another person's legal rights, the rule barring adjudication of generalized grievances more appropriately addressed in the representative branches, and the requirement that a plaintiff's complaint fall within the zone of interests protected by the law invoked.").

298. 2012 U.S. Dist. LEXIS 165723 (D. Me. 2012).

299. *Id.* at *1–2.

300. *Id.* at *3.

301. *Id.* at *12–13.

302. *Id.* at *20–21.

church's injury.[303] Cassidy, furthermore, could not establish that anything stood in the way of the church's filing suit on its own behalf.[304] Though private landowners may challenge land use regulations under RLUIPA if their property is burdened by regulation, they must still demonstrate that their litigation, under RLUIPA, will advance third-party religious exercise rights and why that third party could not pursue its own rights under RLUIPA.[305]

In this vein, courts have repeatedly held that a party "must assert his own legal rights and interests and cannot rest his claim to relief on the legal rights or interests of third parties."[306] As explained by the Supreme Court in *Singleton v. Wulff*:[307]

> Federal courts must hesitate before resolving a controversy, even one within their constitutional power to resolve, on the basis of the rights of third persons not parties to the litigation. The reasons are two. First, the courts should not adjudicate such rights unnecessarily, and it may be that in fact the holders of those rights either do not wish to assert them or will be able to enjoy them regardless of whether the in-court litigant is successful or not. Second, third parties themselves usually will be the best proponents of their own rights. The courts depend on effective advocacy and therefore should prefer to construe legal rights only when the most effective advocates of those rights are before them. The holders of the rights may have a like preference, to the extent they will be bound by the courts' decisions under the doctrine of stare decisis.[308]

This rule is not absolute. There are exceptions where the party seeking third-party standing "has a close relationship with the person who possesses the right" and "there is a hindrance to the possessor's ability to protect his own interests."[309] When an exception to the third-party rules is

303. *Id.* at *23.
304. *Id.* at *26.
305. *Id.* at *30–31.
306. Warth v. Seldin, 422 U.S. 498, 499 (1975).
307. 428 U.S. 106 (1976).
308. *Id.* at 113–14.
309. Powers v. Ohio, 499 U.S. 400, 411 (1991).

being considered, courts consider "the impact of the litigation on third-party interests."[310] In other words, third-party standing inquiry involves both a party-specific and claim-specific assessment. A court reviewing standing must determine whether each claim asserted is entitled to federal court jurisdiction.[311]

Thus, evaluating "standing" is answering the question of whether a case has the constitutional or statutory provision on which a claim can be evaluated within the federal court. Assuming that the constitutional minimum for standing exists, "persons to whom Congress has granted a right of action, either expressly or by clear implication, may have standing to seek relief on the basis of the legal rights and interests of others or, indeed, may invoke the general public interest in support of their claim."[312] What follows is a claim-specific inquiry that applies the Supreme Court's standing rules to a claimant's allegation.

Pleading a claim under RLUIPA is not to be confused with jurisdictional concerns. In *Chabad Lubavitch of Litchfield County Inc. v. Borough of Litchfield*,[313] a Connecticut district court determined that the Chabad Lubavitch of Litchfield County, a Jewish organization led by Rabbi Joseph Eisenbach, lacked standing to bring an RLUIPA action because he did not have a sufficient property interest to satisfy RLUIPA's requirements.[314] The rabbi brought suit against the borough for denying a certificate of appropriateness for a building the Chabad purchased to accommodate its growing membership.[315]

The district court determined that the rabbi lacked standing because he was merely a member of the organization with no property interest and simply felt threatened by the borough's allegedly illegal conduct.[316] The court further rejected Chabad's argument that the rabbi had a sufficient property interest in that he would be able to place a mortgage lien on the property for his unpaid salary, stating that "[a] construction of 'property interest' to

310. Caplin & Drysdale v. United States, 491 U.S. 617, 623 n.3 (1989).
311. *Allen*, 468 U.S. at 752.
312. *Warth*, 422 U.S. at 501.
313. 796 F. Supp. 2d 333 (D. Conn. 2011).
314. *Id.* at 338–39.
315. *Id.* at 337.
316. *Id.* at 338–39.

extend to a creditor of a corporation is so clearly incongruous with the language and purposes of RLUIPA, it barely warrants addressing."[317] Based on these determinations, the court terminated the rabbi as a party to the case.[318]

On appeal, however, the Second Circuit found that the district court erred in its standing analysis insofar as instead of assessing whether the rabbi adequately pled a claim, it treated the question of whether RLUIPA provides a cause of action that encompasses the rabbi's claim as a jurisdictional matter.[319] And at any rate, it was clear that the rabbi satisfied Article III standing requirements, minimally because he was prevented from living on the property, which is a redressable injury.[320]

The absence of a property interest is, generally speaking, a barrier to establishing standing in RLUIPA claims. In *Taylor v. City of Gary*, the city of Gary, Indiana, owned a vacant Methodist Church property.[321] In June 2005, Carlton Taylor, a minister for the "restoration ministry" of The House of the Lord Our God, expressed interest in acquiring the church structure in order to refurbish it and create a house of worship.[322] However, the city refused to give him the property and in January 2006 announced plans to demolish a portion of the church structure in order to build a ruins garden.[323]

In response to the city's decision, Taylor brought a pro se suit against the city, alleging that the city violated his rights under RLUIPA and the Free Exercise Clause of the First Amendment.[324] The district court dismissed his claims when it determined that Taylor lacked standing to sue because he did not have a property interest in the church.[325]

The Seventh Circuit of the U.S. Court of Appeals affirmed. Since Taylor had no interest in the property at issue, he had no standing and his RLUIPA claim was dismissed.[326] The court noted that even if Taylor had standing to

---

317. *Id.*
318. *Id.* at 339.
319. Chabad-Lubavitch v. Litchfield Historic Dist., 768 F.3d 183, 201 (2d Cir. 2014).
320. *Id.* at 201–02.
321. 233 F. App'x 561 (7th Cir. 2007) (unpublished).
322. *Id.* at 562.
323. *Id.*
324. *Id.*
325. *Id.*
326. *Id.*

sue, his complaint still failed under RLUIPA.[327] RLUIPA prohibits land use regulations from substantially burdening a religious practice.[328] However, case law makes clear that a land use regulation is one that restricts a person's ability to use property in which he has a property interest.[329]

B. Ripeness

Ripeness shares a similar conceptual concern with standing in that courts should decline to hear the merits of claims for cases that do not deserve judicial resolution. However, ripeness differs through its specialized focus on preventing premature adjudication. While standing gauges whether a litigant may file suit, ripeness assesses when a suit is appropriate. Ripeness is an especially important issue in the realm of religious land use litigation, as it can be raised at any point in a case.[330] Consequently, even where a defendant fails to raise the issue in an initial response, the argument is not waived. This is true in light of the fact that a ripeness analysis is less stringent in the context of First Amendment litigation where a fear of irretrievable loss exists.[331]

Insomnia Inc. v. City of Memphis[332] reviewed the parameters of ripeness considerations in relation to First Amendment challenges to local land use regulation. The court noted that ripeness is a matter of justiciability, implicating "prudential reasons for refusing to exercise jurisdiction."[333] The doctrine is designed to prevent the courts from addressing, through premature adjudication, the merits of a claim that does not yet present a live case or controversy or otherwise prematurely "entangling themselves in abstract disagreements."[334]

Ripeness evaluations involve three factors:

---

327. *Id.*

328. *Id.*

329. *Id.* (citing Vision Church v. Vill. of Long Grove, 468 F.3d 975, 998 (7th Cir. 2006)).

330. *See, e.g.*, St. Vincent de Paul Place v. City of Norwich, 535 F. App'x 57 (2d Cir. 2013) (reversing a district court's determination that a claim was unripe after plaintiff was later denied a variance application pending appeal).

331. 13A CHARLES A. WRIGHT, ARTHUR R. MILLER & EDWARD H. COOPER, FEDERAL PRACTICE AND PROCEDURE § 3532.3 (1984).

332. 278 F. App'x 609, 2008 WL 2121053 (6th Cir. 2008).

333. *Id.* at *2, 278 F. App'x 609, 612 (quoting Ky. Press Ass'n Inc. v. Kentucky, 454 F.3d 505, 509 (6th Cir. 2006)).

334. *Id.*

> (1) The likelihood that the harm alleged by the plaintiffs will ever come to pass, (2) whether the factual record is sufficiently developed to produce a fair adjudication of the merits of the parties' respective claims and (3) the hardship to the parties if judicial relief is denied at this stage in the proceedings.[335]

Normally, a claim would be unripe under these factors if a religious organization does not, before filing suit, do so much as file an application in accordance with relevant land use regulations. There are, however, exceptions to this rule. *Roman Catholic Bishop of Springfield v. City of Springfield*,[336] as discussed earlier in the equal-terms context, bore important ripeness implications on this point. Again, the case involved a church filing suit after a city ordinance designated its land as a single-parcel historic district, which required the church to seek permission from the city before making future land alterations. Of importance, the church neither submitted an application to make an alteration nor had any specific plans to make one, and it was unclear what if anything the regulation prevented the church from doing.[337] Since the church did not submit an application and could not point to specific plans that the ordinance would disrupt, it presented a mere possibility of future injury, which is usually a textbook case of an unripe claim.[338]

But this was not the church's only argument. Interestingly, it also claimed that the "mere existence" of the ordinance created a ripe controversy. The court was persuaded because having to comply with the regulation created a form of delay, uncertainty, and expense sufficient to show injury.[339] Though the court recognized it was "self-evidently plausible" that there was injury,[340] it later concluded that the regulatory burden was not substantial because it merely involved following general administrative proceedings and

335. *Id.* at *3, 278 F. App'x 609, 612 (quoting Warshak v. United States, 490 F.3d 455, 467 (6th Cir. 2007)).
336. 724 F.3d 78, (1st Cir. 2013).
337. *Id.* at 91.
338. *Id.* at 91–92.
339. *Id.* at 92.
340. *Id.*

because the alleged financial burden was undocumented and only partially traceable to the ordinance.[341]

Thus, an injury does not have to amount to a substantial burden to be ripe, and the possibility of future injury can create a ripe controversy when that possibility creates current hardship. This principle extends to land use regulations that were passed out of discriminatory animus even if not yet applied, according to the Eleventh Circuit in *Temple B'Nai Zion Inc. v. City of Sunny Isles Beach*.[342] In another landmarking case, this one "fortifie[d]" by the reasoning in *Roman Catholic Bishop of Springfield*, Temple B'Nai Zion was a Jewish religious organization operating in Sunny Isles Beach, Florida. Operating as a Judaic temple for a number of years, it switched to Orthodox Judaism not long after 2004. This caused a stir among many members of the congregation, some of whom included powerful members within the city's government, including the mayor and city commissioners.[343]

In 2006, the temple planned renovations for the building and in 2009 applied but was rejected for a permit to begin reconstruction. An application was denied again in 2010.[344] Meanwhile, the city began examining buildings to designate for the first time as historic landmarks. After a hearing, the Preservation Board voted to designate parts of the temple as historic sites, not to be modified without approval. On appeal, the City Commission decided to make the temple a historic site.[345]

Consequently, the temple filed suit. But the district court dismissed the complaint after determining that the question was not ripe, understanding the temple's concern to be an inability to expand when it had not yet requested a waiver or variance to do so.[346] But the Eleventh Circuit held that the district court had misread the temple's complaint. To the Eleventh Circuit, the temple was challenging the enactment of the historic-landmark designation, allegedly done solely for discriminatory purposes. The temple did not indicate concern with the application of the regulation, and thus

341. *Id.* at 99.
342. 727 F.3d 1349 (11th Cir. 2013).
343. *Id.* at 1351.
344. *Id.* at 1351–52.
345. *Id.* at 1353–54.
346. *Id.* at 1355.

the "issue became as ripe as it will ever be."[347] The Eleventh Circuit declined to apply a strict ripeness test because the temple alleged that the city was motivated by discriminatory animus, which makes an injury complete. By declining to address the merits, a court would only be perpetuating the alleged injury.[348]

Similarly, facial challenges to regulations that would effectively block the actualization of a desired land use are generally held to be ripe without a plaintiff's ever even filing a permit. In *Congregation Rabbinical College of Tartikov Inc. v. Village of Pomona*,[349] a group affiliated with a proposed rabbinical college had an interest in constructing a yeshiva—a training and educational facility for rabbis—and large housing facility in the village of Pomona, New York, on a parcel that it claimed was the only available and suitable one in the village.[350]

Starting in the early 2000s, the village enacted regulatory laws to address the "scant" regulations on schools. Though the congregation never submitted a formal plan for the college, it did have a "preliminary concept plan."[351] However, the congregation argued that "collectively," village accreditation, dormitory, and wetlands laws made construction of the college impossible.[352] While to the court it was "debatable" that the laws were passed out of discriminatory animus,[353] the claim was nonetheless ripe because "facial challenges, by virtue of being facial challenges, are ripe and have been ripe" since the challenged laws were passed.[354] The enactment of legislation itself can substantially burden religious exercise. And it was clear that, since the congregation was able to show that it would in fact be prevented from building the college,[355] the court could redress the injury with a favorable ruling.[356]

Otherwise, a bedrock principle of ripeness is finality, which mandates that a government reach a final decision on the application of a land use

347. *Id.* at 1357–58.
348. *Id.*
349. 2015 U.S. Dist. LEXIS 132714 (S.D.N.Y. 2015).
350. *Id.* at *2–3.
351. *Id.* at *10–12.
352. *Id.* at *25–26.
353. *Id.* at *152.
354. *Id.* at *43.
355. *Id.* at *43–44.
356. *Id.* at *33–34.

regulation before a court can concern itself with the merits of a claim. The Third Circuit stressed this point in *Congregation Anshei Roosevelt v. Planning and Zoning Board of the Borough of Roosevelt*.[357] The congregation built its synagogue before zoning regulations went into effect in the New Jersey borough. In 2005, the congregation entered into an agreement with a yeshiva to operate a center within its facility. A neighbor complained, and in response zoning officials visited the property and found that a yeshiva's use was proper within the synagogue. However, the township board overturned the zoning officials' decision and found the yeshiva to be an expansion of a nonconforming use and more comparable to a boarding school than a house of worship. Accordingly, the congregation was required to file a variance application.[358]

The congregation sued, the trial court dismissed, and the Third Circuit affirmed. The court found that the board had simply not issued a definitive conclusion as to the extent that the yeshiva could use the synagogue for a school. Because no variance was sought, no final decision was made. It could not be determined whether the congregation suffered a burden or an injury at all, since having to apply for a variance itself did not impose an injury. Evidently, enforcing the finality requirement prevents courts from acting as "super land-use boards of appeals" that unduly interfere with local affairs.[359]

Particular intermediate actions, such as initial cease-and-desist orders, are not to be misconstrued as a final decision, according to the Ninth Circuit in *Guatay Christian Fellowship v. County of San Diego*.[360] In *Guatay*, the church brought an RLUIPA action without first having filed an application with the county for a modification-of-use permit to use a recreation building for religious assembly. The church owned a recreation building that was in a trailer park in San Diego County. Under the county's zoning ordinance, the land on which the recreation building stood was zoned as a "rural residential" district. The ordinance additionally required a religious assembly use in a "rural residential" zone to obtain a land use permit. The

357. 338 F. App'x. 214 (3d Cir. 2009).
358. *Id.* at 215–16.
359. *Id.* at 219 (quoting Sameric Corp. of Delaware Inc. v. City of Phila., 142 F.3d 582, 598 (3d Cir. 1998).
360. 670 F.3d 957 (9th Cir. 2011).

church had been holding its services in the recreation building since 1986. During that time, the church and property owner twice tried to apply for a use permit with the county, though neither application was approved.[361]

In 2008, the county issued a notice of violation to the trailer park for several infractions of the zoning regulations, one of which was for "illegally convert[ing the recreation hall] for use as a church." The notice also informed the church that the recreation building's use could only be changed with a modification-of-use permit.[362] The church filed suit without first trying to obtain a modification permit, and it alleged violations of RLUIPA and the First and Fourteenth Amendments. While the suit was pending, the church requested that it be able to continue using its building for religious services. The county informed the church that the county would first need to inspect the premises before granting the request, and that if services were held in the building, it would be illegal, since the church did not have a valid certificate of occupancy. Nevertheless, the church commenced its services before such an inspection occurred.[363]

In response, the county obtained a warrant to inspect the church's premises and during the inspection found numerous violations serious enough to require the church to immediately stop holding any sort of assembly in the building. The church eventually remedied the violations and was able to use the structure again for religious assembly. It also began applying for the use permit again, but eventually stopped when its expert informed it that the process would be extremely expensive and time-consuming.[364] The church instead chose to move for partial summary judgment. But the district court rejected its RLUIPA claims as being unripe for review, as the church never completed the use-permit application process.[365]

The Ninth Circuit agreed with the district court's ruling that the RLUIPA claims were unripe.[366] A final decision, the court observed, is not the same thing as a decision that a religious organization is currently violating a land use regulation. Requiring the church to apply for a permit is an important

361. *Id.* at 960–62.
362. *Id.* at 964.
363. *Id.* at 966.
364. *Id.* at 966–68.
365. *Id.* at 968.
366. *Id.* at 976.

part of the ripeness doctrine because it allows courts to refer to full records and better understand the nature of regulatory restrictions. The requirement also provides the opportunity to seek local relief without expending court resources, thereby respecting principles of federalism.[367] On October 9, 2012, the U.S. Supreme Court denied the church's writ of certiorari.

A rare exception to the final-decision requirement is the futility rule, under which a plaintiff must show that seeking a final decision would be a useless exercise. The District Court for the Southern District of New York offered an illustrative discussion of this often-unsuccessful type of challenge in *Sheri Torah Inc. v. Village of South Blooming Grove*.[368] Here, Sheri Torah, a religious corporation that operates a yeshiva, entered into a lease agreement around 2008 for a portion of a larger property in the village of South Blooming Grove, New York. In 2009, Sheri Torah submitted an application to the village for a special-use permit to use the property as a yeshiva.[369] After a number of meetings the Planning Board of the village of South Blooming Grove grew concerned over environmental factors stemming from a belief that the property was once used as an illegal waste transfer station.[370] The board requested a new detailed development plan and an environmental audit of the larger parcel and later voted that it could not make a recommendation without receiving the requested information.[371]

After Sheri Torah failed to submit the information, the board passed a resolution denying the application, leading to a lawsuit under RLUIPA and provisions of the U.S. and New York constitutions.[372] Sheri Torah originally filed its complaint in the Supreme Court of the State of New York, Orange County, before it was removed to the Southern District of New York after the issuance of a ruling that the board was entitled to withhold permits until receiving requested information.[373]

After reviewing the ripeness jurisprudence, the court held that claims should be barred when plaintiffs both fail to obtain a final decision from

367. *Id.* at 980–81.
368. 2013 U.S. Dist. LEXIS 49797 (S.D.N.Y. 2013).
369. *Id.* at *4.
370. *Id.* at *5–6.
371. *Id.* at *7.
372. *Id.* at *8.
373. *Id.* at *8–10.

a local authority and, though they may claim otherwise, cannot show that appeals to the appropriate administrative agency would be clearly futile.[374] In other words, a futility claim must be more than a conclusory assertion. In this case, Sheri Torah did not try to obtain a final decision and accordingly could not demonstrate that the futility exception applied. The board's requests appeared reasonable, and there was no inference from undisputed facts that the board was hostile or acting in bad faith.[375] Though Sheri Torah insisted that much of the board's rationale was a red herring, the board was shown to have been consistent about what it wanted, stated that it would have given consideration to an application when the information was received and, in the court's view, was entitled to the information requested.[376]

C. Exhaustion of Remedies

Ensuring that administrative remedies have in fact been exhausted is often a vital step that has tripped up many successful litigators across the country in RLUIPA cases and other land use disputes. While "ripeness" or "finality" involves a final decision on a land use issue within a community, "exhaustion of remedies" involves a determination that the land use applicant has pursued every internal review within a governmental entity before filing a federal lawsuit. In the context of land use, failure to exhaust administrative remedies at the outset could lead to wasting untold time and money.

In *Grace Community Church v. Lenox Township*,[377] the court explained the exhaustion of remedies doctrine as follows:

> As opposed to finality, the Supreme Court has held that exhaustion "generally refers to administrative and judicial procedures by which an injured party may seek review of an adverse decision and obtain a remedy if the decision is found to be unlawful or otherwise inappropriate and is not required before a plaintiff may bring a suit predicated upon 42 U.S.C. § 1983."[378]

374. *Id.* at *18.
375. *Id.* at *19.
376. *Id.* at *20.
377. 544 F.3d 609 (6th Cir. 2008).
378. *Id.* at 612.

Though not always required, exhausting administrative remedies commonly suffices to establish finality, which is a prerequisite for ripeness. Thus, while finality and exhaustion of administrative remedies can overlap, they are distinct. But the overlap can be slippery, at times creating confusion not exclusively for litigants but for both sides of the bench. Indeed, the Sixth Circuit was divided on this matter in *Miles Christi Religious Order v. Township of Northville*.[379] In 2002, the Miles Christi religious order bought a home on a one-acre plot in Northville Township, Michigan. Six residents lived in the home, which had an 18-person chapel for daily masses and Bible study. After receiving several complaints about traffic and parking, the township requested that Miles Christi submit a site plan for additional parking spaces on the property or seek a variance from the zoning board of appeals. Miles Christi made neither change, and in response the township issued a citation to the religious order.

Miles Christi then filed suit in federal court, alleging the township violated RLUIPA, the Free Exercise Clause and the Michigan Constitution.[380] The township moved to dismiss on the grounds that Miles Christi's claims were unripe because it had not received a final decision regarding the application of the township's zoning ordinances. The district court agreed, and it reasoned that the township's final decision was yet unknown, since Miles Christi had not appealed the township's demand for a site plan to the zoning board.[381]

In affirming the district court's decision, the Sixth Circuit looked to the township's zoning ordinances and found that in the current case, because a variance was needed, finality required the zoning board of appeals to answer three questions: (1) whether Miles Christi put its house to a more intensive use as defined in the code, (2) whether the house could be defined as a church under the code, and (3) whether Miles Christi was obligated to submit a site plan in view of the ordinance and the township's request that it secure a variance.[382]

379. Miles Christi Religious Order v. Twp. of Northville, 629 F.3d 533 (6th Cir. 2010).
380. 629 F.3d at 537.
381. *Id.*
382. *Id.* at 540–42.

The dissent, drafted by Chief Judge Alice Batchelder, is noteworthy because she found that Miles Christi had obtained a final decision.[383] She concluded that the majority's decision did not adequately account for the First Amendment implications of the case and "conflates the exhaustion of administrative remedies with the obtaining of a final decision[.]"[384] She went on to analyze the dearth of cases explaining the applicability of ripeness and finality as well as exhaustion of remedies cases in the context of land use cases. "The line between exhausting administrative remedies and obtaining a final decision is often obscure," she said, "but the two concepts are distinct." Consequences for Miles Christi resulted from the township's decision, which was final and had an immediate, harmful effect. To her, any relief it could provide was merely an administrative remedy whose availability had no bearing on the finality of the intensity determination.[385] Thus, the majority erred in dismissing the claim because Miles Christi effectively failed to exhaust administrative remedies.[386]

Though it may go without saying, partially exhausting administrative remedies is not the same thing as exhausting administrative remedies. A district court in Illinois nevertheless offered this important reminder in *Maum Meditation House of Truth v. Lake County*.[387] In this matter, plaintiff Sheehyung Sung sought to convert his Lake County, Illinois, residence to both a home and a meditation center. Sung claimed that the center would function as an "accessory" to the residence and therefore not require any renovations to comply with the building code.[388] However, the chief engineer and building official of the Lake County Planning, Building and Development Department rejected the new use proposal in an administrative decision, holding that an accessory needed to be functionally related to the primary use.[389]

On appeal, the Zoning Board of Appeals concluded that the proposed use of the property constituted establishing a place of religious worship,

383. *Id.* at 542.
384. *Id.*
385. *Id.* at 543.
386. *Id.* at 544.
387. 55 F. Supp. 3d 1081 (N.D. Ill. 2014).
388. *Id.* at 1084–85.
389. *Id.* at 1085.

meaning it was a mixed use that did not qualify for an exemption from the international building code. If Sung were to comply with applicable regulations, he would have had to complete a long list of renovations costing about $200,000. Instead of doing so, he submitted a complaint containing five counts against Lake County, seeking a preliminary injunction.[390]

The court began its analysis under the customary premise that plaintiffs ordinarily must reach a final administrative decision, often satisfied by exhausting administrative remedies, before a court will address the merits of a complaint.[391] With an eye to Sung's predicament, the court unearthed a yet-untrodden path to administrative remedy. Decisions of the Zoning Board of Appeals were subject to judicial review. But unfortunately for Sung, controlling law dictated that judicial review kick off exclusively in county circuit court. Federal district court would be reserved for overtime. Whatever the virtues of Sung's grievances, the court concluded that he failed to state a claim to permit sidestepping the exhaustion of remedies requirement.[392]

In a typical land use case, a client believes its rights under RLUIPA have been violated because it has either been denied a use permit or it believes it is unfair that it has to apply for such a permit in the first place. It follows that the second step is to ensure that a claimant has actually received a final answer from a final decision-making body. Typically, a land use applicant who seeks a permit might have to apply to the local planning commission. If the permit is denied, the applicant usually can appeal that decision, often to the local board of appeals, city council, or county commission. Under the exhaustion of remedies doctrine, if the Planning Commission denies the permit, it is not until the local board of appeals, city council or county commission has also affirmed the denial of the use permit that the case is ready to be filed. The local government ordinances will specify such appeal methods.

An institution must make sure that it fully and accurately complies with all applicable zoning regulations and has submitted all necessary applications to all local decision-making bodies before delving into litigation, since the consequence for not doing so may be getting the case dismissed before

390. *Id.*
391. *Id.* at 1086.
392. *Id.* at 1086–87.

the court ever gets to the merits. In many cases, the consensus among the various courts seems to be that simply having to apply for a permit likely does not constitute an RLUIPA violation. Instead, one's client should seek to develop a full record before resorting to federal litigation.

D. Mootness

A case is considered moot when the "issues presented are no longer 'live' or the parties lack a legally cognizable interest in the outcome."[393] In this sense, mootness is the flipside of ripeness. Both are concerned with when a lawsuit can be heard, but the former with being late and the latter with being early. "To invoke the jurisdiction of a federal court," controlling precedent commands, "a litigant must have suffered, or be threatened with, an actual injury traceable to the defendant and likely to be redressed by a favorable judicial decision."[394] If an injury is no longer redressable, a claim is moot and a federal court no longer has jurisdiction to hear it.

It is not uncommon for a claim to become moot because a jurisdiction changes its policy to effectively remedy the injury. The Eleventh Circuit held so against an equal-terms claim in *Covenant Christian Ministries Inc. v. City of Marietta*.[395] Covenant Christian Ministries originally entered into a contract in 2004 to purchase about eight acres zoned R-2 residential.[396] When Covenant signed a purchase contract for the land, the city had a provision in its zoning ordinance that allowed religious institutions to build in residential zones as long as the lot size was a minimum of five acres, so as to create a "buffer" between the churches and the residential property.[397] About two weeks later, in response to an RLUIPA challenge, the city eliminated the five-acre requirement from its zoning ordinance and instead imposed a blanket prohibition on all religious institutions in several

393. Cnty. of Los Angeles *v.* Davis, 440 U.S. 625, 631 (1979).

394. Lewis v. Cont'l Bank Corp., 494 U.S. 472, 477–78 (1990); Allen v. Wright, 468 U.S. 737, 750–51 (1984); Valley Forge Christian Coll. v. Americans United for Separation of Church & State Inc., 454 U.S. 464, 471–73 (1982).

395. 654 F.3d 1231 (11th Cir. 2011).

396. *Id.* at 1236.

397. *Id.*

residential districts. Still, the zoning ordinance permitted parks, playgrounds, and recreation centers in R-2 districts.[398]

Covenant finally closed on its land contract in 2005 without researching whether the city ordinance permitted it to build a church on the property.[399] Thus, it was unaware of the ordinance amendment that disallowed building churches in residential districts.[400] When Covenant later tried to obtain a permit to begin construction, the city notified it of the amendment and how churches were no longer permitted in residential zones. The city also advised Covenant to try to rezone its land to be included in either a commercial or institutional district.[401] Covenant applied for rezoning, but the city denied the application. it then filed suit, alleging violations of RLUIPA, the U.S. and Georgia constitutions, and Georgia common law.[402]

The district court granted summary judgment in favor of the city on all of Covenant's RLUIPA claims except under the equal-terms provision. The court determined that the zoning amendment violated RLUIPA because it treated religious institutions on less than equal terms compared to nonreligious institutions.[403] The court then struck the provision that allowed for parks, playgrounds and recreation centers to exist in residential zones while excluding churches, thus prohibiting both religious and nonreligious assemblies in residential zones.[404]

Covenant then submitted another application to the city, which was accepted. Yet, later the same day, the city amended its ordinance by eliminating the flat ban on religious and nonreligious uses in residential areas and instead classified all assembly uses as "special uses" that required city council approval.[405] When the city did not make a decision regarding Covenant's application, Covenant moved for final judgment on the equal-terms violation and for a permanent injunction to require the city to process its application.[406] When the court denied the motion, Covenant tried to amend

398. *Id.* at 1236–37.
399. *Id.* at 1237.
400. *Id.*
401. *Id.*
402. *Covenant Christian Ministries*, 654 F.3d at 1237.
403. *Id.* at 1237–38.
404. *Id.* at 1238.
405. *Id.*
406. *Id.*

its complaint, a move the court deemed untimely since Covenant was on notice of the city's failure to process its application for nearly one year before Covenant tried to amend the complaint.[407] The district court then ruled in favor of the city except on the equal-terms violation. The court awarded nominal damages of $1 to Covenant.[408]

The Eleventh Circuit upheld the district court's determination that the zoning ordinance did not survive a strict scrutiny challenge and thus violated RLUIPA's equal-terms provision.[409] However, the court further agreed with the district court that Covenant was merely entitled to nominal damages in the amount of $1.[410] The Eleventh Circuit further reasoned that—based on the district court's decision to remedy the ordinance's unequal treatment by excluding private parks, playgrounds, and recreation centers from residentially zoned areas along with religious institutions—Covenant had no vested right to build its planned church.[411] The amendment to the city's zoning ordinance that now treats religious and nonreligious institutions alike—as special uses that require city council approval—mooted Covenant's claims for injunctive relief.[412]

However, according to the Fifth Circuit, modifying a regulation by merely changing the category of the restriction will not necessarily moot a claim. As discussed earlier, *Opulent Life Church v. City of Holly Springs*[413] was an equal-terms case involving a jurisdiction that replaced a regulation imposing burdensome requirements on religious land uses alone with a categorical ban on religious land uses in a particular district. Though a church at the time only challenged the regulation that was subsequently repealed, the court found the case not to be moot because the city effectively "doubled down" on its restrictive policy.[414]

Reaching a settlement after filing suit can also render a case moot. For example, in *Merrimack Congregation of Jehovah's Witnesses v. Town of*

407. *Id.*
408. *Id.*
409. *Id.* at 1246.
410. *Id.* at 1247.
411. *Id.* at 1242.
412. *Id.* at 1244.
413. 697 F.3d 279 (5th Cir. 2012).
414. *Id.* at 286.

Merrimack,[415] a court found that mootness arose out of a proposed settlement. A congregation applied for an exception that would allow it to build a church in a residential district. The town's zoning board of adjustment denied the request.[416] In response, the congregation filed suit, alleging violations of RLUIPA and both federal and state constitutional provisions.[417] The parties reached a settlement that ordered the zoning board, inter alia, to grant the congregation's special exception, and the parties together moved to have the consent decree approved.[418]

The district court denied the consent decree for failing to provide sufficient support as to whether the court was authorized to grant the exception.[419] The parties then filed a motion to stay the case for 60 days to allow time for the zoning board to present the settlement at a meeting and to decide whether to grant the exception.[420]

The court determined that the issues were moot, since "the parties los[t] a legally cognizable interest in the outcome" when they chose to address the issue pertaining to the special exception through a zoning board proceeding.[421] The parties were no longer seeking a decision regarding the claims that pertained to the zoning board's earlier rejection of the congregation's application for an exception.[422] Since the congregation's claims were moot, the court dismissed the action without prejudice, unless or until the parties could demonstrate why dismissal should not occur.[423] The court did note that if the parties failed to enter the settlement agreement after the zoning board meeting, any potential claims of the congregation would arise from the circumstances surrounding that proceeding.[424]

415. No. 10-cv-581-JD, 2011 WL 5289869 (D.N.H. Nov. 1, 2011).
416. *Id.* at *1.
417. *Id.*
418. *Id.*
419. *Id.*
420. *Id.*
421. *Id.* (citation omitted).
422. *Id.*
423. *Id.* at *2.
424. *Id.* at *1.

E. Abstention

"Abstention" is the general term given to a variety of doctrines that require or give a federal court the option to refuse to hear a case when hearing the case would usurp powers of another court. Abstention is generally invoked in lawsuits where claims from both a state and federal system are brought at the same time. Quite naturally, with local zoning and land use laws conflating with federal statutory and constitutional law, RLUIPA cases have seen their fair share of abstention challenges.

Abstention involves an examination of whether a federal court can have jurisdiction over a matter where a claimant has standing to sue but also has a state court matter pending before the federal court action is filed.[425] This often involves an analysis of the Younger[426] and the Rooker-Feldman[427] doctrines. In determining the applicability of the Younger abstention rule, the court needs to consider three factors: (1) whether there is an ongoing state proceeding, (2) whether the proceedings implicate an important state interest, and (3) whether an adequate opportunity exists in the state proceedings to raise constitutional challenges.[428]

There are three exceptions to the Younger rule. The first is that the "state proceeding is motivated by a desire to harass or is conducted in bad faith."[429] The second is if the "challenged provision flagrantly and patently violates express constitutional prohibitions."[430] The third is if there is "an extraordinarily pressing need for immediate equitable relief."[431]

One case that addressed this doctrine, previously discussed among the substantial-burden cases, is *Salman v. City of Phoenix*.[432] In review, the case involved a minister who began conducting weekly Bible study meetings in his home and invited neighbors.[433] Salman was later informed that the

425. Hale O Kaula Church v. Maui Planning Comm'n, 2003 U.S. Dist. LEXIS 2451 (D. Haw. 2003).

426. Younger v. Harris, 401 U.S. 37 (1971).

427. Rooker v. Fid. Trust Co., 263 U.S. 413 (1923); D.C. Court of Appeals v. Feldman, 460 U.S. 462 (1983).

428. Middlesex Cnty. Ethics Comm. v. Garden State Bar Ass'n, 457 U.S. 423, 432 (1982).

429. Huffman v. Pursue, 420 U.S. 592, 611 (1975).

430. Moore v. Sims, 442 U.S. 415, 423 (1979).

431. Kugler v. Helfant, 421 U.S. 117, 124–25 (1975).

432. 2011 U.S. Dist. LEXIS 122387 (D. Ariz. 2011). *See also* 2012 U.S. Dist. LEXIS 83305 (D. Ariz. 2012).

433. *Id.* at 2.

activity was considered a "church use," which required a permit.[434] Soon after, he submitted plans for a worship structure on his property, was issued the permit, and then constructed a facility where 40 to 50 people would gather weekly for Bible study.[435] Eventually, city inspectors searched the property and issued a notice of violation, which the minister appealed. He then filed suit, seeking injunctive and declaratory relief while alleging violations of RLUIPA and the U.S. and Arizona constitutions.[436] In response, the city argued that the court was required to abstain from deciding the federal claims under the Supreme Court's Younger abstention doctrine.[437]

Here, the court determined that the state proceedings against the minister for building and zoning violations were still ongoing, as he had appealed the initial convictions and new charges had been filed.[438] The court also determined that his ongoing state criminal proceedings implicated important state interests.[439] Finally, despite the fact that the minister was proceeding pro se, the court found that the Salmans had a chance to raise their constitutional claims in the state matter but did not do so.[440]

The court next outlined two narrow exceptions to Younger abstention that would allow the federal court to take the case: "Where (1) the state proceeding is motivated by harassment or bad faith, or (2) the challenged statute is flagrantly and patently violative of express constitutional prohibitions in every clause, sentence and paragraph."[441] Since all three abstention elements were met and none of the exceptions applied to the Salmans' situation, the court abstained from exercising federal jurisdiction.[442]

The Rooker-Feldman doctrine is something of an offshoot of abstention. While it functions to limit the ability of federal courts to review state court activity, it is, more plainly, a recognition that federal courts have not been granted statutory jurisdiction to hear cases that have already been decided in state courts. Rooker-Feldman thus prevents losing parties in state courts

434. *Id.*
435. *Id.*
436. *Id.* at 4.
437. *Id.*
438. *Id.* at 6.
439. *Id.*
440. *Id.* at 7–8.
441. *Id.* at 9.
442. *Id.*

from using federal courts as review bodies to redress merely unfavorable judgments.[443] Its narrow focus on state court decisions also has important implications for RLUIPA litigation. For instance, in *Holy Ghost Revival Ministries v. City of Marysville*,[444] a family operating religious transactional housing services for released convicts in Marysville, Washington, filed suit against the city because the family believed it was the target of discriminatory land use regulations that disrupted its operations.[445] The city tried to invoke Rooker-Feldman to bar the court from reconsidering an administrative land use decision unfavorable to the family. However, the court noted that Rooker-Feldman does not extend to state administrative agency decisions and denied the request.[446] The doctrine may in some cases stop a claim dead in its tracks, but it is not to be overextended.

443. Exxon Mobil Corp. v. Saudi Basic Industries Corp., 544 U.S. 280, 283–84 (2005).
444. 2015 U.S. Dist. LEXIS 45506 (W.D. Wash. 2015).
445. *Id.* at *2–6.
446. *Id.* at *15–16.

Conclusion

As you have learned over the past 250-odd pages of this book, even a general overview of religious property law is fraught with nuance and exceptions to rules. For those of us whose professional lives are immersed in this legal sphere on a daily basis, speaking with authority can seem, at times, as much an act of faith as religion itself.

As I write this, state and federal courts are likely scrutinizing the legal precedents that have come to shape religious property law as we understand it today and as I have tried to explain in this book. Given the ever-evolving interpretations, this area of the legal system is not for the faint of heart or for the legal neophyte. What I have provided in this book is just a foundational understanding and a first step. Readers would be well-advised to reach out to practitioners who are well-versed in the complexities of church property and zoning disputes.

Admittedly, it's hard to imagine how congregations and their church governing bodies, ostensibly united in their beliefs, can find their relationship degenerating over who owns what piece of property, or that the presence of a house of worship in a community can create tension or not be seen as anything other than good for parishioner and neighbor alike.

If, in fact, the Lord moves in mysterious ways, then man and the laws he erects are no less puzzling.

What I have tried here is to give you a starting point from which to proceed. Good luck in your legal journey. And, of course, keep the faith.

Index

D

E